Sue Kay, Vaughan Jones & Philip Kerr

Inside Out

Student's
Book

Pre-intermediate

MACMILLAN

1 *Me*

Listening

1 🔲 01 You're going to listen to Susan talking about some of the different names that people call her. Which name doesn't she like?

2 Listen again. Match the people (*a–h*) with the names (*1–8*) that they call Susan.

a)	her father and sometimes her sister	1	Mum
b)	her friends and the people she works with	2	Susan
c)	her old friends	3	Suzanne
d)	her son	4	Suki
e)	her mother	5	Sweetheart
f)	her best friend	6	Maggsie
g)	her sister-in-law	7	Bunny
h)	her husband	8	Sue

3 Write down the different names that people call you. Tell your partner. Which of your names do you like best/least?

Lexis: family words

1 Work with a partner. Copy the following table. Under each heading note down the first names of people in your family.

LANGUAGE TOOLBOX

Son / daughter
(Ex-) husband / wife / partner
Boyfriend / girlfriend
Stepfather / stepmother
Half-brother / -sister

Parents	Brothers & sisters	Grandfather & grandmother	Sons & daughters	Uncles & aunts	Cousins	Nephews & nieces

2 Add more headings and names to the table in 1.

3 Discuss the following questions about the names in your table.

a) Which names are typical in your country?
b) Which name is the most unusual?
c) Which name do you like best?

Long vowel sounds

1 🔲 02 In each of the following groups of names one name has a different vowel sound from the others. Listen and spot the odd one out in each group.

1 /ɔ:/ Paul George Sue Dawn
2 /u:/ Julie Ruth Luke Burt
3 /ɑ:/ Charles Laura Barbara Grant
4 /i:/ Peter Eve Margaret Keith
5 /ɜ:/ Shirley Bernard Earl Denise

2 🔲 03 Listen and check your answers to 1. Then listen again and repeat. Rearrange the names so that all four names in each group have the same vowel sound.

What's in a name?

Work in small groups. Discuss the following questions.

a) What name would you give this baby girl?
b) What names do you like for a boy?
c) How did your parents choose your name?

Reading **1** What do you think the following famous people have in common? Read the article and find out.

a) Elton John + Marilyn Monroe
b) David Bowie + Demi Moore
c) Madonna + Bill Clinton

THE NAME GAME

Your name is extremely important. It's how you identify yourself. It's how other people identify you. Elton John was born Reginald Kenneth Dwight. Can you imagine someone famous with a name like that?
5 He had to change it. Marilyn Monroe sounds so much more glamorous than Norma Jean Baker. So how do parents make one of the most important decisions in the lives of their children – giving them a name?

Some parents choose names because they are
10 fashionable. Other parents do the opposite and call their children unusual names, or they even invent names. Helen Petrie, a psychologist at Hertfordshire University, says that people who choose unusual names for their children want to show how special they are.

15 However, the children are not always very happy with their parents' choice. David Bowie's son found the name Zowie so embarrassing that he changed it to Joe. I wonder if Bruce Willis and Demi Moore's children feel good about their names: Rummer Glenn, Scout LaRue
20 and Tallulah Belle!

These days it's fashionable to give your child the name of a place that is important to you: Victoria (Posh Spice) and David Beckham decided to call their son Brooklyn because they were in New York when they
25 discovered that Victoria was going to have a baby. Madonna named her daughter Lourdes after the town in France, and ex-US-President Bill Clinton named his daughter Chelsea after a part of London that he and his wife liked.

30   Personally, I think it's a good idea to give children names of famous people. Leonardo Di Caprio was named after the famous Italian painter, and Liam
35 Gallagher, singer with the band *Oasis*, called his son Lennon after his hero, John.

I wanted to call my first child Elvis, and my husband wanted to
40 call him Pelé. Fortunately she was a girl, so we named her after my favourite aunt – Blodwen.

Reginald Kenneth Dwight (Elton John) ▶

2 Tick (✔) the reasons for choosing a name that the article mentions. Put a cross (✘) by the reasons the article doesn't mention.

a) because it sounds good
b) because it's fashionable
c) because it sounds the same in two languages
d) because it's unusual or original
e) because it's the name of a place
f) because it's a religious name
g) because it's the name of a famous person
h) because it's the name of another member of the family

3 Work with a partner. What other reasons can you think of for choosing a name? Think about your family, your friends, and people in the class.

Lexis **1** Complete the following sentences with words from the text above.

a) I think that my name *sounds* much nicer in my language than in English. (line 5)
b) I won't have to ____ a decision about names. I'm not going to have any children! (line 7)
c) I'd like to have an unusual name – it would make me ____ special. (line 18)
d) I know exactly what I'm going to ____ my children. (line 23)
e) My parents named me ____ a relative. (line 26)
f) I think it's a good ____ to choose a name that's easy to say in different languages. (line 31)

2 Find out if any of the sentences in 1 are true for your partner.

I never forget a face

1 How good are you at remembering people's names? What techniques do you use?

2 Try this memory test. Study these names and faces for thirty seconds. Then turn to page 124 and see which you can remember.

Reading **1** Read this advice for improving your memory. Find an appropriate heading for each paragraph.

a) Repeat it   c) Use it   e) Write it down
b) Visualise it   d) Check the spelling   f) Make associations

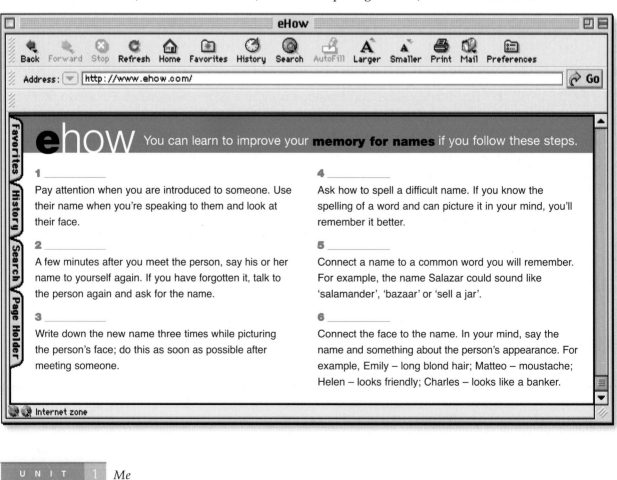

(Based on *eHow to remember names* by Valerie Singer www.ehow.com)

2 Work with a partner. Discuss these questions.

   a) Which of the techniques in 1 have you used for remembering names?

   b) Which of the techniques in 1 could help you to remember new English words and expressions?

   c) What other ways can you think of to help remember and learn new English words and expressions?

Lexis: describing people

1 Look at the nouns, noun phrases and adjectives in the box. Which words can complete sentence *a*? Which words can complete sentence *b*?

> friendly   a banker   a typical mum   intelligent   shy   a doctor   very young
> middle-aged   stressed out   intelligent   about sixty   Greek   a waiter
> a Swedish au pair   a student   fit   a retired police officer   a bit tired   rich

   a) He/She looks ____ .   b) He/She looks like ____ .

'Do you find the accused "looks guilty" or "doesn't look guilty"?'

2 What type of word do you use after *look(s)*? What type of word do you use after *look(s) like*?

3 Write a sentence to describe each person in the six photographs on the previous page. Leave a space (____) for the name.

   For example: ____ *looks about 60. He looks intelligent and quite friendly.*

4 Give your paper to a partner and ask them to complete the sentence with the correct name.

5 Repeat the same exercise for three people in your class. Ask your partner to complete the sentences with the correct name.

Meet A.L.I.C.E.

1 Read the responses in this conversation. Who or what is A.L.I.C.E.?

> Hi. My name's A.L.I.C.E.
>
> **1** *name What your does mean ?*
> It means **A**rtificial **L**inguistic **I**nternet **C**omputer **E**ntity.
>
> **2** *were born you Where ?*
> I was born in Bethlehem, Pennsylvania.
>
> **3** *grow Where did up you ?*
> I think I grew up in San Francisco.
>
> **4** *look do like you What ?*
> I'm blue and I've got one wheel.
>
> **5** *do What do you ?*
> I talk to people on the web.
>
> **6** *like your Do job you ?*
> Yes, I have a passion for my work!
>
> **7** *languages you any speak Can foreign ?*
> No, I only speak English at the moment, but I'd like to learn.
>
> **8** *married you Are ?*
> No, I am single. How about you?
>
> **9** *got children Have any you ?*
> No, but you can download me and make A.L.I.C.E. clones for yourself!
>
> **10** *created you Who ?*
> Dr Richard S. Wallace – he is very clever!

2 Write the words in the questions in 1 in the correct order.

3 🔘 04 Listen and check your answers to 1 and 2.

4 <u>Underline</u> the stressed word in each question. Listen and repeat the questions in the conversation.

LANGUAGE TOOLBOX

What's your favourite … ?
Are you interested in … ?
Have you ever … ?
How often do you … ?

5 Work with someone you don't know very well. Interview them using appropriate questions from 2 and add more questions of your own.

Close up

1 Work with a partner. Look at the table and discuss the questions.

Statement			Question			
subject	(auxiliary) verb			(auxiliary) verb	subject	
You	are ...	→		Are	you ...?	Are you married?
You	can ...	→		Can	you ...?	Can you speak any foreign languages?
Your name	means ...	→	What	does	your name ...?	What does your name mean?

'Can Wolfgang come out and play?'

a) What is the difference in word order between a statement and a question in English?

b) When do you need to use the auxiliary verbs *do, does, did* to form a question?

c) How do you form questions in your language? Is it the same as English?

2 Change the following statements into questions. Then ask your partner the questions.

a) You are hungry. *Are you hungry?*

b) You smoke.

c) You can play the guitar.

d) You've been to Disneyland.

e) You live in Rome. *Where do you live?*

f) Your favourite colour is red. (*What*)

g) You left school in 1997. (*When*)

h) You've got 200 CDs. (*How many*)

3 Rewrite these questions in the correct order.

a) you are old How ?   *How old are you?*

b) life in Do after believe death you ?

c) do much weigh you How ?

d) you anything ever Have stolen ?

e) much earn How you do money ?

f) you many partners How had have ?

4 Work in small groups. In what situations is it okay to ask the questions in 3?

• in your English class • with your best friends • in your family • at work • never!

1 Look at questions A and B below. Question A is an object question because the answer (*A.L.I.C.E.*) is the object of the verb. Question B is a subject question because the answer (*Dr Wallace*) is the subject of the verb. Do you use an auxiliary with a subject question?

Statement			Question	Answer
subject	verb	object		
Dr Wallace	created	A.L.I.C.E.	A What did Dr Wallace create? → A.L.I.C.E.	
			B Who created A.L.I.C.E.? → Dr Wallace.	

2 Work in pairs. You are going to ask and answer some general knowledge questions. Student A turn to page 124. Student B turn to page 126. Follow the instructions.

Language reference: questions

Word order

To form a question in English you put an auxiliary verb before the subject. In the present simple you use the auxiliary *do* or *does*. In the past simple you use the auxiliary *did*. With the verb *be* you put *am, is, are, was* or *were* before the subject.

question word	(auxiliary) verb	subject	
–	Is	your sister	married?
–	Does	she	love him?
Where	do	they	live?
Why	did	she	get married?

Subject questions

When the question word is the subject you do not use *do, does* or *did*. A subject question has the same word order as a statement.

subject	verb	
Who	created	A.L.I.C.E.?
NOT ~~Who did create ...?~~		

subject	verb	
Who	lives	here?
NOT ~~Who does live ...?~~		

Stand By Me

Song **1** Look at the words of the song. On lines *a–f* and lines *g–l* there is an extra word. Find the word and ~~cross it out~~.

a) When the ~~good~~ night has come,
b) And the Disney land is dark,
c) And the moon is the only flashing light we see,
d) No, I probably won't be afraid,
e) Oh, I won't ever be afraid,
f) Just as long as you stand up, stand by me.

So darlin', darlin', stand by me, oh stand by me.
Oh stand now, stand by me, stand by me.

g) If the blue sky that we look upon
h) Should tumble and fall over,
i) Or the rocky mountains should crumble to the sea,
j) I won't cry, I won't cry out,
k) No, I won't shed a big tear,
l) Just as long as you stand up, stand by me.

So darlin', darlin', stand by me, oh stand by me.
Oh stand now, stand by me, stand by me.

And darlin', darlin', stand by me, oh stand by me.
Oh stand now, stand by me, stand by me.
Whenever you're in trouble,
Won't you stand by me, oh stand by me.
Oh stand now, oh stand, stand by me.

Ben E. King

Stand By Me

Recorded by Ben E. King (1961 and 1987), Elvis Presley (1967), and John Lennon (1975).

2 〔▭▭〕 05 Listen and check your answers to 1.

3 Which of the following is the best interpretation of the song?

a) There are going to be a lot of disasters if you stand by me.
b) I won't be able to see very well if you stand by me.
c) If you stand by me, I will feel strong. Nothing will worry me.

4 Tell your partner about a time when you've really needed a friend to 'stand by you'.

Anecdote **1** 〔▭▭〕 06 Listen to Tom talking about somebody who is important to him. Which of the following topics does he talk about?

☐ What is this person's full name?
☐ When did you meet this person?
☐ How old are they now?
☐ Where do they live?
☐ What do they do?

☐ How often do you see them?
☐ Why are they important to you?
☐ What are their best qualities?
☐ Is there anything you don't like about them?
☐ When did you last see them?

2 Work with a partner. Note down as much information as you can remember about the topics Tom talks about. Listen again and check your answers.

3 Think of a person who is important to you. You are going to tell a partner about them. Choose from the list in 1 the things you want to talk about. Think about what you will say and what language you will need.

Tom

2 *Place*

Work with a partner. Look at the four photos and discuss the questions.

- What do you think it's like to live in each of these places?
- Which of these places would you most like to live in?
- Which of these places would you least like to live in?

Lexis

1 Look again at the photos. Find examples of eight of the twelve items in the box.

> high-rise buildings   a river   a hill   a statue   a fountain   a canal
> a park   a church   a bridge   a square   a castle   the sea

2 How many of the things in 1 can you find near your school? Put them in the right order on this line.

Nearest ◄─────────────────────────► Furthest away

a Venice, Italy   b La Bastide, France   c Heidelberg, Germany

d Rio de Janeiro, Brazil

Listening   **1**   ▭ 07 You are going to listen to four people talking about the places in the photos. Match each speaker to a photo. Who likes living where they live? Who doesn't?

2   Use the most appropriate adjective in the box to complete these descriptions from the recording. (Sometimes more than one answer is possible.)

> new   clean   crowded   boring   exciting   polluted   humid

a)   ... a city that's so big and ____
b)   ... people say it's too noisy and ____
c)   ... it's too hot and ____
d)   ... it's a mixture of old and ____

e)   ... the air is lovely and ____
f)   ... I find it so dull and ____
g)   ... the canals are dirty and ____

3   Listen and check your answers to 2. Use these adjective combinations to describe places in your country. Compare your ideas with a partner.

Close up

What's it like?   **1**   Look at the following question. Choose the only possible answer: *a, b* or *c*.

Language reference p15

What's your home town like?
a)   Yes, I do.   b)   It's big and exciting.   c)   The shops.

2   Think of three other possible ways of answering the question in 1.

3   Match the questions from the recording with the most appropriate response.

a)   What's the <u>weather</u> like?   1   It's a mixture of old and new.
b)   What's the <u>architecture</u> like?   2   They're really friendly.
c)   What are the <u>people</u> like?   3   They're too expensive.
d)   What are the <u>shops</u> like?   4   It's hot and humid.

Nouns: countable / uncountable   **1**   Look at the <u>underlined</u> nouns in 3 in the previous section and complete the table.

Language reference p15

Nouns	Countable	Uncountable	Singular form	Plural form
a) weather	✗	✓	*weather*	–
b) architecture	____	____	____	–
c) people	✓	✗	*person*	____
d) shops	____	____	____	____

2   Continue the table in 1 with the nouns in the box. Decide if the nouns are countable or uncountable. Write down the singular form in each case and add the plural form if the noun is countable.

> traffic   restaurant   nightlife   public transport   park   cinema

3   Work with a partner. Discuss these questions.

a)   Which countable noun in the table in 1 has an irregular plural form?
b)   How do you make plural forms of these irregular countable nouns: *a man, a woman, a child, a foot, a tooth*?
c)   How do you make plural forms of regular countable nouns?

4   Work with a partner. Note down the names of two cities or villages you know well. Combine nouns from 1 and 2 with the appropriate question frame below to ask each other questions about the places you have noted down.

a)   'What's the ____ like?'   'It's ...'
b)   'What are the ____ like?'   'They're ...'

First impressions

Writing

1 Read this letter from Rick to a friend. How does he feel about the place he is describing?

Rick

> Hi!
> I've been here a week and my first impressions are not very good. In fact, they are terrible. The city is small and boring. Really boring! The buildings are modern and unattractive, and there are some ugly high-rise office blocks.
>
> The city centre is really dirty and polluted, and public transport is useless. The buses stop at ten o'clock at night, and it's impossible to get a taxi. This probably explains why the streets are completely empty after six o'clock in the evening and the nightlife is terrible. There's nothing to do.
>
> The people look miserable and they're not very friendly. I suppose it could be because the weather is awful – it's cold and hasn't stopped raining since I arrived. Seven days of rain – can you imagine?
>
> But the worst thing is the food – I can't eat it. And the coffee tastes disgusting. Ugh! There aren't many restaurants and they're expensive.
> I want to come home! I really <u>hate</u> it here.
> Love, Rick
> XXX

2 Re-write the letter in 1. Make it sound as positive as you can.

> Hi!
> I've been here a week and my first impressions are really good. In fact, they are fantastic. The city is big and exciting. Really exciting! The buildings are ...

Word stress

1 🔲 08 Complete the following country and nationality sets. <u>Underline</u> the stressed syllable in each word and then listen and repeat to check your answers. What happens to the word stress in each set?

A Country	Nationality	B Country	Nationality	C Country	Nationality
<u>Cu</u>ba	C_____	E_____	E<u>gyp</u>tian	<u>Chi</u>na	C_____
T_____	<u>Tur</u>kish	Italy	I_____	M_____	Mal<u>tese</u>
M_____	Mo<u>roc</u>can	<u>Hung</u>ary	H_____	P_____	Portu<u>guese</u>
Argen<u>ti</u>na	A_____	C_____	Ca<u>na</u>dian	Ja<u>pan</u>	J_____

2 Think of three other countries not mentioned in 1 that you would like to visit. Write down each country and nationality and mark the stress. Tell your partner where you would like to go and what you would like to do there.

Discussion

1 Work in small groups. Decide if you agree with the following statements.

French wine is the best in the world.   *Japanese cars are the best in the world.*

2 Replace the <u>underlined</u> words in 1 in as many different ways as possible. Use topics in the box or think of some of your own.

coffee	watches	women	beer	pop music	fashion	football players
perfume	tea	rice	men	roads	universities	food	mobile phones
shops	films	stereo equipment

3 Write as many sentences as you can which you all agree on. Compare with other groups.

Dream holiday

1 Read through the information about the four destinations on offer in this holiday competition. List them in order (1 = the place you would most like to go to; 4 = the place you would least like to go to). Explain your choices to a partner.

2 You are going to enter the competition. Work with a partner. Read the 'How to enter' section and do parts A and B of the competition.

3 Check your answers to Part A of the competition on page 124. Compare your written summaries for Part B of the competition with other people in the class. Choose a class winner!

WIN A DREAM HOLIDAY FOR TWO!

The winner of our exciting competition can choose a dream holiday for two in one of these fabulous destinations.

New York
Shopping heaven and a great nightlife. Visit Central Park, the Empire State Building, the Statue of Liberty, and shop till you drop!

Karaǧaaç
A tiny village located on the beautiful coast of south-west Turkey. Enjoy the clear seas and white-gold sands of Patara beach, or visit the many archeological sites in the area.

Atlas Mountains
Located in the heart of Morocco, the Atlas Mountains are the perfect place to relax. The people are very welcoming and the air is fresh. You'll feel like a new person.

Havana
The capital of Cuba, famous for its wild music and beautiful people – Cubans know how to have a good time, and so will you.

HOW TO ENTER

Part A
To enter this fabulous competition and win a dream holiday for two, complete the following sentences with option **a**, **b** or **c**.

1 The official language of Brazil is …
 a Portuguese
 b French
 c Italian

2 Ankara is the capital of …
 a Morocco
 b Turkey
 c Malta

3 The third largest country in the world is …
 a China
 b Argentina
 c Australia

4 The zloty is the currency of …
 a Hungary
 b Ireland
 c Poland

5 The Alhambra Palace is in …
 a Egypt
 b Spain
 c Mexico

6 Kyushu is an island in the south of …
 a Thailand
 b Greece
 c Japan

Part B
Now tell us in no more than fifty words which holiday destination you would choose and why you would like to go there.

Send your answers before 1st April to
Dream Holiday, PO Box 437, London NW1 4HB.

Close up

Quantity

Language reference p15

1 Complete the following description of a country with the nouns from the box. Which country do you think it is? Could it be your country? Why / Why not?

| cars | cigarettes | coffee | hours | meat | noise | people | sleep | wine |

Everything's wrong here!

They do everything wrong here!

They eat far too much (1) ____ and they eat it at 11pm.
Yesterday we went out to dinner at 11.30 and we had trouble getting
a table! At 1am we were still eating, and the restaurant was still half-full!

5   They smoke too many (2) ____ . They drink lots of strong (3) ____ and
a lot of (4) ____ .

They spend too many (5) ____ in the sun and they certainly don't
get enough (6) ____ . One Saturday night we went to a disco at 2am
and were surprised to see that there were only a few (7) ____ on the

10   dance floor. Then the DJ arrived at 3am and the party began!

There are far too many (8) ____ in the cities, and there's too much
(9) ____ everywhere!

They do everything wrong here, but the quality of life is great, and
people really know how to enjoy themselves. I don't want to go home!

2 🔊 09 Listen and check your answers to 1.

3 This table categorises the quantity expressions used with the nouns *1–9* in the text in 1.
Choose a suitable heading for each category (A, B, C): *Use with countable and uncountable
nouns; Use with countable nouns; Use with uncountable nouns.*

A	B	C
How many?	How much?	not enough
(far) too many	(far) too much	a lot of
(only) a few	(only) a little	lots of

4 Underline the correct quantity expression in each of these sentences.

a) I don't eat **much** / **many** bread.
b) I eat **a few** / **lots of** fruit.
c) I drink **far too much** / **far too many** beer.

d) I don't eat **much** / **enough** vegetables.
e) I eat **a lot of** / **a little** cakes.
f) I don't drink **enough** / **many** water.

5 How many of the sentences in 4 are true for you? Re-write the sentences so that they are
all true for you. Compare your sentences with a partner.

6 Work with a partner. Use the question frame below to ask each other questions about
daily habits. Add your own nouns and verbs to make different questions.

For example: *How much meat do you eat every day? How many e-mails do you get every day?*

	Nouns		Verbs	
How much How many	chocolate e-mails bad TV programmes sleep money wine friends coffee people meat	do you	eat drink watch get have make phone see send spend	every day?

Language reference: *What's it like?*; nouns & quantity

What's it like?

This question asks about the characteristics of people or things. You usually answer it with an adjective or adjective phrase.

'What's Madrid like?' 'It's big and exciting.'
'What are the people in your village like?' 'They're very friendly.'

Countable nouns

These refer to things which can be counted. You use them with *a/an* or put a number in front of them. You usually form the plural by adding *-s, -es, -ies*.

a car – 500 cars
a church – 3 churches
a country – 12 countries

Note: A few common countable nouns have irregular plural forms.

a child – two children   a person – two people
a foot – two feet   a tooth – two teeth
a man – two men   a woman – two women
a mouse – two mice

Uncountable nouns

These refer to things which cannot be counted. You cannot use *a/an* or put a number in front of them.

advice   food   furniture   information   love
music   rain   traffic   travel   weather   work

Quantity

These are ways you can talk about quantity if you can't or don't want to use an exact number.

With countable nouns: *(only) a few / (far) too many / How many … ?*
*There were only **a few** people who saw them.*
***How many** e-mails do you get every day?*

With uncountable nouns: *(only) a little / (far) too much / How much … ?*
*There's **a little** wine left but no beer.*
***How much** sleep do you get at night?*

With countable and uncountable nouns: *a lot of / lots of / not enough*
*There are **a lot of** problems with this plan.*
*There was **lots of good** food at the party.*
*He did**n't** give me **enough** information.*

Cities of the world

1 Work with a partner. Which of the following cities are capitals? (There are six.)

> Tokyo   Nice   Seoul   Reykjavik   Berlin   Barcelona   Los Angeles   Cairo
> Melbourne   Prague

2 Work with a partner. Student A turn to page 124. Student B turn to page 126. Check your answers to 1 and then follow the instructions.

3 Choose one city you would really like to live in and tell your partner why.

Anecdote   Think about the best city you have ever visited. You are going to tell your partner about it. Choose from the list the things you want to talk about. Think about what you will say and what language you will need.

- ☐ Where is the city?
- ☐ When did you first go there?
- ☐ Were you on holiday?
- ☐ Who did you go there with?
- ☐ What did you do there?

- ☐ How many times have you visited the city?
- ☐ When was the last time?
- ☐ What do you most like about this city?
- ☐ Would you like to live there? Why / Why not?

3 Couples

Reading

1 Look at the photos of four famous Hollywood couples. Which of these celebrities are well-known in your country?

2 Read the information and find out how long each couple was married for. What went wrong with their relationships?

(Based on an article in *The Mirror*)

What went **wrong?**

| Richard Gere and Cindy Crawford | Lyle Lovett and Julia Roberts | Nicole Kidman and Tom Cruise | Bruce Willis and Demi Moore |

got married
in 1991 in Las Vegas.

split up
in 1994.

were married
for 3 years.

What went wrong?
She wanted to have children and he refused.

got married
in 1993 after a six-week romance.

split up
in 1995.

were married
for 2 years.

What went wrong?
The big difference in age became a problem.

got married
on Christmas Eve 1990 in Telluride, Colorado.

split up
in 2001.

were married
for just over 10 years.

What went wrong?
They both wanted to pursue their own careers.

got married
in 1987 in Las Vegas, just four weeks after he asked her out on their first date.

split up
in 1998.

were married
for 11 years.

What went wrong?
It was a stormy relationship, and there were rumours of affairs on both sides.

3 Read the information again and answer these questions.

a) Which couple got married in Las Vegas?
b) Which couple got married on Christmas Eve?
c) Which couple were married the longest?
d) Which couple were married for the shortest time?
e) Which couple split up for professional reasons?
f) Which couple split up because one of them didn't want to have children?

1 Complete the expressions in the sentences below with one word in each case. Look back at the information in the previous section if necessary.

a) The best age to ____ married is twenty-five for women and twenty-seven for men.
b) A big ____ in age should not be a problem for a couple if they are in love.
c) It is impossible for both partners in a marriage to ____ a career.
d) A woman should never ask a man ____ on a first date.
e) A ____ relationship is much better than a boring one.
f) A couple with children should never ____ up. They should stay together.
g) The main reason for getting married is to ____ children.

2 Work in small groups. Do you agree with the statements in 1?

Ross & Jane

Writing **1** Match the words and expressions in the box to an appropriate picture (a–d).

> move in   have a row   chat up   fancy

2 Put the stages of Ross and Jane's relationship in the order that you think best. Add different stages if you think they are necessary. Compare your ideas with a partner.

a) They got married.
b) Ross chatted Jane up.
c) They rang each other up.
d) They fancied each other.
e) They moved in together.
f) They had children.
g) They had a row.
h) They met each other's parents.
i) They kissed.
j) They split up.
k) They went out together.
l) They fell in love.

LANGUAGE TOOLBOX

One day / evening
First / To begin with
Then / Next / After that
After a while
A few weeks later
Finally / In the end

3 Work in pairs. You are going to write the story of Ross and Jane.

• Use the sentences from 2, including any that you have added.
• Use adverbs of time from the Language toolbox as well as appropriate place words.
• Compare your story with other peoples' stories in the class and vote for the best one.

For example: *One evening Ross met Jane at a disco. They fancied each other. To begin with …*

Irregular verb sound groups **1** Complete the following irregular verb tables with the correct forms. What do the verb forms in each table have in common?

A			B			C		
Infinitive	Past simple	Past participle	Infinitive	Past simple	Past participle	Infinitive	Past simple	Past participle
meet	*met*	*met*	*ring*	*rang*	*rung*	*buy*	*bought*	*bought*
keep	a) ____	*kept*	*begin*	*began*	a) ____	a) ____	*brought*	b) ____
mean	b) ____	c) ____	b) ____	c) ____	*drunk*	*catch*	c) ____	d) ____
d) ____	*slept*	e) ____	d) ____	*sang*	e) ____	f) ____	*fought*	g) ____

2 ▭ **10** Listen, check your answers and repeat the verb forms in 1. Add three other verbs to the tables. See page 132.

Let's get personal

Listening

1 🔊 **11** Listen to the first part of a television game show and decide whether the following statements are true or false.

a) The competition is called *Popular*.
b) Bobby Brown is the host.
c) Rosie and David have to answer different questions.
d) They get points for giving the same answers.
e) Rosie and David can hear one another.
f) Rosie and David can hear Bobby Brown.

2 🔊 **12** Write out the questions that Bobby Brown asks Rosie. Listen and check your answers.

Questions	Rosie		David
1 When (**meet David**)? *When did you meet David?*	**a** Nearly three and a half years ago. **b** Over three and a half years ago. **c** Four and a half months ago.		✔ / ✗
2 How (**first meet**)? _____	**a** She was a nurse. He was a patient. **b** She was a patient. He was a nurse. **c** She was a doctor. He was a nurse.		✔ / ✗
3 What time of day (**be it**)? _____	**a** Early morning. **b** Early afternoon. **c** Early evening.		✔ / ✗
4 What (**be the weather like**)? _____	**a** The sun was shining. **b** It was raining. **c** It was snowing.		✔ / ✗
5 What (**both wear**)? _____	**Her** **a** A white coat. **b** A nurse's uniform. **c** A nightdress.	**Him** **a** Blue pyjamas. **b** Green pyjamas. **c** Pink pyjamas.	✔ / ✗
6 Who (**speak first**) and what (**say**)? _____	**a** She said: 'How do you feel?' **b** He said: 'I'm going to be sick.' **c** He said: 'I feel terrible.'		✔ / ✗

3 Listen again and <u>underline</u> the answers (*a*, *b* or *c*) that Rosie gives.

4 🔊 **13** Listen to David answering the same questions. Circle a tick (✔) if he gives the same answer as Rosie and circle a cross (✗) if he gives a different answer.

5 How many points did Rosie and David score out of six?

6 Think about the time that you first met somebody important to you. How many of the questions from *Get Personal* could you answer? Discuss with a partner.

Close up

Irregular verbs p132

Past simple

1 Work with a partner. Look at the verbs in the box and answer these questions.

> buy   stay up   start   hurry   receive   fall   go

a)   Which verbs have irregular past forms?
b)   How do you form the past simple form of regular verbs like *stay up* and *start*?
c)   What happens when the regular verb ends in *e* or a consonant + *y*?
d)   Which auxiliary verb do you use to make past simple negative and question forms?

2 Re-write each of these sentences with past simple affirmative and negative forms.

a)   Yesterday I (**buy**) a CD.   *Yesterday I **bought** a CD. / Yesterday I **didn't buy** a CD.*
b)   Last Saturday I (**stay up**) all night.   e)   This morning I (**receive**) an e-mail.
c)   In January I (**start**) a new diet.   f)   Last night I (**fall**) asleep watching TV.
d)   Today I (**hurry**) to my English lesson.   g)   Last year I (**go**) on holiday abroad.

3 Tick (✔) the sentences which are true for you. Compare your answers with a partner.

Past continuous

1 Look at these extracts from Bobby Brown's interview with Rosie. Choose the present or past continuous by <u>underlining</u> the appropriate auxiliary. Which tense is used for the other verb in each extract?

a)   Well, I **am / was** working as a nurse, and David came into the hospital …
b)   … it **is / was** raining when I arrived at work.
c)   What **are / were** you both wearing when you saw one another for the first time?

2 Which tense do you use to describe something that was in progress when another event happened? Which tense do you use to describe an event that happened at a particular moment?

3 ▣ **14** Listen to the sounds and describe the five situations. Use the past continuous and the past simple.

For example: *He was having a shower when his mobile phone rang.*

4 Work with a partner. Follow these instructions.

a)   Write down three true sentences and one false sentence to describe what you were doing yesterday at each of these times: *7.30 am; 1.00 pm; 6.00 pm; 11.00 pm.*
b)   Ask each other questions beginning *What were you doing at … ?*
c)   Guess which of your partner's answers is false.

Language reference: past tense forms

Past simple

The past simple is used to fix events and situations in the past. You can use it to say when the event or situation happened.

*The last time I **lost** my keys was two weeks ago. They fell out of my pocket on the sofa. I **didn't realise** so I **looked** everywhere. My son **found** them this morning.*

Note: Many verbs have irregular past forms and you have to learn them. There is a list of the most common irregular verbs on page 132.

Past continuous

The past continuous is usually used in contrast with the past simple. You can use it to describe something which was in progress when the main events in the story happened.

*Well, I **was working** as a nurse, and David came into the hospital for an operation.*
*What **were** you both **wearing** when you saw one another for the first time?*

True love

1 Work with a partner. Look at the couples in the article below and decide what you think are the correct answers to these questions.

    a) Who waited too long before asking his lover to marry him?
    b) Who built a monument in the memory of his wife?
    c) Who gave up his kingdom for love?
    d) Who sent red roses to his wife's crypt three times a week until his death in 1999?
    e) Which couple only spent one night apart during thirty years of marriage?

2 Read the article and check your answers.

Great love affairs

a The Duke & Duchess of Windsor
After the death of his father in 1936 Edward VIII became King of England. He was in love with Mrs Wallis Simpson, an American divorcee, and he wanted to marry her. But the British government did not accept her as Queen of England because she was divorced. He had to choose – continue as King of England or marry Mrs Simpson. He chose to stay with the woman he loved.

b Paul & Linda McCartney
When Paul McCartney left the Beatles in April 1970, many people blamed Linda, his American photographer wife. Linda was the love of Paul's life, and in thirty years they only spent one night apart. She died of cancer in 1998 with Paul by her side.

c Marilyn Monroe & Joe DiMaggio
Their marriage lasted less than ten months, but DiMaggio was always there for Marilyn. He organised her funeral, and, until his death in 1999, he sent six red roses to her crypt three times a week.

d Shah Jahan & Mumtaz Mahal
In the 17th century, Emperor Shah Jahan built the Taj Mahal in memory of his wife. He was heartbroken when his wife died after nineteen years of marriage. One year after her death, construction of the Taj Mahal began and it took twenty-two years to complete. Six years later Jahan died and was buried with his true love in one of the most romantic buildings in the world.

e Charles & Camilla
When Charles met Camilla at a polo match in 1970, he fell in love with her. But then he waited too long before asking her to marry him. She got tired of waiting and married somebody else. Now, two marriages and a funeral later, Charles and Camilla are together again.

3 Work in pairs. You are each going to write four comprehension questions on the text in 2. Student A turn to page 125. Student B turn to page 126. Follow the instructions.

4 Work in groups. Discuss these questions.

- Which story do you think is the most romantic?
- Which story do you think is the saddest?
- What famous love stories are there in your country?

Suspicious Minds

Song **1** Look at the title of the song. Do you think a person with a *suspicious mind* …

a) believes what you tell them?
b) doesn't believe what you tell them?

2 Read the song and put the words in the box in the correct place in the song.

hello   dreams   word   tears   trap   never   dreams   again

We're caught in a (1) _____ .
I can't walk out
Because I love you too much, baby.

Why can't you see
What you're doing to me
When you don't believe a (2) _____ I say?

We can't go on together
With suspicious minds.
And we can't build our (3) _____
On suspicious minds.

So, if an old friend I know
Drops by to say (4) _____ ,
Would I still see suspicion in your eyes?

Here we go (5) _____ ,
Asking where I've been.
You can't see the tears are real
I'm crying.

We can't go on together
With suspicious minds.
And we can't build our (6) _____
On suspicious minds.

Oh, let our love survive,
Oh dry the (7) _____ from your eyes.
Let's not let a good thing die
When, honey, you know
I've (8) _____ lied to you.
Mmm, yeah, yeah.

3 **15** Listen to the song and check your answers.

4 Read the song again and complete these sentences with the correct alternative.

a) The singer **wants / doesn't want** to leave.
b) The singer is **happy / unhappy** with the relationship.
c) The singer **thinks / doesn't think** his lover is jealous of his friends.
d) The singer **lies / never lies**.

5 Replace the underlined words with words and expressions from the song.

a) I don't want to leave. (verse 1)
b) I don't believe anything you say. (verse 2)
c) We can't continue together with suspicious minds. (chorus)
d) You say your friend comes to your house to say hello. (verse 3)
e) Please stop crying and believe me. (verse 5)

6 Who said the things in 5: the singer or his suspicious lover?

7 Work with a partner. Describe a time in your life when you had a 'suspicious mind'.

4 Fit

Lexis

Work with a partner. Look at the photos of the sports personalities and complete the table.

> **fit** Someone who is **fit** is healthy and able to do physical activities without getting tired.

- You score six points by completing the 'Personality' column and matching the names to the photos.
- You score six more points by completing the 'Sport', 'Person' and 'Place' columns. Check your answers on page 125. Who scored the most points in the class?

Personality	Sport	Person	Place
A Cathy Freeman	athletics	athlete	track
B Raúl	a) ____	football player	pitch
C Shaquille O'Neal	basketball	d) ____	court
D ____	motor racing	racing driver	race track
E Inge de Bruijn	b) ____	swimmer	f) ____
F ____	c) ____	e) ____	court

Listening

1 🔲 **16** Listen to a discussion between a marketing director and an advertising executive. They want to choose one of the sports personalities in the photos in the previous section to advertise a new isotonic fitness drink. Who do they choose?

2 Listen again and complete these sentences with names or words and phrases from the box. You need to use some words more than once.

> all of them　　Cathy Freeman　　Michael Schumacher　　Raúl　　athletics
> Shaquille O'Neal　　tennis　　Venus Williams　　swimming

a) ____ isn't as good-looking as ____ .

b) ____ is more successful than ____ .

c) ____ is a bit more interesting than ____ .

d) ____ is more famous than ____ .

e) ____ isn't as interesting as ____ .

f) ____ is sexier than ____ .

3 Do you agree with their opinions? Change the sentences in 2 to reflect your own ideas and then compare them with a partner.

4 Work in groups. Decide on a sports personality to advertise an isotonic fitness drink. Who would you choose? Why?

Close up

Comparatives

Language reference p27

1 Test your comparatives! Look at the adjectives in the box and put them in the correct column according to how the comparative is formed. There are three adjectives in each column.

> happy　　successful　　sad　　bad　　strong　　nice　　interesting　　lucky　　far　　wet

+ -er / -r	double letter + -er	– y + -ier	irregular	more + adjective
kind → *kinder than*	*thin* → *thinner than*	*sexy* → *sexier than*	*good* → *better than*	*famous* → *more famous than*

2 Refer to the table of sports statistics. Complete the sentences using the comparative forms of the adjectives + *than*.

a) Shaquille O'Neal (tall) Raúl.
   Shaquille O'Neal is taller than Raúl.

b) Venus Williams (heavy) Michael Schumacher.

c) Inge de Bruijn (young) Cathy Freeman.

d) Raúl (old) Venus Williams.

e) Cathy Freeman (light) Inge de Bruijn.

f) Venus Williams (short) Shaquille O'Neal.

	Born	Height	Weight
Cathy Freeman	16/2/73	1.64m	52kg
Shaquille O'Neal	6/3/72	2.16m	141kg
Michael Schumacher	3/1/69	1.74m	74kg
Raúl	27/6/77	1.80m	68kg
Inge de Bruijn	24/8/73	1.74m	55kg
Venus Williams	17/6/80	1.87m	76kg

3 Add *much* or *a bit* to modify the comparatives in the sentences in 2.

For example: *Shaquille O'Neal is much taller than Raúl.*

4 Use *not as* (*old/tall/heavy* etc.) *as* to compare sports personalities in the table in 2 with people in the class. Make five sentences.

For example: *Michael Schumacher isn't as tall as Marco.*

5 Test your general knowledge! Make sentences comparing the following. Use the adjective given with *a bit / much / not as … as*. The answers are on page 125.

a) London (wet) Rome.

b) The Maracana Municipa Stadium in Rio de Janeiro (large) the Stade de France (Paris).

c) The US Army (small) the North Korean Army.

d) Heathrow Airport (busy) Los Angeles International Airport.

e) Ireland (big) Cuba.

f) The Statue of Liberty (tall) the Eiffel Tower.

The schwa /ə/   **1**   [cassette icon] 17 Complete the following with the correct words to make typical expressions. Then listen and check your answers.

bat   bird   cucumber   feather   fiddle   picture

a) She's as free as a ____ .   c) He's as fit as a ____ .   e) It's as light as a ____ .
b) She's as pretty as a ____ .   d) She's as cool as a ____ .   f) He's as blind as a ____ .

2 In each expression which words contain the schwa sound? Listen again and practise the expressions. Do you have similar expressions in your language?

Fitness test

Reading   Answer the questionnaire below as honestly as you can. Calculate your score and compare your answers with a partner.

ARE YOU DANGEROUSLY **unfit?**

1 In an average day, do you ...
  a climb more than 100 stairs? YES / NO
  b do at least one hour of housework? YES / NO
  c walk or cycle to school or work? YES / NO

2 How often do you walk 5 kilometres or more?
  a Once a month.   **b** Once a week.   **c** Never.

3 How much sport do you do every month?
  a More than 10 hours.   **b** 2–9 hours.
  c Less than 2 hours.

4 How often do you spend 20 minutes or more doing an activity that makes you hot or sweaty?
  a Three or more times a week.
  b Once or twice a week.   **c** Not at all.

5 How long does it take you to walk a kilometre?
  a Less than 10 minutes.   **b** 10–20 minutes.
  c I can't walk that far.

6 How many of the following activities do you do more than once a week?
  a Go for a run. YES / NO   **b** Play a ball game. (football, volleyball, etc.). YES / NO
  c Do some aerobic exercise. (jogging, cycling, etc.) YES / NO

7 Tick the activities you often do when you're on holiday.
  a Go hiking.   **b** Go swimming.   **c** Go sightseeing.   **d** Go dancing.   **e** Lie on the beach.
  f Eat and drink a lot.

8 Do you smoke? YES / NO

just chew it

HOW TO SCORE

1 a YES: 5 NO: 0   **b** YES: 5 NO: 0   **c** YES: 5 NO: 0
2 a 3   **b** 5   **c** 0
3 a 5   **b** 3   **c** 0
4 a 5   **b** 3   **c** 0
5 a 5   **b** 3   **c** 0
6 a YES: 5 NO: 0   **b** YES: 5 NO: 0   **c** YES: 5 NO: 0
7 a 5   **b** 5   **c** 3   **d** 3   **e** 0   **f** 0
8 YES: –10 NO: 0

WHAT YOUR SCORE MEANS

20 or less: Your health and your life are in danger! You must do more exercise.

21–30: Could be worse, but not much worse.

31–40: Not bad, but could be better.

41–50: You are healthier than the average person and you probably find your life more enjoyable as a result.

51 or more: You are super-fit. Are you a professional athlete? (Or are you a liar!)

Lexis: sport

1 Choose the most appropriate alternative in the following sentences.

a) I **do / play / practise** some exercise every day – I don't enjoy it, but it keeps me fit.

b) A lot of my friends **play / go / practise** basketball – I think it's the most popular sport among young people in my country.

c) I'd love to **play / go / practise** snowboarding but I can't even ski.

d) The last time I **did / played / practised** some sport was on holiday – I **did / went / practised** swimming in the sea.

e) I **did / played / practised** a lot of tennis when I was a kid. Now I just watch it on TV.

f) I didn't enjoy **doing / playing / practising** sports at school. Our teacher was horrible.

2 How many of the sentences in 1 are true for you? Compare with a partner.

3 Work in pairs. Complete these collocation lists with either *do, go* or *play*. Add at least one more sport to each list.

a) ____ cycling	b) ____ athletics	c) ____ basketball
fishing	judo	golf
swimming		rugby
windsurfing		tennis
		volleyball

4 Complete the following sentence beginnings with collocations from 3 to make sentences about yourself. Compare your sentences with a partner.

a) I often …   b) I sometimes …   c) I don't …   d) I'd like to …

Lexis: numbers

1 ▪▪ 18 How do you say the numbers in the box? Listen and repeat.

| ¾ | 0.25 | 0.33 | 1½ | ⅛ | ¼ | 1.5 | 0.125 | ⅓ | 0.75 |

2 ▪▪ 19 Work with a partner. Make pairs of numbers with the same value from the numbers in 1. Listen and check your answers.

For example: *¾ is the same as 0.75.*

3 ▪▪ 20 How do you say the following numbers? Listen and repeat.

a) A speed: 205 km/h   128 km/h
b) A sum of money: $59m $17m
c) A big number: 97,002,440   624,112,350

d) A percentage: 8.2%   26.7%
e) A distance: 51.25 km   42.195 km
f) A football score: 4–1   3–0

4 Work with a partner and test your trivia! Which numbers in 3 are the correct answers to the following questions?

a) How fast is Venus Williams' tennis serve?
b) How much money did Michael Schumacher earn in 2000?
c) How many Mars bars do the British eat every year?
d) What percentage of the UK population trust the government?
e) What is the official distance for a marathon?
f) What was the final score in the 1998 World Cup Final when France beat Brazil?

5 ▪▪ 21 Listen and check your answers to 4.

6 Work with a partner. Student A turn to page 125. Student B turn to page 126. Follow the instructions.

Tiger Woods

1 Who is Tiger Woods? Work in groups and note down at least three facts about him.

2 The following numbers come out of a short article about Tiger Woods. Write out the numbers in their full form and then use them to complete the text.

a) 30/12/75 = *30th December 1975*

b) 1st = ____   f) 1½ = ____

c) 16 = ____   g) 50,000,000 = ____

d) ¼ = ____   h) ⅛ = ____

e) 08/04/01 = ____

3 22 Listen and read to check your answers. You can check your spellings in the tapescript on page 135.

Golfing genius

Tiger Woods was born on (1) *30th December 1975* in California, USA, of mixed heritage: he describes himself as (2) ____ black, a quarter Thai, a quarter Chinese, an eighth
5 white and (3) ____ American Indian. His father, Earl Woods, named him Tiger after a friend who saved his life in the Vietnam War.

He was only nine months old when he started to play golf and he played his first game at
10 (4) ____ years old. His father was his first teacher.

At the age of eight, he won a tournament and five more before he was (5) ____ . On (6) ____ Tiger Woods made golfing history. He became the (7) ____ golfer to win all four majors – the most
15 important tournaments – within the same year.

He is helping to make golf more popular with all ages and levels, and most people agree that he is probably the greatest
20 golfer of all time. Certainly, he is already one of the richest.

He now earns more than (8) $____ a year. He has a $100 million deal with Nike and also has
25 deals with American Express, Buick, Rolex and Wheaties.

What advice would he give prospective parents of golf champions? 'Don't force your kids into sports.
30 It has to be fun.'

The best advice he ever got? From his dad: 'Always be yourself.'

1 23 You are going to listen to a radio interview with Pauline Perkins – a big fan of Tiger Woods. Which of the following things does she tell the interviewer?

a) She has a website about Tiger Woods.

b) She writes to Tiger Woods every day.

c) She has a signed photograph of Tiger Woods beside her bed.

d) She always has a party on Tiger Woods' birthday and she puts his pictures all round the house.

e) She watches videos about Tiger Woods every night.

f) She thinks Tiger Woods is a perfect man.

g) She likes the same food as Tiger Woods.

2 Listen again and complete the sentences.

a) I think he's the ____ wonderful person in the world.

b) He's ____ greatest golfer of all time.

c) In fact, he's the ____ player to win four major tournaments in one year.

d) I hear Tiger Woods is ____ of the richest sportsmen on the planet.

e) And is it true that Michael Jordan is one ____ his best friends?

3 Pauline Perkins is mad about Tiger Woods. Work with a partner. Describe somebody or something that you are mad about.

Close up

Superlatives

MARTIN GUHL

1 Work with a partner and complete the following tasks.

a) Write out the superlative forms for the following groups of adjectives.
b) In each group, <u>underline</u> the superlative adjective which is formed in a different way from the other three.

Adjectives
1 old/rich/exciting/great
2 valuable/big/hot/thin
3 funny/interesting/sexy/happy
4 bad/far/good/talented

Superlative forms
the oldest / the richest / <u>the most exciting</u> / the greatest

2 Look at the superlative adjectives you have underlined in 1b. When do you use *most* to form a superlative adjective?

3 Work with a partner. Complete these questions with eight different superlative adjectives. Use the adjectives in 1 or your own ideas.

a) Who is _____ sports person in the world?
b) What is _____ music group of all time?
c) What is _____ place you've ever visited?
d) Who is _____ person you know?
e) What is _____ possession you have?
f) Who is _____ person in the class?
g) Where is _____ nightlife in town?
h) Who is _____ actor / actress in your country?

4 Change partners and take it in turns to ask your questions in 3. Discuss your answers.

Language reference: comparatives & superlatives

Forms with all one-syllable adjectives and some two-syllable adjectives:

1 Adjectives ending in a consonant or e.

great	greater than	the greatest
nice	nicer than	the nicest

2 Adjectives ending in a single vowel followed by a single consonant.

big	bigger than	the biggest
wet	wetter than	the wettest

3 Adjectives ending in y.

happy	happier than	the happiest
sexy	sexier than	the sexiest

4 Forms which are irregular.

good	better than	the best
bad	worse than	the worst
far	further than	the furthest

Forms with adjectives that have two or more syllables:

famous	more famous than	the most famous
interesting	more interesting than	the most interesting

Forms to make negative comparisons:
You can use *not as ... as*.
Raúl is not as tall as Venus Williams.

Forms to modify comparisons
You can use *a bit* or *much*.
Venus Williams is a bit heavier than Michael Schumacher.
Shaquille O'Neal is much taller than Raúl.

Anecdote

Think back to when you did sports at secondary school. You are going to tell your partner about it. Choose from the list the things you want to talk about. Think about what you will say and what language you will need.

☐ How many hours of sport did you do?
☐ What different sports did you do?
☐ Which sports did you like/hate?
☐ What kind of sports facilities did your school have?
☐ What sports kit or equipment did you use?
☐ What was your sports teacher like?
☐ Did you ever play for a school team?
☐ What was your best/worst sporting moment?

5 *Review 1*

Sophie & Paul

Language reviewed: question forms – word order (Unit 1); describing people (Unit 1); expressions to do with relationships (Unit 3)

Questions

blind date A **blind date** is an arrangement made for you to spend a romantic evening with someone who you have never met before.

Sophie

Paul

1 Imagine your friends have fixed up a blind date for you. Do you think they would choose somebody suitable?

2 Work with a partner. Decide on three key questions you would ask about a blind date before agreeing to go out with him or her?

For example: *How tall is he/she?*

Compare your ideas with other people in the class.

3 *Stella*, a monthly magazine for women, prints a regular feature called 'Date of the month'. The magazine arranges a blind date for two people, and then the two people write a report of their date. Work with a partner. Discuss the photos of Sophie and Paul, the two people who are this month's blind date. Do you think their date will be a success?

4 Before Sophie and Paul met, they both had to fill in a questionnaire.

a) Student A read Sophie's answers on page 127 and write out the questions.
b) Student B read Paul's answers below and write out the questions.
c) Compare your questions. Discuss any differences.

1 *(name)* What's your name?	Paul Davies.
2 *(old)*	24.
3 *(do)*	Artist and illustrator.
4 *(star sign)*	Scorpio.
5 *(tall)*	1m 85.
6 *(like)*	Funny, hard-working, romantic, but I think I'm also quite shy.
7 *(films)*	Anything with Penélope Cruz in it!
8 *(favourite)*	Penélope Cruz.
9 *(wear)*	Jeans and trainers.
10 *(free time)*	Clubbing, parties, drinking beer, the cinema, things like that.
11 *(worst fault)*	I've never had a long-term relationship. (Is that a fault?)
12 *(dream weekend)*	Staying in a hotel on an exotic beach with the girl of my dreams and then coming back home to watch England win the World Cup.

5 Student A ask Student B about Paul. Student B ask Student A about Sophie.

For example: *How old is Paul/Sophie? What does Paul/Sophie do?*

6 Does the new information about Sophie and Paul change your prediction about their blind date? Discuss with your partner.

Work with a partner. Sophie and Paul both wrote a report on their evening for *Stella* magazine.

a)   Student A read Sophie's report and answer the questions.
b)   Student B read Paul's report and answer the questions.
c)   Compare your answers to the questions. Do you think they'll see each other again?

Questions:
1   What were their first impressions of one another?
2   How do they describe each other's character?
3   How did they think the date went?

Paul's report

When I first met Sophie, I couldn't believe my eyes. She was amazing – the best-looking woman I've ever met. I thought she looked like a model. She
5   looked very fashionable, even glamorous, in a short black dress, so I was really glad I'd put my best suit on. I fancied her straight away and I think she found me attractive too.
10   I felt a bit embarrassed at first, but after a few drinks we started chatting, and then I felt more relaxed. I don't think we've really got the same sense of humour – Sophie is actually quite serious and rather difficult to
15   get to know. She wasn't very talkative and she didn't tell me much about herself. But I think she liked my jokes.

I really enjoyed the meal and the service was excellent. The waitress was very
20   helpful, and I left her a generous tip. I'll definitely go back to that restaurant again.

Sophie got tired towards the end of the meal. I wanted to go dancing, but she said she had to get up early the next day, so I
25   got her a taxi.

I think the evening went very well and I'm looking forward to seeing her again. She says she's busy for the next three months, but I'll call her then and hopefully,
30   something will happen between us.

Something funny happened when I said goodbye to her – she called me John.

Sophie's report

Paul didn't look like his photograph – I think it must be an old one. His hair was shorter, and he was wearing rather unusual clothes – a sort of stripey suit with
5   a pink shirt. At first, I thought he was wearing his pyjamas. Anyway, I thought he looked kind and friendly and he had a nice smile, but I definitely didn't fancy him!
10   He's very talkative. In fact, I didn't get a chance to say anything really. He laughed a lot at his own jokes too. At first, I thought he was really funny, but then I got a bit tired of his jokes and I wanted to
15   talk about more serious things – you know, get to know him a bit better.

During the meal, Paul paid a lot of attention to the waitress. That really put me off him and put me in a bad mood.
20   When I get angry, I go very quiet so I didn't talk very much for the rest of the evening and I was glad when the meal was finished. It was a miserable evening. I couldn't wait to get a taxi and go home. I
25   discovered one thing, though – I'm never going on a blind date again!

1   Read the advert that Paul put in the lonely hearts column of a newspaper six months later. On a piece of paper write your own advert for a lonely hearts column.

2   Fold the paper and give it to your teacher. Then take another paper and guess which student it belongs to.

time! Photo and handwriting please. South. PO Box 294.

SINGLE ARTIST, early-twenties, fit, funny, hard-working and romantic wants to meet warm, generous, attractive person for friendship and fun. PO Box 3776

BORED TEACHER 36 needs athletic partner for tennis, golf,

Vinnie & Tanya

Language reviewed: *looks* + adjective v. *looks like* + noun (Unit 1); comparison structures (Unit 4); past simple and past continuous (Unit 3); nouns and quantity expressions (Unit 2)

Listening

1 Work with a partner. You are going to hear about the man in the photograph. Before you listen, look at the picture and describe him using the four sentence beginnings and the ideas in the box.

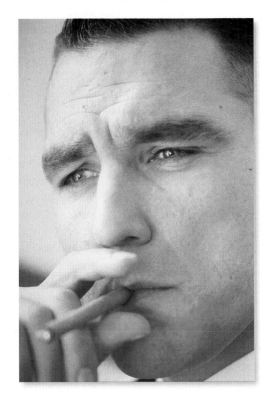

a) He looks …
b) He doesn't look …
c) He looks like …
d) He doesn't look like …

> a chat show host   a film star
> fashionable   a family man   tough
> a soccer player   fit   middle-aged
> romantic   sexy   a gangster

2 What other ways can you think of to complete the sentences?

3 ▭ 24 Listen to a radio programme about this man. In what ways were your impressions in 1 and 2 correct? In what ways were they wrong?

4 Listen again and complete these sentences. The number of words you need is indicated, and the word in brackets at the end of each sentence will give you a clue.

a) Well, yeah, he's [2] *much better known* in Britain than he is over here. (*well-known*)
b) I'd say he's still __[2]__ for his soccer skills than as an actor. (*famous*)
c) Yes, they're __[4]__ Manchester United, but … (*successful*)
d) The __[1]__ guy on the pitch? In what way? (*tough*)
e) Not really, no, but Vinnie was __[4]__ other soccer players. (*violent*)
f) … he's __[4]__ many people think. (*nice*)
g) … and he's __[5]__ people I've ever met. (*generous*)
h) Obviously, he's __[4]__ Brad Pitt, but he's a great character actor. (*good-looking*)

5 Would you like to meet Vinnie Jones? Why / Why not?

Comparison structures

1 Look at the adjectives in the box. What are the comparative and superlative forms?

> tall   emotional   good-looking   talented   sexy   punctual   optimistic
> lucky   young   generous   flexible   ambitious

2 Complete the following sentences about yourself using the comparative and superlative forms of the adjectives from the box in 1. Write down four true sentences and one false one. Swap your paper with a partner and see if they can guess which sentence is false.

For example: *I'm better-looking than my brother.*

- I'm …
- I'm a bit …
- I'm much …
- I'm not as …
- I'm the …

1 You are going to read about how Tanya got together with Vinnie. Read the article once and decide if it was 'love at first sight'.

Love at first sight?

Vinnie and Tanya first met at a cricket match when they were twelve, but they lost touch with each other soon afterwards.

5 (1) **Much / A few** years later they met again in a pub, but then their lives (2) **took / were** taking different directions. Vinnie spent (3) **many / some** time in Sweden
10 playing soccer before returning to London, where he continued his soccer career. He had a son with his girlfriend, Mylene, but the relationship (4) **didn't work out /**
15 **don't work out**. Meanwhile, Tanya (5) **got married / was getting married** to a soccer player called Steve Terry, and they had a daughter, Kaley.
20 (6) **Many / Much** years later, Vinnie was sitting in his living room with a friend. The friend, who (7) **stood / was standing** by the window, said to Vinnie,
25 'There's the most amazing-looking woman outside. Come and have a look.' Vinnie (8) **got up / was getting up**, looked out of
30 the window, and there was

Tanya, looking more beautiful than ever. She was now living in the same street as Vinnie, and (9) **a few / a little** days later Vinnie knocked on
35 the door. They got on really well and (10) **spent / were spending** the whole night talking. Tanya was now separated from her husband, and she and Vinnie became good friends. After
40 a while, the friendship changed into love, and they've been together ever since.

2 Read the article again and choose the correct alternatives.

3 25 Listen and check your answers to 2.

4 How many couples do you know who first met when they were at school? Tell your partner about them.

Vinnie Jones usually plays 'hard men' in films. Think of a character in a film you have seen recently. You are going to tell your partner about it. Choose from the list the things you want to talk about. Think about what you will say and what language you will use.

☐ What was the name of the film and who was the director?
☐ What did you know about the film before you went to see it?
☐ What was the name of the character you saw in the film?
☐ What was the character like?
☐ What happened to the character in the film?
☐ Were they the main character or did they have a supporting role?
☐ What did you particularly like or dislike about the character?
☐ Which actor played the part of the character?
☐ What did you think of the actor's performance?
☐ Would you go and see this actor in another film?

Neighbours

gossip Informal conversation, often about other people's private affairs.

Language reviewed: *looks* + adjective v. *looks like* + noun (Unit 1); past simple and past continuous (Unit 3); expressions to do with relationships (Unit 3)

1 Work in groups of four. Discuss the following questions.

- How many neighbours have you got?
- How much do you know about each neighbour?
- What do your neighbours usually like talking about?

2 Look at these pictures of the scene and the characters in a sketch called *Gossip*. Compare the pictures to your own street and your own neighbours. How different are they? Tell your partner.

Mrs Jones	**Mr Jones**	**Miss Fox**	**Mrs Kray**	**Mrs Maggs**
She lives in number 1 with Mr Jones. They don't have any children.	He works in an office. His company sells carpets.	She lives alone in number 2. She has never found a man that was good enough for her.	Her husband died ten years ago. She lives in number 3 with her mother. She loves to gossip.	She's a friend of Mrs Jones. She calls round for coffee every Monday morning.

3 🔲 26 You are going to listen to and read the sketch. What is the confusion between Mrs Jones' cat and Mrs Jones' husband?

4 Work in groups of four. You are going to perform the sketch.

a) Decide who is going to play each character. (Mr Jones and Mrs Maggs can be played by the same person.)

b) Practise your parts individually. Think about what voice your character will have, what they will look like and how they will act.

c) Perform the sketch for the rest of the class.

5 Work in groups of four. Imagine a final scene inside Miss Fox's house where the confusion is explained. Write a dialogue and compare it with other groups in the class. Perform your final scene for the rest of the class.

Gossip

Scene	A street	
Characters	Mrs Jones, from number 1	
	Mrs Maggs, a friend of Mrs Jones	
	Mrs Kray, from number 3	
5	Miss Fox, from number 2	
	Mr Jones, Mrs Jones' husband	

*Mrs Maggs rings doorbell at number 1. Mrs Jones comes
to the door crying. Mrs Kray is cleaning her doorstep at
number 3 … She tries to listen to the conversation*
10 *outside number 1.*

	Mrs Jones	(*Crying*) Oh hello, Mrs Maggs.
	Mrs Maggs	Oh dear, what's the matter?
	Mrs Jones	(*Crying*) I've lost my Sammy.
	Mrs Maggs	Who's Sammy?
15	**Mrs Jones**	My cat.
	Mrs Maggs	Where's he gone?
	Mrs Jones	(*Crying more*) I don't know – he's lost!

Mrs Maggs puts her arm round Mrs Jones.

	Mrs Maggs	Oh dear – don't cry. He'll come back.
20		When did you last see him?
	Mrs Jones	He had his dinner last night, and that's the last time I saw him. (*Crying loudly*) He often stays out at night but he always comes home for breakfast … boo hoo.
25	**Mrs Maggs**	What does he look like?
	Mrs Jones	(*Crying loudly*) He's gorgeous. He's black with white ears and a white tail. And I love him!
	Mrs Maggs	Have you any idea where he could be?
30	**Mrs Jones**	Well, the last time I saw him, he was running after that cat from the post office.
	Mrs Maggs	Right, listen to me. You go in and have a nice cup of tea, and I'll go and look for Sammy.

35 *Mrs Jones goes inside and Mrs Maggs goes off-stage.
Miss Fox comes out of number 2.*

	Mrs Kray	Did you see Mrs Jones from number 1? She looks very upset this morning.
	Miss Fox	Oh dear. It's that husband.
40	**Mrs Kray**	(*Thinks for a moment and then looks as if she's found the answer to a problem*) Ah, now I understand.
	Miss Fox	What do you mean? What do you understand?
45	**Mrs Kray**	Well, I wasn't sure what they were talking about – I couldn't hear everything, but now I understand! She was talking about her husband.

	Miss Fox	(*In a gossipy voice*) And what did she say
50		about her husband?
	Mrs Kray	She says she loves him – and she thinks he's gorgeous!
	Miss Fox	Gorgeous? How can she think he's gorgeous? He looks like a little frog.
55	**Mrs Kray**	Anyway, he's gone away with that woman from the post office.
	Miss Fox	The woman from the post office? No!
	Mrs Kray	Yes, he came home for dinner last night, and then he left.
60	**Miss Fox**	Then he left? No! (*Enjoying the story*)
	Mrs Kray	Yes. And it's not the first time.
	Miss Fox	Well, I know it's a stormy relationship. I can hear through the wall when they have a row.
65	**Mrs Kray**	Apparently, he often stays out at night. But she says he always comes home for breakfast.
	Miss Fox	(*Enjoying the story more and more*) That's terrible!!
70	**Mrs Kray**	Oh look – here he comes.

Mr Jones arrives home carrying a bunch of flowers.

	Mr Jones	Morning, ladies.
	Miss F & Mrs K	(*Innocently*) Morning, Mr Jones.

Mr Jones goes into number 1 and off-stage.

75	**Miss Fox**	He looks pleased with himself, doesn't he? Did you see the bunch of flowers he was carrying?
	Mrs Kray	Well, he feels guilty, doesn't he?

Mrs Jones comes out onto the street smiling. She is
80 *holding Sammy, her cat, in her arms.*

	Mrs Jones	He's back!

*Miss Fox and Mrs Kray look at one another and raise
their eyebrows.*

	Miss Fox	Look, I know it's none of our business, but
85		we think you'd be better off without him.
	Mrs Jones	Without who? My cat?
	Mrs Kray	Your husband.
	Mrs Jones	(*Confused*) My husband?
	Miss Fox	Look, we know how you feel, but there are
90		plenty more fish in the sea. Come along, let's go inside, and I'll make you a nice cup of tea.

*Miss Fox and Mrs Kray put their arms around
Mrs Jones and lead her into number 2.*

---

upset (adj) (line 38) = unhappy

he feels **guilty** (adj) (line 78) = he feels unhappy because he has done something wrong

it's none of our business (line 84) = it doesn't concern us

there are plenty more fish in the sea (lines 89–90) = there are many more people you can have a relationship with

6 Shop

Work in small groups. Discuss the following questions.

- When do you give presents?
- What's the best present you've ever given?
- What's the best present you've ever received?
- Do you think it's easier to buy presents for men or for women?

Reading **1** Read this article about giving and receiving presents and answer the following questions.

- a) Did a man or a woman write the article?
- b) Does he or she think men are good at choosing presents?
- c) Does he or she think women are good at choosing presents?
- d) What do women and men really want for their birthday? Do you agree?

What people really want for their *birthday*

IT was my birthday recently, and as usual I didn't get what I really wanted. I usually get a bunch of flowers, a book, a box of chocolates and electronic gadgets. My family
5 always ask me what I want, and I always tell them the same thing – I want a surprise. So this year I got flowers, books, chocolates and gadgets.

Flowers are lovely, but they hardly ever last for more than a week, and a real present is
10 something you can keep. I always look for the diamond ring hidden in the flowers, but it's never there.

Books are a waste of time, and I hate getting chocolates because I'm normally on a diet.
15 But gadgets are the worst. Most women are not interested in gadgets. Men buy gadgets for women because men love gadgets. For my birthday my husband bought me a gadget that makes bubbles in the bath, like a jacuzzi. Last
20 year he got me one of those things you put on the back of your seat and it massages your back. What's he trying to tell me? That I deserve some little luxuries? I agree with that, but the little luxuries I like are made of gold or silver.

25 But women are sensitive and intuitive so they always know the right thing to buy. Right? Wrong.

The big mistake that women make is that they usually buy clothes. They buy clothes because
30 they like them and they want other people to wear the clothes they like. 'You always wear dark colours, and I want to change you, so I'm going to buy you a brightly coloured tie or a pair of Mickey Mouse socks.'

35 This is a big mistake. Men don't usually want brightly coloured ties or silly socks. The word to remember when you're buying a present for a male is *Gadgets*. Men like anything digital or electronic. Like one of those watches that tells
40 scuba divers the time in Atlantis.

For his last birthday, I gave my husband a small torch and a Swiss army knife, the same present that I once gave to a 12-year-old nephew. He was overjoyed.

45 It's very simple. You can't go wrong if you always remember the 'G' word for men and the 'J' word for women – and that's 'J' for jewellery not 'J' for jacuzzi.

2 Rearrange the words below to make six statements from the article. You have been given the first word.

- a) A ...   can real you something is present keep
- b) Books ...   time of waste a are
- c) Most ...   in are interested women gadgets not
- d) Women ...   and intuitive are sensitive
- e) Men ...   usually silly or coloured want socks don't ties brightly
- f) Men ...   anything like electronic digital or

3 Do you agree with these statements? Discuss with a partner.

Lexis: collocation

1 *A bunch of flowers* is a phrase from the article in the previous section. Match words from column A with words from column B to make similar phrases.

A		B	
a)	a bunch of	1	socks / scissors / jeans
b)	a box of	2	cake / furniture / wood
c)	a pair of	3	cigarettes / crisps / biscuits
d)	a packet of	4	flowers / grapes / keys
e)	a piece of	5	wine / perfume / whisky
f)	a bottle of	6	chocolates / matches / tissues

2 Work with a partner. Which things in 1 are common presents in your country? Which things would be very strange or unusual presents?

Close up

Verbs with two objects

1 Re-write the following sentences as in the example. Check your answers in the article on page 34.

	subject	verb	direct object	for/to	indirect object	
	Men	buy	gadgets	for	women.	*Men buy women gadgets.*
a)	My husband	bought	a gadget	for	me.	_____ (line 18)
b)	He	got	one of those things	for	me.	_____ (line 20)
c)	I	gave	a small torch	to	my husband.	_____ (line 41)

2 Translate the sentences in 1. Identify the subject, verb, direct object, etc. in your translation. What is the most common word order for sentences like these in your language?

3 On a piece of paper write three true sentences and one false one using words and phrases from the boxes. In each sentence include a subject, a verb, an indirect object and a direct object. Exchange your piece of paper with a partner. Check the word order. Guess which sentence is false.

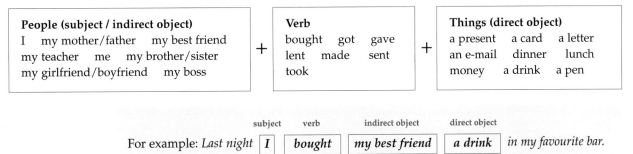

People (subject / indirect object)
I   my mother/father   my best friend
my teacher   me   my brother/sister
my girlfriend/boyfriend   my boss

\+

Verb
bought   got   gave
lent   made   sent
took

\+

Things (direct object)
a present   a card   a letter
an e-mail   dinner   lunch
money   a drink   a pen

	subject	verb	indirect object	direct object	
For example: Last night	I	bought	my best friend	a drink	in my favourite bar.

Language reference: verbs with two objects

Several common verbs can have two objects: *bring, buy, get, give, lend, make, send, show, take, teach, tell.*
With these single-syllable verbs there are two possible sentence structures:

1 Subject + verb + direct object + for/to + indirect object

*My husband + bought + a gadget + **for** + me.*
*I + gave + a small torch + **to** + my husband.*

2 Subject + verb + indirect object + direct object

My husband + bought + me + a gadget.
I + gave + my husband + a small torch.

Verbs + **for**: buy, get, make.
Verbs + **to**: bring, give, lend, send, show, take, teach, tell.

Note: With two/three-syllable verbs such as *demonstrate, describe, explain* or *suggest* you can only use sentence structure 1.

The teacher explained the exercise to us.   NOT ~~The teacher explained us the exercise.~~

Anecdote   Think about the last time you went shopping to buy a present for somebody. You are going to tell your partner about it. Choose from the list below the things you want to talk about. Think about what you will say and what language you will need.

☐ Who was the present for?

☐ What was the occasion: a birthday, an anniversary, … ?

☐ Where did you go shopping for the present?

☐ Did you know what you were going to buy or did you have to look around?

☐ What did you buy?

☐ How much did you spend?

☐ Did you buy a card too?

☐ Did the person like the present?

☐ Was it the sort of present you would like to receive?

Close up

Adverbs of frequency

1   Complete this sentence from the article on page 34 (lines 10–12) by inserting the adverbs of frequency *always* and *never* in the correct positions.

I look for the diamond ring hidden in the flowers, but it's there.

2   <u>Underline</u> all the examples of adverbs of frequency in the article on page 34. Do adverbs of frequency come before or after the main part of the verb? Is this true for *be*?

3   Find more adverbs of frequency in this word snake. Put them in order starting with *always* and finishing with *never*.

normallysometimeshardlyeveroftenoccasionallyusuallyrarely

4   How well do you know the person sitting next to you? Add an adverb of frequency from 3 to the sentences below to make true sentences about your partner.

For example: *She occasionally gets what she wants for her birthday.*
            He doesn't usually get what he wants for his birthday.

a) He/She spends more than £25 on a present.
b) He/She is positive about life.
c) He/She goes out at the weekend.
d) He/She is on time.
e) He/She has lunch at home during the week.
f) He/She goes to bed before 10.00 pm.

5   Compare your sentences in 4 with your partner and check how many are actually true. How similar/different are you?

6   Work with a partner. Use the same ideas in 4 to make sentences about your life when you were a child. Include an adverb of frequency in each sentence. Add your own ideas. Discuss how different your life is now compared to then.

For example: *When I was a child I always got what I wanted for my birthday.*

Language reference: adverbs of frequency

always, often, usually, normally, sometimes, occasionally, rarely, hardly ever, never

The most usual positions are:
- Before the main part of the verb.
  *I **always** tell them the same thing.*
  *Men don't **usually** want brightly coloured ties.*

- After the verb *be*.
  *She's **hardly ever** on time.*
  *I'm **normally** on a diet.*

How much is she wearing?

Reading **1** Look at these photographs of four famous women. Which ones do you recognise? Whose clothes do you like best? Match the photographs (a–d) with the texts (1–4).

1 Gwyneth Paltrow

- Top £2,500
- Trousers £500
- Shoes £2,000
- Bag £1,250
- Watch £3,000
- Earrings £800

Total £10,050

2 Jennifer Aniston

- Evening dress £3,000
- Bag £500
- Shoes £400
- Necklace £28,500
- Bracelet £28,000
- Earrings £10,000
- Ring £25,000
- Wedding ring £50,000

Total £145,400

3 Kylie Minogue

- Coat £22,000
- Top £400
- Trousers £400
- Belt £200

Total £23,000

4 Catherine Zeta Jones

- Evening dress £7,500
- Bag £3,000
- Silk wrap £1,500
- Shoes £400
- Earrings £725
- Bracelet £1,200
- Engagement ring £180,000

Total £194,325

2 Read the captions again and note down who is wearing the most expensive …

a) dress   b) trousers   c) top   d) shoes   e) ring   f) earrings

Check your answers with a partner.

LANGUAGE TOOLBOX

Designs:
leopard-skin   plain
patterned   striped   check

Materials:
leather   cotton   denim
woollen   silk   synthetic

Jewellery:
a necklace   a bracelet
a (wedding/engagement)
ring   earrings

3 Test your memory! Cover up the photographs and decide whether the following are true or false. Check your answers and correct the wrong information.

a) Jennifer Aniston is wearing a blue evening dress.
b) Kylie Minogue isn't wearing any jewellery.
c) Gwyneth Paltrow is carrying a bag.
d) Catherine Zeta Jones is wearing a pink silk wrap.
e) Jennifer Aniston isn't wearing a watch.
f) Kylie Minogue is wearing a striped top.
g) Gwyneth Paltrow is wearing a leopard-skin mini-skirt.
h) Kylie Minogue is wearing a matching coat and top.

4 Work with a partner. Discuss the following issues.

a) Where did you buy the clothes you are wearing today?
b) When did you last buy an item of clothing? Describe it.
c) Where is the most expensive clothes shop in your city?
d) Describe the most expensive item of clothing you've ever bought.
e) Do you think it's right to spend tens of thousands of pounds on clothes and jewellery? Why / Why not?

Close up

1 Work with a partner. Complete the statements with *Men* or *Women* as you think appropriate.

a) _____ can't stand shopping for clothes.
b) _____ don't mind spending hours and hours shopping for clothes.
c) _____ spend a lot of time going from shop to shop, comparing prices and quality.
d) _____ don't bother looking at the price tag before they buy.
e) _____ don't waste time shopping unless they really need something.
f) _____ prefer going to the dentist's to going shopping.

2 Look at the statements in 1. <u>Underline</u> all the verbs and verb phrases that are followed by a verb in the *-ing* form.

For example: *a)* Men <u>*can't stand shopping*</u> for clothes.

3 You are going to read interviews with two men about their attitudes to shopping. There are twelve cases where a verb or verb phrase should be followed by an *-ing* form. Correct the mistakes.

	Russell, 26, a writer, single	Billy, 32, a designer, engaged
1 Do you mind ~~go~~ *going* round the shops?	Not really. But after about an hour I want to go home.	It depends. I don't mind go shopping, but on Saturdays I prefer watch football on TV.
2 What kind of shops do you like go into?	Book shops. I could spend a whole day in a book shop.	I love listen to music, so music shops are my favourite.
3 Are there any kinds of shops you hate go into?	I hate supermarkets so I don't bother go into them any more. I do my shopping on the internet.	I can't stand go into shoe shops with my girlfriend. She tries on ten pairs and then buys the first pair.
4 Do you enjoy buy clothes for yourself?	Not really. I don't waste time shop for clothes unless I really need something.	I like have new clothes, but I don't enjoy try them on.

4 [cassette] 27 Listen and check your answers to 3. Do you know any men with similar attitudes to shopping?

5 Work with a partner. Take it in turns to ask and answer the questions in 3.

Language reference: verbs + *-ing* form

You usually use the *-ing* form after the following verbs and verb phrases: *can't stand, don't mind, enjoy, hate, like, love, not bother, prefer, spend time, waste time.*

I don't mind shopping.
I love listening to music.
I don't bother going into supermarkets anymore.

I'll take it

Listening **1** Russell wants to buy a present for his girlfriend. You are going to listen to the conversation he has with the shop assistant. Before you listen look at the following sentences. Put *R* if you think Russell says them. Put *SA* if you think the shop assistant says them.

a)	Can I help you?	f)	What size is she?
b)	I'm just looking, thanks.	g)	I'll take it.
c)	What sort of thing are you looking for?	h)	How would you like to pay?
d)	What colours have you got?	i)	Here's your receipt.
e)	Purple suits people with green eyes.	j)	Can she exchange it if it doesn't fit?

2 ▣ **28** Listen and check your answers.

3 How would you describe Russell's feelings? Do you feel the same way when you buy clothes for a man/woman?

4 Work with a partner. You are going to read and listen to a conversation between Roz (*R*) and a shop assistant (*SA*). Roz wants to buy a new mobile phone. Complete the conversation with an appropriate word.

SA: Can I (1) _____ you?

R: Yes, I'm (2) _____ for a mobile phone.

SA: And what (3) _____ of mobile phone are you looking for, madam?

R: Um – what do you mean?

SA: Well, what do you want to do with your mobile phone – do you want to access the internet, send text messages, play games … ?

R: No, no. I just want to make telephone calls.

SA: Right. Something like this perhaps? This model comes with a Call Register facility which keeps track of the calls you have received, missed and dialled – also, if you take our pre-pay option, you can find out how much credit you still have.

R: No, no I'm not interested in all that. I just want to make telephone calls.

SA: Fine. How about this basic model? It's very easy to use.

R: Yes … (4) _____ colours have you got?

SA: Well, we have this rather nice red one.

R: Red doesn't (5) _____ me.

SA: Red doesn't (6) _____ you??

R: That's right. I wear a lot of pink.

SA: I see. Um, well, we haven't got pink but we have this one in blue. Does blue (7) _____ you?

R: Yes, I like blue. I'll (8) _____ it.

SA: Fine. I don't suppose you're interested in the clock function.

R: No.

SA: … or voice and speed dialling …

R: No. I just want to pay!

SA: Okay, that'll be £60. How would you (9) _____ to pay, madam?

R: In cash. Here you are.

SA: Thank you madam. Here's your (10) _____ . Oh, and don't forget this catalogue that tells you all about our mobile phone accessories. I'm sure you'll …

beep

beep

beep

079046345

5 ▣ **29** Listen and check your answers.

6 Work with a partner. Do you think Russell and Roz are typical men and women?

7 Work with a partner. You are going to write your own shopping dialogue.

a) Decide on the shop and what the customer is buying.

b) Decide on the character/personality of the shop assistant and the customer.

c) Include at least six of the following eight words.

fit	help	just	pay	receipt	size	sort	suit

d) Practise your conversation and perform it for the rest of the class.

7 Job

LANGUAGE TOOLBOX

I think she works outside /
   in an office.
He probably does a manual
   job / an office job /
   a factory job.
They look like a young
   woman's / an elderly
   man's / an artist's hands.

Work with a partner. Discuss the following questions.

- Do you notice people's hands when you meet them?
- What do you think hands can tell you about a person or their life?
- Look at the three pairs of hands (*1, 2* and *3*). What can you say about each person's age, sex or job?

Listening

1 ▪▪ **30** Listen to the three people whose hands appear above. They are describing their jobs. Which speaker (*A, B* or *C*) is a midwife (= a nurse who delivers babies), a farmer, a guitarist?

2 Listen again and note which speaker …

a) has a very stressful job.
b) has never had a day off through illness.
c) works nights.
d) dropped out of school.
e) gets up very early.
f) has made loads of money.
g) works outdoors.
h) works long hours.

3 How many part-sentences from 2 can you complete by adding the name of a person you know as the subject? Tell your partner about the people you have noted down.

For example: *My friend, Peter, has a very stressful job. He's an airline pilot, and …*

Lexis:
expressions
with *hand*

1 The words and expressions in the box were used by the speakers in the previous section. Replace the <u>underlined</u> words or phrases in these sentences with an appropriate alternative from the box.

time on my hands   gives a hand   hands   On the other hand   second-hand

a) I don't think it's a good idea to buy a <u>used</u> car – they always break down.
b) I'm the kind of person who likes to be busy all the time. I get bored if I have too much <u>spare time</u>.
c) I don't like it when someone <u>gives</u> me a baby to hold – I don't know what to do!
d) I love going to the city for shopping. <u>But</u> I'm very happy I live in the country.
e) My father rarely <u>helps</u> with the housework.

2 Are any of the sentences true for you? Compare your answers with a partner.

Reading

1   Work in small groups. Check the meaning of these jobs in a dictionary. You are going to read an article entitled *Nightmare jobs*. Discuss the sort of bad experiences you could have in these jobs.

actor	au pair	factory worker	hairdresser	telesales person	vet

2   Read the article and compare your ideas in 1 with the stories each person tells. Were any of your ideas similar?

Nightmare jobs

Sally: a vet

What's the worst thing that has ever happened in your job?
Probably the dog that bit me. It
5   wasn't a big one – I don't mind the big ones. The small ones are the worst. It gave me a very nasty bite.

Have you ever done any other jobs?
Yes, I did various jobs when I was a student. One
10   summer I did fruit-picking in France, Spain and Greece.

What's the worst job you've ever done?
I worked as an au pair for a rich family in New York. I never had a day off and I had to do
15   everything – cooking, cleaning, shopping – *and* look after their horrible children. I left after two weeks and got a job as a waitress in an Italian restaurant.

William: a hairdresser

20
What's the worst thing that's ever happened in your job?
The first time I cut somebody's hair, I cut one side too short, so I had to cut the other side to match.
25   When the woman saw how short her hair was, she started crying. I felt terrible.

Have you ever done any other jobs?
Yes, I've done lots of stupid ones! For instance I've sold ice-cream on the beach and handed out
30   publicity flyers in the street.

What's the worst job you've ever done?
Telesales! You have to telephone people and try to sell them doors and windows. Work conditions are terrible – you can't have a break, and if you
35   want to go to the toilet, you have to ask for permission, and then they time you! Nightmare.

Rob: an actor

What's the worst thing that's ever happened in your job?
40   So many bad things have happened – but I think my worst moment was when I read my first bad review in the newspaper. They wrote terrible things about me, and I was so upset. Now I don't read my reviews any more.

45   **Have you ever done any other jobs?**
Oh yes. I've done hundreds of jobs over the years. Before I got my first big part, I was working as a waiter.

What's the worst job you've ever done?
50   The worst job I've ever done was at an egg-packing factory. I stood for hours and hours at the end of a conveyor belt, putting eggs
55   into boxes. It was noisy, boring, and worst of all, the smell was disgusting – I've never eaten an egg since.

3   Read the article again and find words to complete the sentences below. The first letter of each word has been given to you.

   a)   The boss had a very n____ temper and he was always shouting at me.
   b)   I never had any time o____ : I even had to work at weekends!
   c)   I had to work non-stop from nine to six without having a proper b____ .
   d)   I wasn't allowed to do anything at all without asking the boss for p____ .
   e)   The machines were so n____ that I couldn't hear myself speak.
   f)   The conditions were d____ ! I had a shower every day as soon as I got home.

4   Work with a partner. Discuss these questions.

* Do you know anybody who has had to work under conditions like these?
* What are the worst conditions you've had to work under?
* What do you think is the worst job in the world?

Close up

Language reference p43

Verb structures p129

Present perfect simple

1 Work with a partner. Look at these two sentences from the article in the previous section and answer the questions.

1 'Yes, I did various jobs when I was a student.'
2 'Oh yes. I've done hundreds of jobs over the years.'

a) Which sentence refers to a completed action in 'finished' time. What is the name of the tense used?
b) Which sentence refers to a completed action in time 'up to now'. What is the name of the tense used?
c) How do you form the affirmative, negative and question forms of the tense you identified in *b*?

2 Put the time expressions in the box under the appropriate heading. Add three more time expressions of your own under each heading.

when I was a student   over the years   recently   a few years ago   last week
today   never   yesterday   in 1999   this week

'Finished' time	Time 'up to now'
when I was a student	*over the years*

'Really, thanks a lot. It's the best party we've been to all night.'

3 Complete these sentences with a time expression from 2, or one of your own. Choose the appropriate tense and try to make all the sentences true for you. Compare your sentences with a partner.

For example: *a) I met a lot of interesting people when I was in Tokyo.*

a) I **'ve met / met** a lot of interesting people …
b) I **haven't been / didn't go** to the beach …
c) I **'ve bought / bought** a great CD …
d) I **'ve spent / spent** too much money …
e) I **haven't seen / didn't see** any good films …
f) I **'ve done / did** a lot of silly things …

4 Divide the irregular verbs in 3 into two groups: Group A where the past simple and past participle forms are the same; and Group B where they are different.

Group A			Group B		
Infinitive	Past simple	Past participle	Infinitive	Past simple	Past participle
meet	*met*	*met*	*go*	*went*	*been*

5 Add the following verbs to the appropriate group in 4. There are a total of eight verbs in Group A and twelve verbs in Group B.

bite   choose   drive   eat   feed   give   hear   hide   sell   sleep   stick
take   wear   write

6 Work with a partner. Make questions from the following prompts.

a) best or worst / holiday / go on   *What's the best holiday you've ever been on?*
b) best or worst / meal / eat
c) best or worst / joke / hear   e) best or worst / T-shirt / wear
d) best or worst / car / go in   f) best or worst / party / go to
                                          g) best or worst / bed / sleep in

7 Choose three questions from 6 and ask your partner. Find out as much as you can.

Language reference: present perfect simple

The present perfect has several uses, but in all cases it shows a connection between the past and now. You can use the present perfect simple to describe completed actions that have taken place in time 'up to now'. In contrast, if you want to describe a completed action in 'finished' time then you must use the past simple.

Time 'up to now'

The past	Now

*I've done a lot of silly things **in my life**.*

Here are some time expressions which describe time 'up to now': *today, this week, recently, never, over the years.* When these time expressions refer to the time up to now, we usually use the present perfect.

*My brother's **never been** to a pop concert.*
*I **haven't seen** any good films **recently**.*

'Finished' time

The past	Now

*I did a lot of silly things **when I was a child**.*

Here are some time expressions which describe 'finished' time: *yesterday, last month, when I was a student, in 1990, a few minutes ago.* With these time expressions we always use the past simple.

*She **called** you **a few minutes ago**.*
*I **didn't go** to the beach **last summer**.*

Class experience

1 Read through *At least once in their lifetime ...* and complete the sentences with the names of people in the class. You must use everybody's name at least once. Write more sentences if you need to.

At least once in their lifetime ...

1 ____ 's been to an opera.
2 ____ 's travelled to two other continents.
3 ____ 's been to the cinema alone.
4 ____ 's given a speech in public.
5 ____ 's worked abroad.
6 ____ 's bought an original piece of art.
7 ____ 's broken someone's heart.
8 ____ 's broken the speed limit.
9 ____ 's changed a baby's nappy.
10 ____ 's organised a party for somebody.
11 ____ 's ...

2 Are your sentences true? Ask the people whose names you have written down.
For example: *Verónica, have you ever been to an opera?*
Paul, how many other continents have you travelled to?

3 Which person in the class wrote the largest number of true sentences?

4 How many things on the list have *you* done?

Youth versus experience

Listening

1 Work with a partner. You are going to listen to a radio interview with Mr Reynold. Look at the photograph and discuss possible answers to the following questions.

a) What sort of company does Mr Reynold work for?
b) When did he start working for the company?
c) How old is he?

2 31 Listen and check your ideas in 1.

3 Listen again and decide if these statements are true or false. Correct the false statements.

a) Mr Reynold never forces anybody <u>to retire</u>.
b) The oldest <u>employee</u> at Reynold's is 97.
c) Reynold's pays <u>a decent salary</u>.
d) Employees get five <u>weeks' paid holiday</u>.
e) All the staff are over the <u>retirement age</u>.
f) Mr Reynold's secretary Edith <u>handed in her notice</u> because she wanted to get married.
g) Mr Reynold has never had any reason <u>to fire</u> anyone.
h) Mr Reynold's brother is going to <u>run</u> the business from next year.

Lexis: employment

1 Use appropriate words and expressions <u>underlined</u> in 3 above to complete these statements.

a) Everybody should get six ____ a year.
b) Nurses and teachers don't get ____ . The government should pay them more.
c) The official ____ should be the same for men and women.
d) If you don't want ____ you should be able to continue working.
e) Managing directors who ____ large corporations earn far too much money.

2 Work in small groups. Discuss the statements in 1. Do you agree or disagree?

Anecdote

Think about a retired person you know well. You are going to tell a partner about them. Choose from the list below the things you want to talk about. Think about what you will say and the language you will use.

☐ What is their name?
☐ How do you know them?
☐ How long ago did they retire?
☐ How old were they when they retired?
☐ What did they do for a living?

☐ How many different places did they work during their career?
☐ What sort of things have they done since they retired?
☐ Do you think they are happier in retirement than in work?

Presentation

Letter of application

1 Read this letter of application for a job at Reynold's Department Store. Use the words and expressions in the box to improve the parts of the letter that are <u>underlined</u>.

> (enclosed)   Sir or Madam   a new challenge   look forward to hearing
> would like to apply for   reached retirement age

45 Walpole Rd
Bournemouth BH1 4EH

Reynold's Department Store
100–105 Wimbourne Rd
Bournemouth BH2 6TG   6th July 2002

Dear (1) <u>Mr or Mrs</u>
I saw your advertisement for a job as sales assistant in your garden furniture department and I (2) <u>want</u> the job.

   I am an experienced shop assistant and I have worked in many different departments. Please see my curriculum vitae (3) <u>in the same envelope</u> for more details.

   I started working in shops when I was twenty-one, forty-five years ago. I left my last job six years ago when I (4) <u>got too old</u>, but I get terribly bored at home. I feel I am ready for (5) <u>new things</u> now.

   I would be available for an interview at any time, even at short notice.

   I (6) <u>can't wait to hear</u> from you.

Yours faithfully,

Edna Smith

Edna Smith (Miss)

2 Write your own letter of application for your dream job.

Presenting yourself

1 Read this self-introduction. Imagine you are attending a training course and you are going to introduce yourself to everybody in the group. Think about how you will say the information.

Good morning. Let me introduce myself. My name's Lourdes Rivas and I work for British Airways. As you probably know we are a major international airline. I'm based at Sondika airport in Bilbao where I'm in charge of sales and promotion. I'm looking forward to doing this course.

2 Work with a partner. You are going to re-write this self-introduction in order to make it easier to say. Follow these instructions. The first few lines have been done for you.

> Good <u>mor</u>ning. //
> Let me introduce myself //
> My name's Lourdes / Rivas //
> and I work for British Airways //

a) Insert / / where you think there should be a pause and start a new line.
b) <u>Underline</u> the stressed word(s) or syllable(s) in each line.
c) Insert / between words that you need to say very clearly.

3   32 Listen and repeat after the recording.

4 Prepare your own self-introduction or invent one. Write out the information using the techniques above. Introduce yourself to the rest of the class.

8 *Rich*

Money

Song

1 Work with a partner. Look at the lines of the song, *Money*. Choose the most appropriate alternative to complete the first two lines of each verse.
(Note: *it don't = it doesn't*)

2 ▭ **33** Listen to the song and check your answers to 1.

3 Which sentence best describes the singer's attitude to money.

 a) Money can buy love.
 b) Love is more important than money.
 c) Money is the most important thing in life.

4 Work with a partner. Discuss these questions.

 a) What is your opinion about the singer's attitude to money?
 b) Do you know anybody with similar opinions?
 c) How would you describe your own feelings about money?

5 What do the following sayings mean? How many 'money' sayings can you think of in your language? Which sayings do you like best?

 'Money talks.'
 'Money doesn't grow on trees.'
 'Time is money.'

The best things in life are
 (1) **expensive / free / dangerous**.
But you can keep them for the birds and
 (2) **bees / flies / ants**.
Now give me money.
That's what I want.
That's what I want, yeah.
That's what I want.

Your lovin' gives me a
 (3) **thrill / headache / lift**.
But your lovin' don't pay my
 (4) **rent / bills / taxes**.
Now give me money.
That's what I want.
That's what I want, yeah.
That's what I want.

Money don't get everything, it's
 (5) **true / interesting / funny**.
What it don't get, I can't
 (6) **believe / use / understand**.
Now give me money.
That's what I want.
That's what I want, yeah.
That's what I want.

Now give me money.
Whole lot of money.
Yeah, I want to be free.
Whole lot of money.
That's what I want.
That's what I want, yeah.

The Beatles

The Beatles (1960–70) were the most successful band of all time. They sold over one billion records. *Money* was one of their earliest songs.

Millionaires

Reading 1 Work in small groups. Discuss these questions.

- What different ways are there of becoming a millionaire?
- How many millionaires can you name?
- How did they make their money?

2 Read the article about three millionaires and match the adjectives in the title (*good, bad, extremely generous*) to the people in the photos.

The good, **the bad** and
the extremely generous

When do you have enough money? How many yachts, limousines and luxury homes can one millionaire use? What can rich people do with all that money? They can't take it with them when they die ... or can they?

5 **Brian Williamson**, one of Britain's richest men, thinks he can. He has spent £40 million on building a palace inspired by Versailles and the White House. But he isn't planning to live in it 10 – not while he's still alive anyway. When he dies, he will be buried in it with his art and furniture collection. It is a monument to himself. Williamson managed to make his money by investing in property. He was a millionaire by the age of 22. He 15 has five children by three different mothers, but his children will not inherit any of his fortune. 'The purpose of Arlington Palace,' says Williamson, 'is to take my money with me when I die and 20 to make sure that nobody else gets their hands on it.'

Eric Miller has a rather different attitude to money. 25 When he retired, he sold his business and made a very large profit. He then moved out of his seven-bedroom house and moved into a caravan at the end of his garden. He donated the 30 house to the Catholic church, so that it could be used as a holiday home for disabled children. 'All my life I've been worried about the poor,' explains Mr Miller. 'I don't want to be selfish. I'm quite happy living in my caravan.'

35 For **Mike and Kathy Dawson** it's simple: the more they earn, the more they give away. Ten years ago, they were earning enough to own three 40 large houses, several expensive cars and still save some money each month. Then their employer doubled their salary making them into millionaires. At this point they decided that 45 they didn't need any more money to live on and chose to give it away. Each month they give away any extra money they make to children's charities around the world. 'I believe you become a millionaire,' says Mike Dawson, 'when you give away £1 million.'

3 Which millionaire do you most sympathise with? Discuss with your partner.

Lexis: money expressions 1 Read through the article again and <u>underline</u> all the words and expressions that are associated with money.

2 Use the words and expressions you have <u>underlined</u> in 1 to complete these questions. The first letter of each missing word has been given to you.

a) What's the most money you've ever s____ on an item of clothing?
b) Is it possible to m____ a lot of money in your job (or the job you want to do)?
c) Have you ever sold something and m____ a large profit?
d) Do you e____ more than you spend or spend more than you e____ ?
e) Do you try to s____ some money every month or do you spend it all?
f) Mike Dawson believes that you become a millionaire when you g____ away £1 million. Do you agree?

3 Work with a partner. Ask and answer the questions in 2.

Going solo

1 Work with a partner and discuss these questions.

- What is the most popular band at the moment in your country?
- What sort of music do they play and how many hits have they had?
- What sort of future do you think the band has? Will they stay together or split up? Why?

2 Read the extract from a TV guide. Who is Matt McKay and why is he giving an interview?

PICK OF THE DAY
Channel 7, 8.30 pm

A hole in the Ozone

At first, it was a dream come true for Matt McKay, lead singer of chart-topping boy band, *Ozone*. Matt McKay always wanted to be a pop star. He was only 17 when he joined boy-band, *Ozone*, as lead singer. A year later, *Ozone* had their first number one hit. By the time he was 20, Matt was a millionaire. *Ozone* concerts sold out overnight and the future looked rosy.

Then Matt announced that he was leaving the band. At the height of their success, he suddenly gave it all up.

In Matt's first interview since the split, he talks openly about his decision to leave *Ozone* and his plans for the future.

Rick   Dean   Matt

3 [cassette] 34 Listen to the first part of the interview with Matt McKay. Tick (✔) the reasons he gives for leaving the band.

a) He didn't like the other members of the band.
b) He didn't have any freedom.
c) He was bored with singing and dancing.
d) He couldn't go out or have relationships.
e) He didn't make any money.
f) The people he met were only interested in his money.

4 In the second part of the interview, Matt talks about his plans for the future, and the lessons he has learnt from the past. Before you listen, match each verb in column A with the most suitable phrase from column B. In some cases more than one answer is possible.

A		B	
a)	carry on	1	a solo career
b)	pursue	2	money on stupid things
c)	employ	3	singing
d)	waste	4	my own songs
e)	spend	5	the kind of music I like
f)	forget	6	a decent manager
g)	write	7	the same mistakes again
h)	play	8	more time with my family
i)	make	9	my real friends

5 [cassette] 35 Work with a partner. Tick (✔) the things in the list in 4 you think Matt is going to do. Put a cross (✗) by the things you think he is not going to do. Listen and check your answers.

6 Which would you prefer to be: a) rich; b) famous; c) rich and famous. Tell your partner and give reasons.

Close up

(be) going to

Language reference p50

Verb structures p130

1 Correct the mistakes in these sentences.

a) 'I going to carry on singing.'
b) 'I'm definitely not go to forget my real friends.'
c) 'What kind of music are you going play?'

2 Work with a partner. Complete the following situations by answering the questions in *italic* with your own ideas. Read out one of your completed situations to the class.

a) Last year's holiday was a disaster. *What happened?*
    This year, we've decided to go somewhere else. *What are you (not) going to do?*

b) My last exams were a disaster. *What happened?*
    This year, I've decided to prepare for them properly. *What are you (not) going to do?*

c) The last party we held was a disaster. *What happened?*
    This time we've decided to prepare it differently. *What are you (not) going to do?*

d) My last relationship was a disaster. *What happened?*
    This time I've decided to do things differently. *What are you (not) going to do?*

3 Work with a partner. How many decisions have you already made about the rest of today / this week / this month / this year / your life? Use the prompts below and your own ideas to ask and answer questions about the decisions you have made.

Question				Answer	
What	are you going to	do	after the lesson		I've no idea.
Where		go	this evening	**✗** (You don't know.) →	I haven't
		be	tomorrow	**?**	decided yet.
			this weekend		
			next summer	**✓** (You know.) ⟶	I'm going to …
			for the New Year		

Listening **1** 📼 36 The poster advertising Matt McKay's European concert tour has some mistakes in it. Listen to the radio interview and write *Cancelled* by the three concerts Matt is *not* doing.

In Europe MATT McKAY

UK 4, 5, 6 Nov
~~IRELAND 8 Nov~~ Cancelled
GERMANY 9, 10, 11 Nov
HOLLAND 12 Nov
BELGIUM 13 Nov
LUXEMBOURG 14 Nov
DENMARK 15 Nov
FRANCE 24, 25 Nov
SWITZERLAND 26 Nov
CROATIA 28 Nov
SPAIN 29, 30, Nov

Single out today: 'I'M THE ONE' available now in all good music stores www.mattmckay.com

2 Use words from the interview in 1 to complete these sentences. Listen and check your answers.

   a) I can't remember when I last bought a s____ . I usually download songs from the internet these days.
   b) When I buy a new a____ , I usually like only one or two of the songs on it.
   c) I don't like g____ where you have to sit down – I prefer to dance.
   d) The last time my favourite band went on t____ , I saw two of their concerts.
   e) I'll never be one of Madonna's biggest f____ . I just don't like her music.
   f) I have no idea what's top of the c____ at the moment.

3 Find out how many of the sentences in 2 are true for your partner.

Close up

Present continuous

Verb structures p130

1 Look at the three quotes in the present continuous. Which sentences refer to arranged future events? Which sentence refers to a present event?

   a) 'Your first solo single **is coming out** tomorrow.'
   b) 'Matt McKay … **is sitting** here with me in the studio today.'
   c) 'We**'re starting** a European tour next week.'
   d) 'We**'re having** a short holiday the following week.'

2 You are extremely rich and famous! Below is your diary for next week. Copy it and fill it in with at least one appointment for each day of the week. Use your imagination.

3 Work as a whole class. Follow these instructions, using your diary from 2.

   • Choose three times in the week when you would like to arrange to do something with other students.
   • Go round the class and find out who is free at these times.
   • Make arrangements to do something with the people who are free and note the arrangements in your diary.
   • Tell the class what you are doing and who you are doing it with.

4 Work with a partner. How different is your life from the life you described in 2 and 3? Think about your real arrangements for next week and say what you are doing.

MONDAY
10.30am Massage

TUESDAY
7pm – fly to Paris for dinner at the Ritz

WEDNESDAY
1pm – lunch with Madonna and Guy

THURSDAY

FRIDAY

SATURDAY

SUNDAY

Language reference: future forms

(be) going to and the present continuous are common ways of talking about the future.

(be) going to

You use this to talk about your future intentions (things you have decided to do).
I'm going to carry on singing.
I'm not going to forget my real friends.

Present continuous

You use this to talk about future arrangements (eg appointments and organised events).
Are you doing anything for lunch today?
We're starting a European tour next week.

Note: You can also use *(be) going to* to talk about future arrangements.

Now give me money (that's what I want)

Reading　**1**　Read the information on the Prince's Trust website. What can the Trust help you to …

　　a)　get?　b)　improve?　c)　do?　d)　learn?　e)　buy?　f)　start?

Prince's Trust

Address: http://www.princes-trust.org/

The Prince's Trust
get help and a grant

If you are aged 14–30 and looking for a chance to improve your skills or get into work . . .

The Prince's Trust could pay for you to do a training course to help you learn new skills. We could buy you the equipment you need. Talk to us – we'll help you move forward with your plans. Since 1983, over 40,000 young people have started their own businesses with our support. Film and TV celebrities help the Prince's Trust as 'Ambassadors'*. They help us by attending events and visiting our programmes and courses. (*Geri Halliwell, The Corrs, Ricky Martin, Phil Collins, Pierce Brosnan.)

2　Can you apply for this kind of help in your country? Where?

Writing　**1**　Work with a partner. Imagine you want to start a business together and you want to apply for a grant from the Prince's Trust. Discuss the following questions.

> **grant** Some money that the government or an organisation gives you for a specific purpose and does not ask you to pay back.

　　a)　What sort of business would you like to start? Choose from ideas in the box below or choose your own idea.

> a band　　a website for English students　　a sports club　　a photography studio
> a window-cleaning business　　a baby-sitting service　　a pizza delivery shop

　　b)　What would you need to set up the business? Equipment? Training?

2　Three people made applications for grants from the Prince's Trust. Read their summaries about what they want to achieve. Which is the best application? Why?

a　I'm going on holiday to Ibiza in four weeks. Before I go, I want to earn some cash. My idea is to clean people's windows in the neighbourhood. My mate, Dave, has got a van, but we haven't got any ladders. Does the Prince's Trust pay for things like that?

b　I dance in an Irish folk group that is based in North London. We are giving a charity performance for the local old people's home at the end of the month and we need new shoes. There are twenty-four of us! Can you help?

c　I have completed a three-year course in computer skills and web design and I have gained some work experience in the UK, Holland and the USA. I would like to apply for a grant to set up an international employment agency on the world wide web. This agency would specialize in finding jobs for young people who want to gain work experience abroad. To do this, I need to rent an office, buy computer hardware and software and employ one person as a marketing manager. Please see my detailed business plan attached. I believe there is a big market for the kind of services my company would provide and I would be grateful if you could give serious consideration to my application.

3　Work with the same partner as in 1. Plan out and write your own summary about what you want to achieve to complete your application.

4　Decide which application in the class is most likely to succeed.

9 Rules

Reading

1 Work with a partner. Have you ever read a 'self-help' book? Did it help? What is the most important book you have ever read?

2 Read this page from an online bookshop about a 'self-help' book called *The Rules*. Who is the book for?

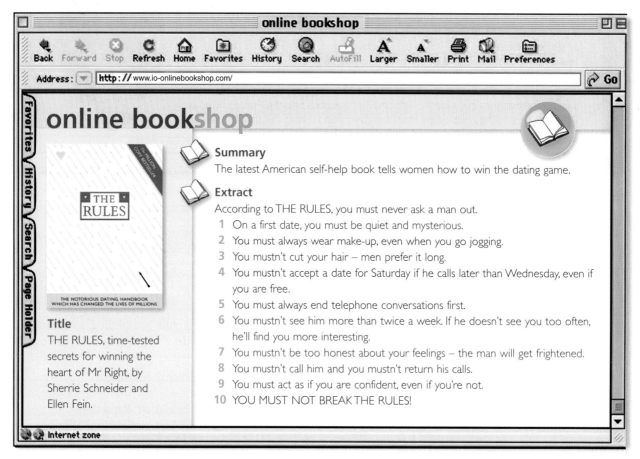

online bookshop

Title

THE RULES, time-tested secrets for winning the heart of Mr Right, by Sherrie Schneider and Ellen Fein.

Summary

The latest American self-help book tells women how to win the dating game.

Extract

According to THE RULES, you must never ask a man out.
1 On a first date, you must be quiet and mysterious.
2 You must always wear make-up, even when you go jogging.
3 You mustn't cut your hair – men prefer it long.
4 You mustn't accept a date for Saturday if he calls later than Wednesday, even if you are free.
5 You must always end telephone conversations first.
6 You mustn't see him more than twice a week. If he doesn't see you too often, he'll find you more interesting.
7 You mustn't be too honest about your feelings – the man will get frightened.
8 You mustn't call him and you mustn't return his calls.
9 You must act as if you are confident, even if you're not.
10 YOU MUST NOT BREAK THE RULES!

3 Do you agree with any of the rules from the extract of *The Rules*? Do you know anybody who would like to buy this book? Would you like to buy this book? Discuss with a partner.

Lexis: describing character

1 Find opposite adjectives in the extract from *The Rules* to complete these pairs.

a) cheerful ≠ miserable
b) talkative ≠ ____
c) sensible ≠ silly
d) open ≠ ____
e) ____ ≠ boring

f) hard-working ≠ lazy
g) ____ ≠ dishonest
h) optimistic ≠ pessimistic
i) sensitive ≠ insensitive
j) ____ ≠ insecure

2 37 Listen and check your answers. Underline the stressed syllable in each word. Practise saying the words.

3 Which of the adjectives in 1 describe your Mr or Ms Right and which ones describe your Mr or Ms Wrong? Add more adjectives if necessary.

4 Compare your answers with a partner. Do you have the same ideas?

Reading   **1**   Read these readers' reviews of *The Rules* and match an appropriate heading (*a–d*) with each review (*1–4*).

a)   *The Rules* are dishonest.   c)   *The Rules* are sexist.
b)   *The Rules* are old-fashioned.   d)   *The Rules* are right.

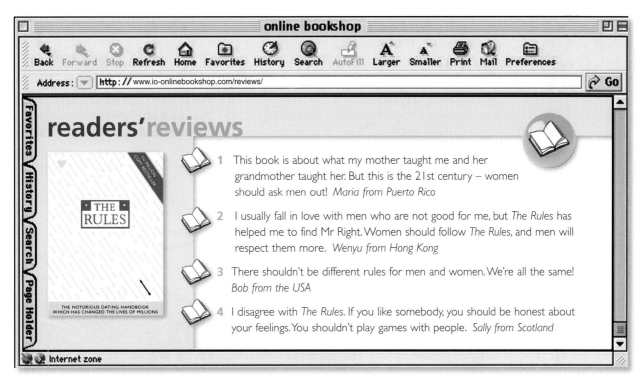

2   Which review do you agree with most? Compare with your partner.

Close up

must &   **1**   Work with a partner. Read the sentences below. Which sentence offers advice or a
should   suggestion? Which sentence expresses an order or an obligation?

Language reference p55

Verb structures p130

a)   You must follow *The Rules*.
b)   You should follow *The Rules*.

2   Write the negative and question forms of the two modal sentences in 1.

3   Work with a partner. Imagine a popular men's magazine has asked you to write men's rules for successful dating. Complete *The Men's Rules* with *must* or *mustn't* as appropriate. Add one more rule of your own.

a)   You _____ arrive on time for dates – women hate it when you keep them waiting.
b)   On her birthday, you _____ give a woman a gold ring – she'll think you want to marry her and that's exactly what she wants. Be safe – give her flowers.
c)   You _____ pay when you go out. Women want to be equal, but not that equal!
d)   You _____ be funny. You may be good-looking, well-dressed and have the brains of Einstein, but if you can't make them laugh, forget it.
e)   You _____ talk about other beautiful women, even famous ones. She'll remember, and years later, when you make a comment about her cooking, she'll tell you to get Julia Roberts to make your lunch.

4   Work with a partner. Do you agree with any of *The Men's Rules* in 3?

5   Work in small groups. Discuss your real opinions about what makes a successful date. Write down a list of good advice for men and women. Include at least six things you think they should or shouldn't do. Compare your list with other students in the class.

Linking

1 🔊 **38** Listen and repeat the sentences below. What happens to the pronunciation of the last 't' in *must* and *mustn't* when the following word starts with a vowel? What happens when it starts with a consonant?

a) You must be quiet and mysterious.
b) You must always wear make-up.
c) You mustn't accept a date for Saturday.
d) You mustn't cut your hair.

e) You must end telephone conversations first.
f) You must pay when you go out.

2 🔊 **39** Practise saying the sentences below. Listen and check your answers.

a) You must stay in bed for a few days.
b) You mustn't open it until your birthday.
c) You must ask if you don't understand.

d) You mustn't call me at work.
e) You must stop writing now.
f) You must indicate before overtaking.

3 Who do you think is speaking to whom in 2? What is the situation? What other things could these people say to each other using *must*?
Discuss your answers with a partner.

Listening

1 🔊 **40** You are going to listen to Barbara talking about her relationship with Michael after she had read *The Rules*. What happened to the relationship? What is the title of the book she is reading now?

2 Listen again and complete these sentences with the correct alternative.

a) Barbara decided to do *The Rules* because she wanted (1) **a proper relationship** (2) **a new relationship**.
b) Barbara (1) **was too busy** (2) **had to say she was too busy** to talk to Michael on the phone.
c) The real Barbara is (1) **warm and friendly** (2) **cold and hard**.
d) Michael thought she was (1) **mysterious and fascinating** (2) **behaving like a cow**.
e) When Barbara fell in love with Michael, she (1) **wanted to** (2) **didn't want to** continue to follow *The Rules*.
f) When Michael saw the book he was (1) **angry** (2) **happy**.
g) Now Barbara wants to (1) **find a new man** (2) **stay single**.

3 What advice would you give to Barbara? Do you think she should read *The Joy Of Being Single?*

Close up

Past modals: obligation & permission

(Language reference p55)

1 Complete what Barbara said in the previous section. Use past modal structures from the box.

> I didn't have to   I could   I had to   I couldn't

Present time	**Past time**
The Rules say:	Barbara said:
'You mustn't phone him.' →	(1) ____ phone him.
'You must finish the conversation first.' →	(2) ____ finish the conversation first.

2 Work with a partner. Which modal structure in 1 means:

a) It wasn't possible for me to …
b) It was necessary for me to …

c) It was possible for me to …
d) It wasn't necessary for me to …

3 Use *had to*, *didn't have to* and *couldn't* to complete this account of a rock star's schooldays.

(Adapted from *Best of Times, Worst of Times, Sunday Times Magazine*)

Schooldays of a rock star

Bill Wyman, now in his sixties, was a member of The Rolling Stones, one of the most successful rock bands in the world. Here he tells us about his childhood.

5 'I was one of three kids out of my primary school to get a place at grammar school. I was delighted because I liked learning, but my father wasn't very pleased because I (1) ____ wear a uniform. The uniform was expensive, and we were
10 very poor. Also, I (2) ____ get a bicycle because the school was a long way from where I lived.

One day, a boy from school invited me to his house. It was a lovely house – a palace compared with mine. My father said I (3) ____ invite my
15 friend back to my house. In fact I didn't want my friends to come to my house – it was too embarrassing. We had no electricity or running water, and the toilet was in the garden.

There was no heating in the house. In winter
20 there was ice on the inside of our bedroom windows, so getting out of bed was really hard. The only good thing about it was that we (4) ____ have a bath every night. The water was too cold.

School was going well: I was about sixteen and
25 about to take my exams. But one day my father said, 'Right, I've had enough of you in that school. You're leaving.'

I (5) ____ leave school and start earning some money
30 for the family. The headmaster asked my father to let me take the exams, but he refused, and after that I (6) ____
35 go to college.

Anyway, that was the end of my education but I can't complain – after that I got into
40 music, and the rest is history!'

4 🔊 41 Listen and check your answers.

5 Work with a partner. Discuss in what ways your own schooldays were different from (or similar to) Bill Wyman's.

6 Write a short account of your partner's schooldays. Include at least one example of each of the following sentence beginnings: *He/She couldn't … , He/She had to … , He/She didn't have to …*

Language reference: obligation & permission

must & should

You use *must* when you want to give an order or express strong obligation. You use *should* when you are giving advice or expressing an opinion.
*You **must** arrive on time for school.* (= I order you to arrive on time.)
*You **mustn't** break The Rules.* (= I order you not to break The Rules.)
*You **should** be honest about your feelings.* (= I advise you to be honest about your feelings.)
*There **shouldn't** be different rules for men and women.* (= I don't think it's a good idea if there are different rules for men and women.)

Modal structures: obligation & permission

The table below summarizes some present and past modal verb structures for obligation and permission. Note that *must/mustn't* has no past form.
*I **had to** wear a uniform.*
*I **couldn't** invite my friend back to my house.*
*We **didn't have to** have a bath every night.*

	Possible	Not possible	Necessary	Not necessary
Present	*You can do*	*You mustn't (can't) do*	*You must (have to) do*	*You don't have to do*
Past	*You could do*	*You couldn't do*	*You had to do*	*You didn't have to do*

Geisha

Reading **1** Makiko is training to be a geisha. You are going to read about her training. Before you read, look at the sentences below and decide if you think they are true or false.

  a) A lot of women in Japan today want to become a geisha.
  b) A geisha has to have a different kimono for every month of the year.
  c) To become a geisha you have to study for many years.
  d) A geisha has to sing and dance for her customers.
  e) A geisha can't speak to her customers.
  f) 'A trainee geisha can go to High School.
  g) A geisha can't have relationships or get married.

2 Read the article and check your ideas in 1.

TRAINING TO BE A

Geisha

The white face, dark eyes and hair, and blood red lips: both foreigners and the Japanese are fascinated by these beautiful and mysterious women.

5 Makiko is training to be a geisha. Not many girls want to become a geisha in Japan today. Makiko's parents wanted her to go to university, study medicine and become a doctor. But Makiko's grandfather paid for her training and bought the 10 kimonos she needed. It's very expensive to become a geisha. You have to have a different kimono for each month of the year, and today a kimono costs three million yen, that's about $30,000.

15 It's a hard life for a trainee geisha. She has to leave her family and move into a special boarding house called a 'maiko house'. Here, she has to learn traditional Japanese arts such as playing instruments, the tea ceremony, flower arranging, 20 singing and dancing. She has to take many difficult tests and exams. Only the best will pass everything and become geishas many years later.

We asked Makiko to describe exactly what a geisha does.

25 'A geisha has to serve customers and also entertain them. She has to sing and dance, and make good conversation.'

Did she enjoy her life as a trainee geisha?

'I love it, but it's hard work. Sometimes I get 30 tired of wearing the kimonos and I want to put on a pair of jeans and go to school like a normal teenager. But I can't have a normal life now. I don't mind. I feel very lucky.'

And what about later – can she have a family?

35 'Of course. A geisha can have relationships like anybody else and she can get married when she chooses.'

In Japan today there are fewer than a thousand geisha, but they play an important role in 40 preserving Japanese culture and history.

3 Are there any specialist schools that train students for particular jobs in your country? What sort of qualifications do you need to get into these schools? Do you know anyone who goes to a specialist school? Tell your partner.

Lexis: education

1 Complete the following statements using words from the text.

a) More and more people are *training* to be computer programmers. (line 5)
b) Not many people want to ____ teachers nowadays. (line 6)
c) If you ____ medicine, it takes seven years to become a trainee doctor. (line 7)
d) It ____ a lot of money to go to university. (line 13)
e) When they go to university, most students leave home and ____ into student accommodation. (line 16)
f) If you fail your end of year exams, you can usually ____ them again a few months later. (line 20)
g) You can't go to university unless you ____the entrance exam. (line 21)
h) University students play an important ____ in the future of the country. (line 39)

2 Work in small groups. Do you think the statements in 1 are true of your country?

Word stress

1 Match an appropriate stress pattern with the correct column of school subjects.

a) ■ ▪ ▪   b) ▪ ▪ ■ ▪   c) ■   d) ■ ▪   e) ▪ ■ ▪ ▪

1 ■	2	3	4	5
Art Maths	English History Music Physics	Chemistry Literature Politics Geography	Biology Philosophy Technology	Economics

2 📼 42 Listen, check and repeat the answers to 1.

3 Work with a partner. Look at the school subjects in 1 and discuss which ones were …

a) the hardest to learn / the easiest to learn
b) the most boring / the most interesting
c) the least useful / the most useful.

Anecdote

Think about your favourite subject at secondary school. You are going to tell your partner about it. Choose from the list the things you want to talk about. Think about what you will say and the language you will need.

☐ What was your favourite subject at school?
☐ What was particularly special about this subject?
☐ What was the teacher's name and what were they like?
☐ What were the other students like?
☐ What was the classroom like?
☐ How many lessons did you have a week?
☐ What sort of activities did you do in the lesson?
☐ How much homework did you have to do?
☐ What sort of marks did you get in the subject?
☐ Did you learn anything which is useful to you today?

10 Review 2

Fact or fiction?

> **Language reviewed:** adverbs of frequency (Unit 6); present perfect simple (Unit 7); future forms – *(be) going to* & present continuous (Unit 8); numbers (Unit 6); verbs with two objects (Unit 6)

Appropriate language

1 An English magazine carried out a survey to find out how English people lie. Look at the six most common lies and choose the correct structure in each sentence.

   a) 'Sorry I'm late, darling. I **could / had to / should** work late at the office.'
   b) 'I **couldn't / didn't have to / mustn't** get here earlier – the bus was late.'
   c) 'You sent it last month? I **hardly ever / never / occasionally** received it!'
   d) 'I **gave up / give up / 'm going to give up**. Tomorrow. Next week. Soon.'
   e) 'You can trust me. I **always keep / often keep / never keep** a secret.'
   f) 'Thank you. That was the best meal we **ever have / had ever had / 've ever had.'**

2 ▭ 43 Work with a partner. Look at the lies and decide for each sentence who is speaking to whom. What is the situation? Listen and check your answers.

3 Work in small groups. Discuss these questions.

- Have you ever given false information to: a) your parents? b) your boss? c) an official?
- Have you ever lied about: a) your age? b) your qualifications? c) your experience?
- In what situations (if any) do you think it's okay to lie?

Listening

1 Work with a partner. <u>Underline</u> any words or phrases that you associate with the job of a customs officer.

> alcohol   blackboard   contraband cigarettes   conveyor belt   inside information
> ladder   legal limit   search   tractor

2 ▭ 44 (Parts 1 & 2) You are going to listen to a radio programme about a customs officer who works in the port of Dover in England. Listen and mark the following statements *T* (true) or *F* (false).

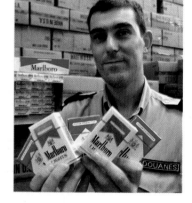

   a) The driver has driven a long way.
   b) The driver has been to a little town near Calais.
   c) The driver is getting married next week.
   d) The driver has bought some whisky for the wedding.
   e) The driver hasn't broken the law.
   f) Customs officers often have inside information.
   g) Customs officers can usually tell if someone is lying.
   h) Customs officers always catch the real professionals.

3 Rearrange these comments about liars from the radio programme so that they make sense. Then listen again to Part 2 and check your answers.

   a) look They you usually don't at   *They don't usually look at you.*
   b) hide hands often They their
   c) face a their lot touch sometimes People
   d) They little say very often

   e) too start They much sometimes saying
   f) negative use Liars more usually verbs
   g) often up voice goes Their

Speaking

1 Read the questions. Prepare two answers for each question – one true and one false.

    a) What are you doing next weekend?
    b) How often do you help with the housework at home?
    c) How much chocolate did you eat yesterday?
    d) How many foreign capital cities have you been to?
    e) When was the last time you did some exercise?
    f) Who's your favourite singer of all time?
    g) When was the first time you kissed somebody?
    h) How many times have you lied to your mother?

2 Work with a partner. Follow these instructions using the questions in 1.

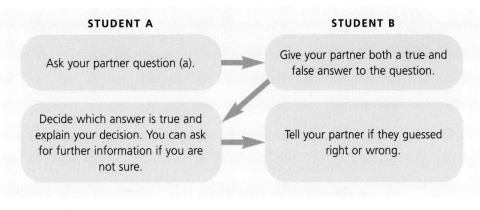

STUDENT A	STUDENT B
Ask your partner question (a).	Give your partner both a true and false answer to the question.
Decide which answer is true and explain your decision. You can ask for further information if you are not sure.	Tell your partner if they guessed right or wrong.

3 Continue taking turns until you have both asked and answered all of the questions. Who is the most successful liar?

Numbers

1 Work with a partner. Look at the following table and guess the missing numbers and countries in each category.

Top 3 whisky drinkers
(Bottles per year)
1 __(a)__ : 145,000,000
2 France: 137,000,000
3 The USA: __(b)__

Top 3 beer drinkers
(Litres per person per year)
1 __(c)__ : 160
2 Ireland: 141.3
3 Germany:
    __(d)__

Top 3 coffee drinkers
(Cups per person per year)
1 __(e)__ : 1,356
2 Denmark: __(f)__
3 Finland:
    1,293

Top 3 Coca-Cola drinkers
(Glasses per person per year)
1 __(g)__ : 343
2 Mexico: 322
3 Germany:
    __(h)__

2 45 Listen and check your answers to 1. Who made the best guesses in the class?

3 Listen again and repeat each number. Which statistic do you find the most / the least surprising?

Verbs with two objects

1 Complete the following sentences by putting the words in brackets in the correct order.

    a) The last time I went abroad ... (my family I lots of presents bought)
    b) The last time I went to dinner with friends ... (took I them a box of chocolates)
    c) The last time I went to a wedding ... (got a very expensive gift the couple I)
    d) The last time I went on holiday ... (all my friends I a postcard sent)
    e) On my last birthday ... (me my mother a big cake made)
    f) On Valentine's Day ... (gave my sweetheart me a beautiful bunch of flowers)

2 Guess how many of the sentences in 1 are true for your partner. Ask your partner to find out how many correct guesses you made.

Growing up

Language reviewed: modals of advice, obligation and permission (Unit 9); expressions to do with work and education (Unit 7, 8 & 9)

Reading   **1**   Work in groups of three. You are going to read about three generations of the Bennett family. Discuss what each of them probably said about the following topics. Write *GF* (grandfather), *S* (son) or *GS* (grandson) next to a quote under each topic.

1 Fathers	2 Family life	3 Education	4 Relationships
a 'We couldn't disturb him.'	**a** 'I didn't have to come home at a certain time.'	**a** 'My parents didn't have to support me financially.'	**a** 'We should get married one day.'
b 'I don't have to hide anything from him.'	**b** 'We had to make our own entertainment.'	**b** 'I think colleges and universities should be free.'	**b** 'We couldn't bring girlfriends home.'
c 'We had to obey him without question.'	**c** 'I could only watch TV at the weekend.'	**c** 'I had to walk to school.'	**c** 'We had to get married.'

2   Student A read about the grandfather. Student B read about the son. Student C read about the grandson. Check your answers to 1 and take it in turns to explain the reasons behind each quote.

For example: Student A – 1c) *The grandfather had to obey his father without question because he was a very strict man.*

Three generations

Three men from the Bennett family talk about how life has changed over three generations.

The grandfather (65)

When I see my son and his son
together, I think they have a
lovely relationship – it wasn't
like that in my day. My father
was very strict, and we had to
obey him without question.
   When I was a boy, I had to walk five kilometres
to school. There was no other way of getting there.
   At home we didn't have a television, so we had
to make our own entertainment. I spent all my
free time outside playing football.
   But we couldn't play football on Sundays
because we had to go to church.
   I left school when I was fourteen and went to
work in a bakery. That's where I met Mabel.
   We couldn't bring girlfriends home in those
days. We had to meet in public places. I suppose
that's why so many people got married young. I
was only nineteen, and Mabel was eighteen.

The son (44)

When I was growing up, my
father was always at work,
and when he came home we
couldn't disturb him because he
was tired.
   Because my father left school
very early and regretted it afterwards, he wanted

me to do well at school. I had to show him my
homework every night and I could only watch
television at the weekend.
   When I was eighteen I got a place at university.
My parents didn't have to support me financially
because the government gave me a grant to study.
   I didn't go home very often, even during the
holidays. I preferred spending time with my
friends, especially my girlfriends. In my last year
of university I met Louise, and we got a place
together. We had to get married when Louise
found out she was pregnant.

The grandson (19)

I've always had a very close
relationship with my dad and I
don't have to hide anything
from him.
   When I was at school, I had
a lot of freedom. When I went
out, I didn't have to come home at a certain time
– my parents trusted me.
   I'm at college now, and my parents have to pay
for my studies, but I have to work in the evenings
to pay for any luxuries I want.
   I think it's wrong that my parents have to pay
for my studies. I think colleges and universities
should be free for everybody.
   My girlfriend often stays at my parents' house,
and I sometimes go and stay with her parents.
Both our parents think we should get married one
day, but we're definitely not in a hurry.

3 Read about all three men. For each generation, note down three ways in which you think their lives were the same or different to your own, your father's and your grandfather's. Compare with a partner.

Lexis: *work* or *job*?

1 Work with a partner. Complete the following questions with *work* or *job* and then ask each other the questions.

   a) Have you ever <u>had</u> a full-time ____ ?
   b) Would you like to ____ <u>abroad</u>?
   c) Do you know anybody who has a <u>dangerous</u> ____ ?

2 Write down six more questions by replacing the <u>underlined</u> words in 1 with appropriate alternatives. Use words and phrases from the box or your own ideas.

For example: *Have you ever looked for a full-time job?*

> with children   outdoors   boring   part-time   looked for   applied for
> well-paid   from home   resigned from

3 Ask your partner your questions from 2. Find out as much information as you can.

Lexis: work expressions & collocations

1 Look at the word snake. How many different jobs can you find?

drummerfactoryworkerfinancialadvisergeishamanagingdirectorshopassistanttelesalespersonvet

2 Complete the following quotes with one of the verbs in the box. Match each quote with a job in 1.

> have   make   run   spend   take

   a) 'I ____ a living by telling people how to invest their money.'
   b) 'I didn't have to ____ any exams to get this job. It's noisy, smelly and very badly paid.'
   c) 'Sometimes I have to ____ very difficult decisions about whether or not to operate.'
   d) 'I ____ all my time on the telephone. Sometimes I can ____ over three hundred phone calls a day.'
   e) 'I can't ____ a day off during the weekend: Saturdays and Sundays are our busiest days.'
   f) 'The most important objective when you ____ a business is to ____ a profit. Nothing else matters.'
   g) 'You can ____ a lot of money if you have a hit single. Unfortunately, straight after our first hit we split up.'
   h) 'I don't mind serving the customers. But I also have to ____ good conversation, and that's really hard.'

Discussion

1 Work together as a class. Write up the names of all the jobs that you, your parents and your grandparents have done.

2 Work in small groups. Look at all the jobs you have written down in 1 and discuss the following questions.

   a) In which job can you earn the most money?
   b) In which job do you get the most days of paid holidays?
   c) Which job do you have to study longest for?
   d) In which job do you get the most training?
   e) Which job is the most stressful?
   f) Which job is the most useful to society?

Language reviewed:
All the main structures from Units 1–9.

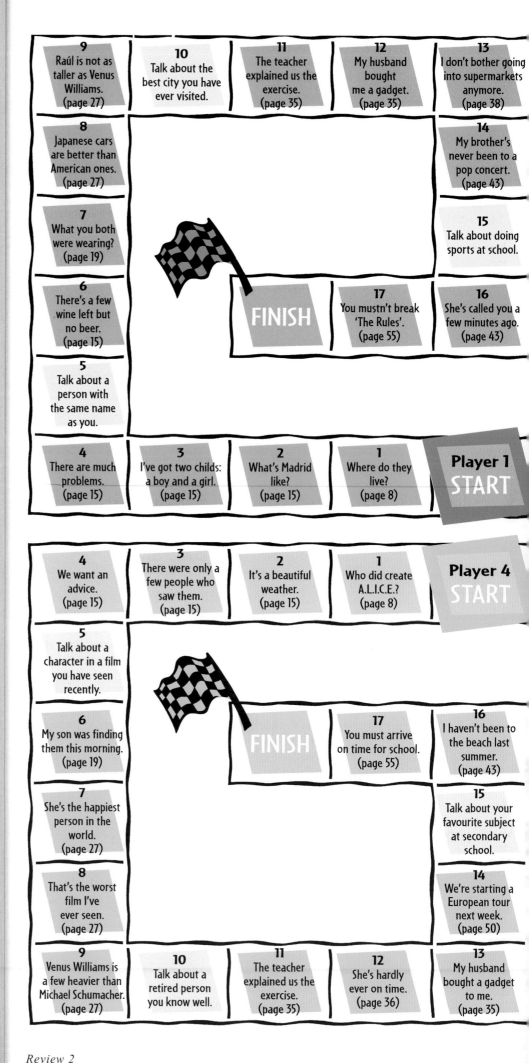

9
Raúl is not as taller as Venus Williams.
(page 27)

10
Talk about the best city you have ever visited.

11
The teacher explained us the exercise.
(page 35)

12
My husband bought me a gadget.
(page 35)

13
I don't bother going into supermarkets anymore.
(page 38)

8
Japanese cars are better than American ones.
(page 27)

14
My brother's never been to a pop concert.
(page 43)

7
What you both were wearing?
(page 19)

15
Talk about doing sports at school.

6
There's a few wine left but no beer.
(page 15)

FINISH

17
You mustn't break 'The Rules'.
(page 55)

16
She's called you a few minutes ago.
(page 43)

5
Talk about a person with the same name as you.

4
There are much problems.
(page 15)

3
I've got two childs: a boy and a girl.
(page 15)

2
What's Madrid like?
(page 15)

1
Where do they live?
(page 8)

Player 1
START

4
We want an advice.
(page 15)

3
There were only a few people who saw them.
(page 15)

2
It's a beautiful weather.
(page 15)

1
Who did create A.L.I.C.E.?
(page 8)

Player 4
START

5
Talk about a character in a film you have seen recently.

6
My son was finding them this morning.
(page 19)

FINISH

17
You must arrive on time for school.
(page 55)

16
I haven't been to the beach last summer.
(page 43)

7
She's the happiest person in the world.
(page 27)

15
Talk about your favourite subject at secondary school.

8
That's the worst film I've ever seen.
(page 27)

14
We're starting a European tour next week.
(page 50)

9
Venus Williams is a few heavier than Michael Schumacher.
(page 27)

10
Talk about a retired person you know well.

11
The teacher explained us the exercise.
(page 35)

12
She's hardly ever on time.
(page 36)

13
My husband bought a gadget to me.
(page 35)

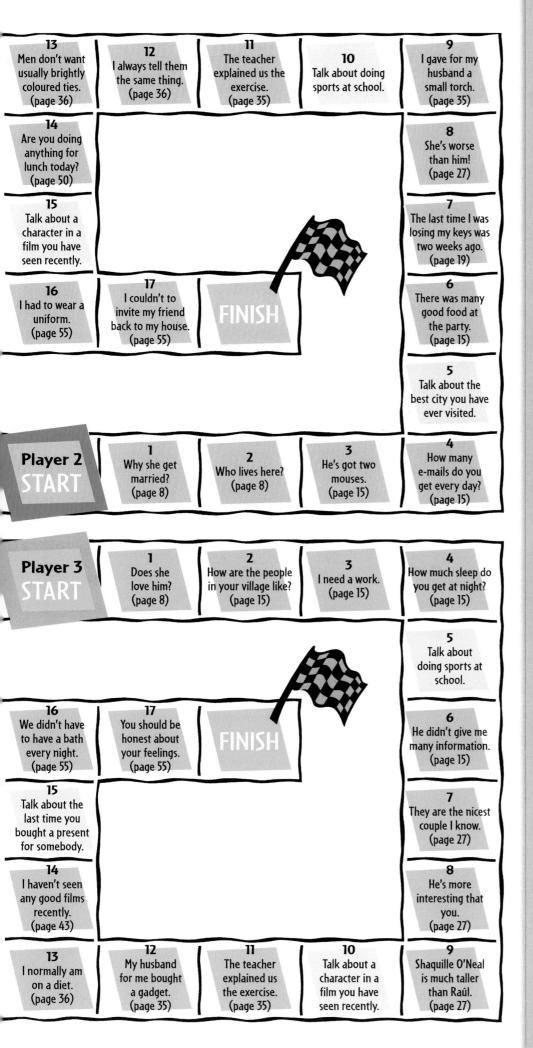

13 Men don't want usually brightly coloured ties. (page 36)

12 I always tell them the same thing. (page 36)

11 The teacher explained us the exercise. (page 35)

10 Talk about doing sports at school.

9 I gave for my husband a small torch. (page 35)

14 Are you doing anything for lunch today? (page 50)

8 She's worse than him! (page 27)

15 Talk about a character in a film you have seen recently.

7 The last time I was losing my keys was two weeks ago. (page 19)

16 I had to wear a uniform. (page 55)

17 I couldn't to invite my friend back to my house. (page 55)

FINISH

6 There was many good food at the party. (page 15)

5 Talk about the best city you have ever visited.

Player 2 START

1 Why she get married? (page 8)

2 Who lives here? (page 8)

3 He's got two mouses. (page 15)

4 How many e-mails do you get every day? (page 15)

Player 3 START

1 Does she love him? (page 8)

2 How are the people in your village like? (page 15)

3 I need a work. (page 15)

4 How much sleep do you get at night? (page 15)

5 Talk about doing sports at school.

16 We didn't have to have a bath every night. (page 55)

17 You should be honest about your feelings. (page 55)

FINISH

6 He didn't give me many information. (page 15)

15 Talk about the last time you bought a present for somebody.

7 They are the nicest couple I know. (page 27)

14 I haven't seen any good films recently. (page 43)

8 He's more interesting that you. (page 27)

13 I normally am on a diet. (page 36)

12 My husband for me bought a gadget. (page 35)

11 The teacher explained us the exercise. (page 35)

10 Talk about a character in a film you have seen recently.

9 Shaquille O'Neal is much taller than Raúl. (page 27)

HOW TO PLAY

Play the game with three, four or five players. One person in each game is the *Checker*. They don't play the game. You will need a coin and counters and an extra copy of *Inside Out* Pre-intermediate Student's Book.

1 Each player places their counter on a different square marked START.

2 Decide which player is going to start the game. The first player then tosses the coin and moves the counter along their 'road' as follows: 'Heads' = two spaces. 'Tails' = one space.

3 Players then play in turns, moving along their 'roads'. If a player lands on a grammar square (darker colour) they must read the sentence on that square. They must say if the sentence is grammatically correct or incorrect. If the sentence is incorrect, they must correct it.

4 The *Checker* will then turn to the Language reference on the page given and see if the player is right. If the player is right, they can now wait for their next turn. If the player is wrong, they must miss a turn.

For example:
Student A:
'*11 The teacher explained us the exercise. (page 35)*'
Er … I think it's correct.

Checker:
Wrong! It should be 'The teacher explained the exercise to us.' You miss a turn.

5 If a player lands on a speaking square (lighter colour), they must talk about the topic for sixty seconds. Players should be timed from the point at which they start talking so that they can have a little thinking time before they start.

6 The first player to reach their FINISH is the winner.

11 Smile

Work in small groups. Look at this expression and discuss the questions.

> Say 'cheese'!

- When do people say this?
- What do you say in your language?
- Do you find it easy to smile for photographs?

Lexis: the face **1** Use words from the photograph below to complete the following article about smiling. Choose an appropriate singular or plural form for each word.

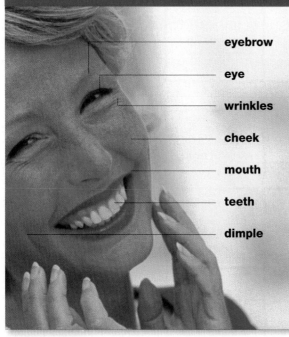

'Smile and the world smiles with you.
Cry and you cry alone.'

eyebrow

eye

wrinkles

cheek

mouth

teeth

dimple

According to research from the USA, we smile for many different reasons.

- There's the listener/response smile. When two people are having a conversation, the listener smiles to encourage the speaker.
- There's the polite smile. This is the sort of smile you make when your aunt gives you a horrible birthday present.
- There's the miserable smile. For example, when you go to the dentist, and he tells you that you need to have a (1) _____ taken out.

Very often, these social smiles are not real: they are 'fake' smiles. Fake smiles are easy to do – you just have to tighten the muscles on your (2) _____ .

But there's only one smile that is the smile of true enjoyment. This smile is extremely hard to fake. It involves the muscles at the corners of the (3) _____ and the muscles around the eyes.

When someone gives a true smile, the (4) _____ get smaller, and you see little (5) _____ around the edge. The (6) _____ go up, and on some people, (7) _____ appear in their cheeks.

The genuine smile of enjoyment not only makes us feel good, but it makes others feel good too.

2 ▭ 46 Listen and check your answers. How many different smiles are mentioned? Can you do all these smiles? Show your partner.

3 Look at the photo in 1 again and tick (✓) the features you can see.

| bags under the eyes beard beautiful teeth false eyelashes freckles |
| moustache pale skin wavy hair |

4 Which of these features do you like on a man or a woman? Describe your ideal face to your partner.

5 Work with a partner. Look at the pairs of eyes on the left. According to the text, which ones do you think are smiling? How can you tell? Look at page 125 to see the complete faces. Which ones did you guess correctly?

a
b
c

/s/, /z/ or /ɪz/? **1** 🔊 **47** Listen and repeat these nouns. In each set, <u>underline</u> the noun where the final 's' is pronounced differently from the others.

a) ears eyes cheeks legs
b) lips hands toes arms
c) dimples freckles wrinkles eyelashes

2 Put the nouns from the box into the appropriate column depending on the sound of the final 's'. Add the nouns from 1. The first ones have been done for you.

backs knees noses chins moustaches wrists heads shoulders stomachs beards

+ /s/	+ /z/	+ /ɪz/
backs	knees	noses

3 🔊 **48** Listen, repeat the words and check your answers. Which of the nouns in 2 would you not expect to use in the plural when describing someone?!

Lexis: describing character

1 The way you smile can show what sort of person you are. Read the article below and match one of the headings (a–d) to each paragraph (1–4).

a) Shy and sensitive   b) Cheeky   c) Confident   d) Sociable

What's in a smile?

1 This is the smile of a joker. The raised eyebrows and dimples in the cheeks show a good sense of humour and a warm personality. This sort of person is often a bit of a rebel – they have little respect for authority.

2 The wide, toothy smile shows that this person is easy-going and friendly. They enjoy being in a crowd and are good fun to go out with. They're always looking for the next party.

3 The smile is in the eyes. This is a sensitive person, and a loyal friend. This sort of person thinks before they speak and is a good listener. They don't like to be the centre of attention in a crowd.

4 This is a smile that says, 'I know it all.' This type of person is very sure of themselves. They like a good argument, and they usually win. They're hard-working and very ambitious. And they can be quite bossy.

2 🔊 **49** Listen and check your answers.

3 🔊 **50** Listen to six different people talking and use the most appropriate adjective in the box to describe each one.

ambitious   bossy   confident   sensitive   sociable   easy-going

LANGUAGE TOOLBOX

affectionate cold dark deep frightening independent loyal mysterious selfish stormy strong nasty sweet unpleasant

4 Use any of the adjectives in the Language toolbox, or your own ideas to do this personality test.

Write one word to describe each of the following.

• a dog ____   • a cat ____   • a rat ____   • coffee ____   • an ocean ____

5 Turn to page 125 to find out the meaning of what you have written. Do you think it's accurate? Tell your partner.

What are you like?

1 Answer the questionnaire below. For each situation, choose *a*, *b* or *c* according to what you are most likely to say. Then calculate your score, read what it means on page 127 and compare with a partner.

Optimist or pessimist — what are you?

1 It's Sunday, and you're in the middle of a long walk in the country. It starts to rain.
a It always rains when I go for a walk.
b It could be worse – it could be snowing.
c Great! I really enjoy walking in the rain.

2 You arrive home after a great holiday.
a I don't want to go back to work.
b I'm going to start planning my next holiday. I want to have something to look forward to.
c The holiday was great, but now I'm looking forward to sleeping in my own bed.

3 It's your 40th birthday.
a The best years of my life are over.
b I'm getting older – so what? It happens to everybody.
c Life begins at 40 – where's the party?!

4 You've got a cold.
a I need to see a doctor as soon a possible.
b I need to buy some tissues.
c It's just a cold – it won't kill me.

5 Your partner has ended your relationship.
a I've had enough of men/women. I'm never going to fall in love again.
b I know I'll get over it, but it might take a long time.
c He/She wasn't the right one for me.

6 You have to make an important life decision.
a Whatever I decide to do, it will be the wrong decision.
b I'm going to take my time and think carefully about my decision.
c Whatever I decide to do, it will be the right decision.

7 It's autumn.
a I don't like autumn because it will soon be winter.
b It's just another time of year.
c It's a beautiful time of year.

8 You unexpectedly inherit £5,000.
a £5,000 isn't going to change my life.
b Great! I can buy a few luxuries that I couldn't afford before.
c This must be my lucky day – I think I'll buy a lottery ticket.

How to score   Each time you answer **a** score 1.   Each time you answer **b** score 2.   Each time you answer **c** score 3.

2 Who got the highest or lowest score in the class?

1 Complete these statements by choosing the appropriate structure. Refer to examples in the questionnaire if necessary.

a) I want **to be / being** extremely rich.
b) I'm looking forward to **go out / going out** tonight.
c) I always try **to get up / getting up** early even at the weekend.
d) I enjoy **to speak / speaking** English.
e) I need **to spend / spending** more time at home.
f) I've decided **to grow / growing** my hair long.

2 Do you think any of the sentences are true for your partner? Ask questions to find out.

3 Use the same verb structures to write six more sentences that are true for you. Compare them with a partner.

For example: *I don't want to get married until I'm thirty.*
I'm looking forward to finishing my studies.

Don't Worry, Be Happy

Song

1 Make word pairs by matching a word from list A with a word from list B that rhymes.

A	B
style	bed
trouble	smile
head	note
frown	double
late	down
wrote	litigate

(style is linked to smile; trouble is linked to double)

2 🔲 **51** You are going to listen to a song called *Don't Worry, Be Happy*. Read the song and complete each verse with the word pairs from 1. Then listen and check your answers.

3 Find at least three reasons for worrying that are mentioned in the song.

4 Work with a partner. Discuss what you think the biggest worries are for the following people.

a) a child
b) a 14-year-old girl
c) a 16-year-old boy
d) a university student
e) a parent
f) a grandparent

How does this song make *you* feel? What music makes you feel happy. Tell your partner.

Don't Worry, Be Happy

A massive hit in 1988 for singer, composer and conductor, Bobby McFerrin.

Here's a little song I (1) _____ .
You might want to sing it note for (2) _____ .
Don't worry, be happy.

In every life we have some (3) _____ .
When you worry you make it (4) _____ .
Don't worry, be happy.

Ain't got no place to lay your (5) _____ ?
Somebody came and took your (6) _____ ?
Don't worry, be happy.

The landlord says your rent is (7) _____ ?
He may have to (8) _____ .
Don't worry, be happy.

Ain't got no cash, ain't got no (9) _____ ?
Ain't got no girl to make you (10) _____ ?
Don't worry, be happy.

'Cos when you worry, your
    face will (11) _____ .
That will bring everybody
    (12) _____ .
Don't worry, be happy.

Close up

Imperatives

1 Choose a correct alternative way of saying 'Be happy' from the following.

a) Be not sad.   b) Don't sad you.   c) Don't be sad.   d) Don't you sad.

2 Look at the following imperatives. Give an alternative way of saying the same thing by using the adjectives in brackets.

a) Be good. (naughty) *Don't be naughty.*
b) Be quiet! (noisy)
c) Be on time. (late)
d) Be nice. (mean)
e) Behave yourself. (rude)
f) Cheer up. (miserable)
g) Say what you think. (shy)
h) Calm down. (angry)
i) Act your age. (childish)

3 Work with a partner. Choose an imperative from 2 and write a three-line dialogue to show a typical situation where it could be used.

For example: A: *I'll see you at 8.30 outside the cinema.*
B: *Don't be late!*
A: *Don't worry. I'm never late.*

Language reference: imperatives

You use an imperative form when you are telling somebody to do something or not to do something: orders, advice, encouragement, etc.
Come here.   Be quiet!   Don't be shy.   Come on.   Hurry up!

Take it easy

1 Imagine that today is 'No-Stress Day'. Read the article on the right and answer the questions. Discuss your answers with a partner.

a) Which suggestion is the easiest for you to do?

b) Which suggestion is the most difficult for you to do?

c) Which is the best or worst suggestion?

2 Work with a partner. Add three of your own suggestions to the list.

Lexis: phrasal verbs

1 Complete the sentences using these phrasal verbs from the article.

> give up   hang up   put on
> switch off   switch on   take off
> throw away

a) I always *take off* my shoes before I go into my house.

b) If I want to relax I ____ all the lights and sit in silence.

c) When I want to look my best, I ____ a suit.

d) I could never ____ smoking – it's the only thing that helps me relax.

e) The first thing I do when I get to the office is ____ my computer.

f) I never ____ plastic bags, because they're so useful.

g) I never do any ironing. I just ____ my clothes very carefully when they come out of the washing machine.

2 Are any of the sentences true for you? Discuss with a partner.

---

16 ways to
de-stress

1 Take off your watch.

2 Switch off your mobile phone.

3 Don't eat your breakfast on your feet – sit down and enjoy it.

4 Put on your most comfortable clothes.

5 Don't run after the bus – let it go.

6 Smell the roses.

7 Give up the gym.

8 Fall in love.

9 Only switch on your television if there's something you really want to watch.

10 Throw away any clothes you haven't worn for the past two years.

11 Have a laugh.

12 Hang up your clothes when you take them off.

13 Spend ten minutes doing absolutely nothing.

14 Walk.

15 Only do the ironing if you love it.

16 Put on your favourite music and turn up the volume.

(Adapted from The Guardian)

Close up

Phrasal verbs

1 Work with a partner. Look at the three phrasal verbs used in these sentences and answer the questions.

subject	verb	object	particle		subject	verb	particle	object	
I	*took*	*my shoes*	*off*	*and*	*I*	*ran*	*after*	*the bus.*	*But it didn't stop.*

subject	verb	particle	
So I	*sat*	*down*	*and cried. I hate bus drivers.*

a) Which phrasal verb does not take an object?
b) Which phrasal verb can have the object between the verb and the particle? (SEPARABLE)
c) Which phrasal verb always has the object after the particle? (NOT SEPARABLE)

2 When the object is a pronoun such as *it, them, her*, where do you always put it when the phrasal verb is: a) separable? b) inseparable?

3 Put the words in the right order to make answers to the questions. Look the phrasal verbs up in a dictionary if you are not sure.

a) What shall I do with this banana skin? (away throw it) *Throw it away.*
b) What shall I do with this mess? (it up clear)
c) What shall I do about this problem? (it deal with)
d) What shall I do with this application form? (fill in it)
e) What shall I do with my grandmother's wedding ring? (after it look)
f) What shall I do about my party? Nobody can come. (it call off)

Language reference: phrasal verbs

The term 'phrasal verb' usually refers to all multi-word verbs, consisting of a verb + particle(s). Phrasal verbs can be divided into three basic types.

1 verb + particle
Some phrasal verbs are intransitive and so do not take a direct object.
Sit down and enjoy it.   When are you going to grow up?

2 verb + object + particle (SEPARABLE)
The biggest group of phrasal verbs are transitive. When the direct object is a noun, you can put it before or after the particle.
Take off your shoes.   Take your shoes off.
When the direct object is a pronoun, you must put it between the verb and the particle.
Switch it off, please. NOT *Switch off it*

3 verb + particle + object (NOT SEPARABLE)
With this type of phrasal verb you always put the direct object – noun or pronoun – after the particle.
She looks after her grandmother.   I ran after it, but the bus didn't stop.

Laughter – the best medicine

1 🔲 52 Listen to a report about laughter – without laughing. What are the benefits of laughter?

2 Work with a partner. Sit facing each other. Student A tries to make student B smile and/or laugh by saying funny things. Student B tries to keep a straight face. Take it in turns to make each other smile and/or laugh.

12 *Rebel*

May Day

Reading

1 Work with a partner. Look at the photograph below and discuss the following questions.

a) What do you think is happening?
b) What things do people demonstrate about in your country?
c) Have you ever seen or taken part in a demonstration? What was it about?

2 Read the article. Are the following statements true or false?

a) Many of the protesters disagree with globalisation.
b) Twelve protesters were arrested in Sydney, Australia.
c) There was some fighting in the German capital, Berlin.
d) In Norway, a protester threw a bottle at the foreign minister.
e) In London, most of the protesters demonstrated peacefully.

3 Do you think demonstrations are a good way of making a point?

Seattle 2000

Global May Day protest

Around the world, thousands of people took part in protest marches and demonstrations today. Many
5 of the protesters were demonstrating against globalisation. Demonstrations were peaceful in most places, but in Sydney, Australia,
10 violence broke out, and dozens of protesters were arrested.

Fighting also broke out in the German capital, Berlin, where protesters threw stones
15 and bottles at police.

In Norway, a protester threw an apple-pie in the face of foreign minister, Thorbjoern Jagland.
20 In London, a small group of protesters broke away from peaceful demonstrators. They smashed shop windows and tried to set fire to a
25 supermarket. Fifty people were arrested.

What are you doing here?

Listening

1 At the May Day demonstrations in London not everybody was demonstrating against globalisation. Match the slogans (*a–f*) with the causes (*1–6*).

a) NO TO MULTINATIONALS 1 Against nuclear weapons
b) SAVE THE TREES 2 Against cruelty to animals
c) STOP STAR WARS 3 Against globalisation
d) BAN ANIMAL TESTING 4 Against student fees
e) EQUAL WORK MEANS EQUAL PAY 5 Against destruction of the environment
f) FREE EDUCATION FOR ALL 6 Against unequal pay for women

2 [cassette] **53** You are going to listen to radio interviews with the four protesters in the photos on the right. Before you listen, look at the photos and try to match the people with the slogans and causes in 1. Listen and check your answers.

Lexis: protest

1 Complete the sentences below, using these words from the recordings in the previous section.

> against   anti-   supporter of   don't feel
> in favour   really care   support

a) I'm a ____ peaceful action.
b) I'm ____ of many of the causes here.
c) I'm not ____men – I just want a fairer system.
d) I'm ____ animal testing.
e) I ____ animal rights.
f) I ____ strongly about politics – too boring.
g) I don't ____ about globalisation and stuff.

2 Work with a partner. Discuss the statements in 1. Which ones are true for you?

3 What causes do you feel most strongly about? Compare with a partner.

Lexis: word families

1 What are the noun forms for the following verbs: *pollute, globalise, demonstrate, inform*?

For example: *pollute – pollution*

2 [cassette] **54** Add each verb and noun pair from 1 to the table according to their stress pattern. Listen, repeat and check your answers.

Jake, 23, factory worker

Debbie, 27, housewife

Ronny, 27, cook

Caroline, 18, schoolgirl

A		B		C		D	
Verb	Noun	Verb	Noun	Verb	Noun	Verb	Noun
▪■	▪■▪	▪■	▪▪■▪	■▪▪	▪▪■▪	■▪▪	▪▪▪■▪
pollute	pollution	____	____	____	____	____	____

3 [cassette] **55** Listen and repeat eight more verb/noun pairs. Add them to the appropriate column of the table in 2. On which syllable does the stress fall when a noun ends in *-ion*?

Close up

Dynamic & stative meanings

'Dad, you're shaving with my mobile phone'

1 Work with a partner. Look at the verbs in these three extracts from the radio interviews in the previous section. Discuss the questions.

'People are playing music.'
'We're demonstrating for equal pay.'
'I'm having fun with my friends.'

a) Do the verbs describe actions or states?
b) What is the name of the tense used in all three extracts?

2 Re-write these sentences by putting the verb in brackets in the present continuous tense.

a) A phone (ring). *A phone is ringing.*   d) A clock (tick).
b) A teacher in another class (talk).   e) A student (laugh).
c) The traffic (make) a lot of noise.   f) People (chat).

3 Work as a class. Listen in silence for fifteen seconds and tick (✓) the actions in 2 that are true. Note down other things that are happening.

4 Work with a partner. Look at the verbs in three more extracts from the radio interviews in the previous section. Discuss the questions.

'I just want a fairer system.'
'I have three dogs, two cats and a pet mouse.'
'I don't know much about it.'

a) Do the verbs describe *actions* or *states*?
b) What is the name of the tense used in all three extracts?
c) Is it possible to use a continuous tense with verbs when they describe a state?

5 From the extracts in 1 and 4, which verb has two different meanings and describes both an action and a state?

6 Work with a partner. Decide if the verbs in brackets describe an action or a state. Put the verb into an appropriate form to complete the sentences.

a) Jane (like) James Bond films.   e) Brian (look) like his father.
b) Tony (know) how to play the piano.   f) Ryan (look) for a new place to live.
c) Marta (have) a television in her bedroom.   g) Sue (think) of going out tonight.
d) Julie (have) difficulty with this exercise.   h) Rosa (think) war is stupid.

7 Replace the names in 6 with names of students in the class to make as many true sentences as you can. Ask questions to help you.

For example: *Do you like James Bond films?   Are you thinking of going out tonight?*

Language reference: dynamic & stative meanings

Dynamic meanings: 'actions'

Most verbs have dynamic meanings. They describe actions: something 'happens'. You can use them with continuous forms to talk about activities in progress.

*People **are chatting**.*

Stative meanings: 'states'

Some verbs connected with knowledge, emotion or possession have stative meanings. They describe states: nothing 'happens'. You cannot use them with continuous forms.

*I **don't feel** strongly about politics.*

Note: some verbs such as *have*, *look*, and *think* can have both dynamic and stative meanings.

*Rosie **is looking** for a new place to live. (look = dynamic meaning)*
*Brian **looks** like his father. (look = stative meaning)*

Celebrity rebels

Reading   **1**   You are going to read an article about three famous people who have all rebelled against their family in different ways. Read the article and find out who …

     a)   <u>joined</u> a political group.   d)   <u>coloured</u> their hair.
     b)   <u>committed a crime</u>.   e)   had <u>inappropriate</u> relationships.
     c)   <u>started</u> smoking as a teenager.   f)   <u>left home to live with</u> the circus.

REBEL **REBEL**

Princess Stephanie of Monaco

Princess Stephanie is the younger daughter of Prince Rainier of Monaco. She is known as the 'rebel royal', mainly because of her unsuitable relationships. She married one of her bodyguards and had two children. She then divorced him and had a relationship (and a third child) with another bodyguard.

After that she was photographed in a circus caravan with Franco Knie, an elephant trainer – in other words, the rebel royal ran away with the circus!

Patty Hearst

On February 4, 1974, Patricia Hearst, the 19-year-old daughter of a very wealthy businessman, was kidnapped by a revolutionary political group called the Symbionese Liberation Army (SLA).

She was held prisoner for 57 days while the kidnappers waited for her parents to pay the ransom.

But they didn't pay the ransom and so Patty decided to rebel against her family. She became a member of the SLA and was renamed Tania.

Then she broke the law: five members of the SLA, including 'Tania', were photographed robbing the Hibernia Bank in San Francisco.

Patricia was later charged with bank robbery but she was released after three years in prison. She was finally pardoned by President Clinton in 2001.

Macaulay Culkin

Macaulay Culkin was born on August 26 1980 in New York, the third of seven children. 'Mack', as his friends call him, starred in the film, *Home Alone*, which made him one of the most famous and richest child stars of all time.

In 1995, his parents separated and started fighting over Mack's money. Disgusted with his parents' behaviour, Mack refused to accept any film roles until they stopped fighting.

Then, at the age of 17, he took up smoking, dyed his hair pink and got married.

2   Replace the <u>underlined</u> words in 1 with words or expressions from the text.

3   Work with a partner. Discuss the following questions.

- Who do you think is the most rebellious of the three people?
- In what other ways do people rebel against their families?
- In what ways did you rebel against your family when you were younger?

Anecdote   Think about a time when you got into trouble as a child. You are going to tell your partner about it. Choose from the list the things you want to talk about. Think about what you will say and the language you will need.

☐ How old were you?   ☐ Did you know it was wrong?
☐ Where were you?   ☐ What did you feel like afterwards?
☐ Were you alone or with other people?   ☐ Who caught you?
☐ What did you do?   ☐ What happened to you?
☐ Why did you do it?   ☐ Did you ever do the same thing again?

Close up

Language reference p75

Passives

1 Work with a partner. Look at the question and two alternative answers (*1* and *2*) below. Discuss why the second answer is the more natural alternative. Then choose the correct explanation (*a* or *b*).

What happened to
Patty Hearst on
February 4, 1974?

subject	verb	object
1 A revolutionary political group	kidnapped	her.

subject	verb	by	agent
2 She	was kidnapped	by	a revolutionary political group.

a) Because the question is about Patty Hearst. We usually start sentences with the person or thing that we are interested in.
b) Because Patty Hearst was a very rich and important woman.

2 Work with a partner. Refer to answers 1 and 2 in the last exercise. Discuss the following.

a) Which tense are both answers in?
b) In which answer is the verb in the passive form?
c) Which auxiliary verb combines with a past participle to form the passive?

3 Here are the main events from the Patty Hearst story. Complete the following task.

a) Put the verbs in the most appropriate form: active or passive.
b) Put the events in the correct order and re-tell the story.
c) Check your answers in the text on page 73.

( ) a) She (**charge**) with bank robbery.
( ) b) She (**rename**) 'Tania'.
( ) c) She (**hold**) prisoner for 57 days.
( ) d) She (**photograph**) robbing a bank.
( ) e) She (**decide**) to rebel against her family.
( ) f) She (**pardon**) by President Clinton in 2001.
( ) g) She (**release**) after three years in prison.
( ) h) She (**become**) a member of the SLA.
(1) i) She (**kidnap**) by a revolutionary political group.   *was kidnapped*
( ) j) She (**break**) the law.

4 Use past simple passives to complete the article about Che Guevara.

IMAGE OF A REBEL

IT is an image that became a legend of the twentieth century. It is tattooed on Diego Maradona's arm. A Che poster (1 **pin**) *was pinned* on Mick Jagger's wall when he was a student, and millions of T-shirts are still decorated with the image today. The picture (2 **take**) on 5 March 1960 at a memorial service in Havana, Cuba. Cuban photographer, Alberto Korda (3 **send**) by the magazine *Revolución* to take photographs of the Cuban leader, Fidel Castro.

'Che was standing behind Fidel Castro on the platform,' said Korda. 'You couldn't see him. Then suddenly he stepped forward to the edge of the platform. I managed to take a photo. Then he was gone.'

Seven years later, in October 1967, Che Guevara (4 **kill**) in Bolivia, and Korda's photograph became an icon for revolutionaries everywhere. Korda's photographs (5 **exhibit**) in Paris in Spring 2001. It was while he was attending the exhibition of his work that Korda died.

5 ▭ 56 Listen and check your answers.

6 Think of famous people that you admire. Whose picture would you like to have …

    a) on a poster on your wall   b) on your T-shirt   c) tattooed on your arm

Language reference: passives

In passive sentences, the object of the active verb becomes the subject of the passive verb. You can mention the person or thing ('agent') which performs the action, but it's not necessary.

		subject	verb	object
Active	In 1974,	a revolutionary political group	kidnapped	Patty Hearst.

		subject	verb	by	agent
Passive	In 1974,	Patty Hearst	was kidnapped	by	a revolutionary political group.

You use the passive when you want to say what happened to a subject rather than what a subject did.

*Patty Hearst **was renamed** 'Tania'.   Where **was** Che Guevara **killed**?*
*Korda's photos **were exhibited** in Paris in Spring 2001.*

How green is the class?

Report writing

1 Work in small groups. Look at the activities below and discuss which ones are good and which are bad for the environment.

    a) Travelling into town by car.
    b) Buying fresh, organic fruit or vegetables.
    c) Using public transport.
    d) Taking bottles to a bottle bank.
    e) Recycling paper.
    f) Wearing a fur coat.
    g) Picking up litter and putting it in a bin.
    h) Buying a hamburger in a plastic container.
    i) Paying more for something because it is environmentally friendly.
    j) Using plastic bags for your shopping.

2 Work in small groups. You are going to do a survey to find out how many people have done the activities in 1 in the last two weeks. Follow these instructions.

    a) Prepare the question you are going to ask for each activity.
    For example: a) *Have you travelled into town by car in the last two weeks?*
    b) Decide who is going to ask which questions.
    c) Go round the class and ask the questions and note down the answers.
    d) In your groups, write down the results of the survey for each activity.

3 Using the results from 2, write up a survey report which is true for your class by replacing the underlined expressions in the model text on the right. Change other parts of the model if necessary.

Survey report

A survey was carried out in Newtown, California, to find out how green people are.

The results of the survey
5 show that only a few people have used public transport in the last two weeks but everybody has travelled into town by car.

Most of the people
10 interviewed have bought a hamburger in a plastic container and several people have picked up litter and put it in a bin.

A small number of people
15 have taken bottles to a bottle bank or recycled paper but none of the people interviewed has paid more for something because it is environmentally
20 friendly.

A large number of people have worn a fur coat and everybody has used plastic bags for their shopping.

25 Nobody has bought organic fruit or vegetables in the last two weeks.

The results of the survey suggest that the inhabitants of
30 Newtown, California are not very green.

13 Dance

Reading

Do the questionnaire and compare your answers with a partner.

Lexis: *on* & *at*

1 Test your prepositions! The questionnaire talks about being *on stage* or *at a club*. Add *on* or *at* to the noun phrases in the box.

> the phone   a concert   holiday
> a plane   the doctor's   the internet
> a business trip   the hairdresser's
> a night club   a training course

on the phone, …   at a concert, …

2 Write down two true sentences and one false sentence about yourself using prepositions + noun phrases in 1. Read your partner's sentences and guess which sentence is false.

1   *I was on the phone just before the lesson began.*
2   *I was at a night club on Saturday.*
3   *I was …*

DISCO DIVA
OR TWO LEFT FEET?

1 Your favourite place for dancing is …
a on stage.
b at a club or a party.
c in your own bedroom.

2 Tick the music you know how to dance to.
Pop   Rock 'n' roll (Jive)   House
Reggae   Salsa   Flamenco
Classical or ballroom (eg waltz)
Traditional music of your country

3 Which sentence best describes your attitude to dancing?
a I hate it.
b I love it and I'm pretty good.
c I love dancing but I'm not particularly good.

4 Which sentence best describes the way you dance?
a I don't care what other people think.
b I feel uncomfortable.
c I want people to look at me.

5 When I dance …
a I stay more or less in one place.
b I need a lot of space to move around.
c I do the same as my partner.

6 At a pop concert, I usually …
a get up and dance to the music.
b stay sitting down.
c I don't go to pop concerts.

7 How often do you dance all night?
a About once or twice a year.
b Never. Don't be ridiculous!
c Every weekend.

8 At a party …
a I'm usually the last to get up and dance.
b I'm usually the first to get up and dance.
c I don't go to parties where people dance.

How to score
1 a 3, b 2, c 1   5 a 2, b 3, c 1
2 1 point for each tick.   6 a 3, b 2, c 1
3 a 1, b 3, c 2   7 a 2, b 1, c 3
4 a 3, b 1, c 2   8 a 2, b 3, c 1
Turn to page 127 to find out what your score means.

The clubbing capital of the world

Work in small groups. Discuss the questions.

- Which town or city in your country is famous for its nightlife?
- Where do people go dancing or clubbing where you live?
- Which is your own favourite place for a night out?

Reading **1** You are going to read an article about the island of Ibiza. Read the first part of the article (*Party island*) and answer the questions.

a) What kind of people go to Ibiza?
b) How many tourists visit the island every year?
c) How long has Ibiza been a party island?
d) What happened in 1987?
e) What kinds of music do the DJs play?

Party island

The beautiful Mediterranean island of Ibiza has a population of 80,000. But in summer two million tourists visit the island. Why? Because Ibiza is the clubbing capital of the world.

Top DJs play the latest dance music in 400 clubs and bars situated around the island's two main towns, San Antonio and Ibiza town.

Ibiza has been a party island since the sixties when hippies first started coming to the island.

But it became famous for clubbing with the arrival of Acid House in 1987.

Since then, DJs have been playing dance music for all tastes: dance, trance, techno, garage, pop, rock and funk.

Ibiza

2 Have you ever been to a club which has any of the following? Compare with your partner.

a) 'live' music
b) several different dance-floors
c) foam parties
d) space for 10,000 people
e) a swimming pool
f) trees planted inside

3 Read the second part of the article (*The clubs*). Match the clubs with the features in 2.

For example: a) 'live music' – *Privilege*

The clubs

Amnesia

(www.amnesia.es)

When it opened in the 70s, *Amnesia* had an open-air dance-floor, but in 1990 noise laws forced the owners to build walls and a roof. The club is best-known for its foam parties. The music is a mix of house and trance, with some rock and pop. *Amnesia* has always been one of the island's favourite clubs for end-of-season parties.

Privilege

(www.privilege-ibiza.com)

The owners of a restaurant called *Ku* decided to build a mini-disco (125 people maximum) back in 1978. It was here that Bob Marley, Grace Jones and Freddie Mercury performed 'live', and many international stars have followed in their footsteps since then. In 1994, they built a new disco and called it *Privilege*. It is the size of a football pitch – it has room for 10,000 and has everything: several different dance-floors, palm trees in the main room, a DJ suspended over the swimming pool and on some nights there's even a DJ in the toilets!

4 Would you like to go to Ibiza? Why / Why not? Tell your partner.

My Ibiza

Listening

1 Work with a partner. You are going to listen to a radio programme called *My Ibiza*. Look at the photos of the three people interviewed and guess who said each of the following.

a) 'I haven't been home for a couple of years now.'
b) 'I've been living in Ibiza town since 1995.'
c) 'I've spent all my money.'
d) 'I haven't been to the beach yet.'
e) 'I've been a resident DJ at *Amnesia* for two years.'
f) 'I've been dancing all night.'

2 57 Listen and check your answers to 1. Which person do you think enjoys their life most?

Lexis: informal language

1 Replace the underlined words in these statements with informal expressions from the interview with Josh.

| how come   I'm skint   knackered   clubbing   reckon |

▲ Josh, 18, student

a) I'm usually so <u>tired</u> after a night out that I don't get up till after lunch.
b) I often wonder <u>why</u> I never meet anybody interesting when I go out.
c) I've been <u>going to night clubs</u> since I was fifteen.
d) I <u>think</u> it costs far too much to get into clubs these days.
e) When <u>I haven't got any money</u> I usually get my friends to pay for me.

▲ Saskia, 29, DJ

2 Find out if any of the statements in 1 are true for your partner.

Anecdote

Think of a time recently when you went to a place where people were dancing and having a good time. You are going to tell your partner about it. Choose from the list below the things you want to talk about. Think about what you are going to say and how you are going to say it.

▲ Antonio, 36, restaurant owner

☐ Where were you? A club? A party? A concert?
☐ What kind of music was playing?
☐ Who was playing the music? A 'live' band? A DJ?
☐ How loud and clear was the music?
☐ How crowded was the place?

☐ What kind of clothes were people wearing?
☐ Did you dance or did you watch other people dancing?
☐ Were people dancing alone or with a partner?
☐ How long did you spend there?
☐ Did you have a good time?

Close up

for & since

Language reference p80

1 Look at the way *for* and *since* are explained in the diagram. Then complete the table so that the information is correct counting from today.

	Since	For
yesterday	=	*24 hours*
1999	=	____ *years*
Sunday	=	____ *day(s)*
my last birthday	=	____
I started studying English	=	____

2 Add more examples of your own to the table in 1.

been

Language reference p80

1 Work with a partner. Read the following sentences about the people in the radio programme, *My Ibiza*, on page 78. Then discuss the questions.

1 Josh <u>has been</u> in Ibiza for nine or ten days but he <u>hasn't been</u> to the beach yet.
2 Saskia <u>has been</u> in Ibiza since 1997. She is Dutch but she <u>hasn't been</u> home for a couple of years.

a) What tense are the <u>underlined</u> verbs?
b) In which case is *been* the past participle of *go*?
c) In which case is *been* the past participle of *be*?

2 Make true sentences about yourself using the following prompts and an appropriate time expression with *since, for* or *never*. Compare your answers with a partner.

a) not go to London
    For example: *I haven't been to London since I was sixteen. / I haven't been to London for years. / I've never been to London!*
b) not go to a good party
c) not go to the beach
d) not go to a rock concert
e) not go to a wedding
f) not go out for dinner
g) not go skiing
h) not go abroad

'David likes going somewhere hot for his holidays.'

3 Note down the names of some good shops, restaurants, pubs or night clubs in your city. Ask your partner if they know them or if they have been to them recently. Find out as much as you can.

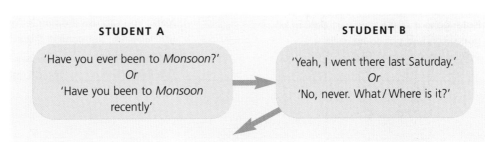

1 Look at the table based on information from the radio programme, *My Ibiza*, on page 78. Which 'facts' tell us *how long* an activity has continued?

1 Past facts	+	2 Present facts	→	3 Present perfect facts
Saskia started as a DJ at *Amnesia* two years ago.	+	Saskia is a DJ at *Amnesia*.	→	She's been a DJ at *Amnesia* for two years.
Tourists started coming to Ibiza in the sixties.	+	Tourists come to Ibiza every year.	→	They've been coming to Ibiza since the sixties.

2 Underline the main verbs in column 3 of the table in 1. Discuss these questions with your partner.

a) Which verb describes a state?
b) Is it in the present perfect simple or continuous?
c) Which verb describes a single or repeated action?
d) Is it in the present perfect simple or continuous?

3 Write the name of ...

a) a foreign person you <u>know</u>.
b) a type of music you <u>like</u>.
c) a subject you <u>are</u> interested in.
d) a café or bar you <u>go</u> to.
e) a shop you <u>buy</u> clothes in.
f) a favourite possession you <u>have</u>.
g) the house you <u>live</u> in.
h) the place you <u>work</u> or <u>study</u>.

1 Decide if each <u>underlined</u> verb describes a state or a single/repeated action.
2 Write eight present perfect facts which answer the question *How long ...?*
3 Compare your facts with a partner.

For example: *I've known Max for seven years. I've been going to Bar Isa since 1999.*

4 Work as a class. Find out who has done or who has been doing the things in 3 the longest. Follow these instructions.

a) Each student choose one 'fact' from 3 and practise the questions you will ask.
   For example: *a) Do you know anybody foreign? → How long have you known him/her?*
b) Ask everybody in the class and record the answers.
c) Report the results back to the class.

Language reference: present perfect simple & continuous

for & since

for + a period of time and *since* + a point in time are two ways of saying the same thing.

for a few days / for three years / for ages
since Monday / since I left school / since 1997

been

been is the past participle of *go* as well as *be*.

He **hasn't been** to the beach yet. (go)
Have you **been** abroad this year? (go)
I've been ill since last night. (be)
How long **have you been** here? (be)

Note: *gone* is also a past participle of *go*.
gone = go and <u>not</u> come back.
been = go and come back.

Present perfect simple & continuous

You can use the present perfect when you want to say how long something has continued from a point in the past up to now. For verbs with stative meanings you always use the simple form.

I've been a DJ for two years.
She's known Tommy since they were at school.

For verbs with dynamic meanings you usually use the continuous form.

I've been clubbing every night.
My mother's **been playing** tennis since she was eight.

Note: You can use the simple form for very unchanging, 'permanent' situations. Compare:

I've been living here since May. (Temporary)
I've lived here all my life. (Permanent)

Billy Elliot

1 Read this introduction to an extract from a book based on the film, *Billy Elliot*. What is the problem? What do you think will happen?

> Billy's mother is dead. His father and brother are miners and they are on strike. Billy's father wants his son to learn to box, like he did and his father before him, but Billy becomes fascinated by the magic of ballet. In secret, Billy starts having ballet lessons every Saturday. In this extract from the story, Billy describes what happens when his father comes to watch him boxing but instead finds him in a ballet class.

2 ▣ **58** Read and listen to the extract. Who do you sympathise with: Billy or his dad?

nan (line 6): informal word for *grandmother*
telly (line 7): informal word for *television*
wind me up (line 10): informal expression for *annoy me*
lads (line 14) informal word for *boys*
I had him there (line 17): informal expression for *I caught him in a difficult situation*

(From Billy Elliot, by Melvin Burgess)

Back home he pointed at a chair behind the table, staring at me all the while he was taking his coat off. Then he sat down opposite me.
  I knew what he wanted. He wanted me to say sorry. Well, I wasn't going to. He could wait for ever. It was stupid! What had I done wrong?
5 'Ballet,' he said at last.
  'So what's wrong with ballet?' I said. My nan was sitting on a chair by the window eating a pork pie and watching us like we were on the telly. I looked at her. It was easier than having to look at him. I could see him turning red again out of the corner of my eye.
10 'What's wrong with ballet? Look at me, Billy. Are you trying to wind me up?'
  'It's perfectly normal,' I said, turning to face him.
  'Normal?' I was scared. He'd gone all white around the lips.
  'I used to go to ballet,' said my nan.
  'See?' I said.
15 'For your nan. For girls, Billy. Not for lads. Lads do football or boxing or wrestling or something.'
  'What lads do wrestling?' I asked and I had him there because no one I know does wrestling round here.
  'You know what I mean.'
20 'I don't know what you mean.'
  The thing is, all right, I knew what he meant. At least, I used to know. Ballet isn't what boys do. It's not football and boxing and being hard. It's not what we do. But once I've done it, it is what we do.
  Just because I like dancing, it doesn't mean I'm turning into someone else.
25 Does it?

3 Here is a brief summary of the extract. Put the lines of the summary in the correct order.

( ) a) at his father. He looked
(2) b) off and without saying anything sat
( ) c) up. Billy knew what his father meant.
( ) d) down opposite Billy. Billy didn't look
(1) e) His father took his coat
( ) f) at his nan instead. Billy said there was nothing wrong
( ) g) with doing ballet, but his dad thought he was winding him

4 What interests did you have when you were twelve? What did you want to be? Tell your partner.

14 *Call*

Work in small groups. Discuss these questions.

- How many phone calls do you make/receive in a typical day?
- What do you use your phone for most?
- Who do you call most?

Reading **1** Work with a partner. List any things that you dislike about phones. Read the magazine article and check if it mentions any of the things on your list.

PHONE MOANS

Audrey: 'I hate it when the person I'm speaking to starts drinking a cup of tea or eating something. It sounds disgusting!'

Ben: 'It's so boring when you go out with somebody who spends half the time talking on their mobile. When I go out with somebody, I switch my phone off and listen to my voicemail when I get home.'

Cathy: 'I think there should be places where mobile phones are banned. For instance, when I'm on a train or in a restaurant, I hate listening to people talking about things that are quite private! It should be against the law! Call me old-fashioned, but I like to travel or eat in peace.'

Dan: 'I've given up phoning my friends since they had children. Every time I phone them, they ask me to talk to their two-year old boy. I have to speak to him in this silly voice, and he never speaks so I have to listen to him breathing down the phone. Fortunately, they haven't asked me to speak to the baby yet, but she's usually screaming in the background, so you can't have a proper conversation anyway.'

Ellen: 'I like to talk to a real person on the phone, but nowadays you get a recorded message which gives you all these options to choose from. If you don't hear everything the first time, you can't ask them to repeat. You have to start again. Oh, and the music that they play while you're on hold – awful.'

Frank: 'I hate it when you telephone a company or an office and you can never get through to the person you want to speak to. The operator puts you through to an extension, and the person you want is not there, so you have to wait for ages. Then, you get another extension, and it's still the wrong one, so you have to wait again. And again and again until you get bored of trying.'

2 How many of the things mentioned in the article sometimes happen to you?

1 Complete the questions with words and expressions from the article on page 82.

a) Do you think it should be against the law to use a m____ while you're driving?

b) Have you ever been in an embarrassing situation because you forgot to s____ your phone o ____ ?

c) When somebody leaves a message on your v____ m____ , how long do you wait before you return the call?

d) When was the last time you listened to a r____ m____ and had to choose from different o____ ?

e) While you are o____ h____ , do you prefer to listen to music or to silence?

f) Have you ever had a problem getting t____ to the right e____ ?

2 Choose three questions from 1 to ask your partner.

Domestic crisis

1 📼 59 Listen to the first part of Lorna's telephone conversation. Which of the following problems does Lorna mention?

a) My back is hurting.
b) The house is untidy.
c) The car has broken down.
d) The cat has died.
e) The Kids are annoying me.

f) I've had a row with my partner.
g) The fridge is empty.
h) I'm bored.
i) I've got no money.
j) I've lost my keys.

2 Lorna uses the words and expressions in the box to talk about the five problems mentioned in 1. Re-write the problems using the words and expressions that Lorna uses. Listen and check your answers.

a mess	run out of	killing me	bare	driving me mad

3 📼 60 Listen to the second part of the telephone conversation. Who is Juliet?

4 📼 61 After the first conversation, Lorna tries to get help. She makes two more phone calls. Listen to the two conversations and say if the sentences are true (*T*) or false (*F*).

a) Lorna's mother is out.
b) Lorna's father offers to help with the children.
c) Lorna asks Jackie to baby-sit for a couple of hours.
d) Jackie asks if her sister can come with her.
e) Lorna offers to drive over and pick Jackie up.

5 Have you ever had any of the problems in 1 above? Did you call anybody for help? Who? Tell your partner.

Close up

Offers & requests

'I said, would you mind turning down your fan?'

1 Listen again to Lorna's two conversations in 4 in the previous section. Match the opening phrases (*a*–*g*) with the sentence endings (*1*–*7*).

a) Can I
b) Shall I
c) Could you
d) I was wondering if you could
e) Would you mind
f) Is it okay if I
g) Would you like me to

1 drive over and pick you up?
2 come over and baby-sit?
3 bring my boyfriend?
4 call you back later?
5 tell her it's urgent?
6 hanging on a moment, please?
7 leave a message for your mother?

2 Put the opening phrases in 1 (*a*–*g*) into three groups.

Offers: asking someone if you can do something for them	b
Requests: asking someone if they can do something for you	c
Requests for permission: asking someone if it's okay for you to do something	a

3 Work with a partner. Look again at the opening phrases in 1. Do you usually use more or fewer words if you want to be formal?

4 Look at the following mini-situations. Think of a person you would phone for each situation. Tell your partner.

A You want someone to choose a film for you to see together.	**B** You want someone to look after your pet while you are on holiday.	**C** You want someone to write a job reference for you.
D You want someone to check an important letter you've written in English.	**E** You want someone to help you buy a new outfit for a friend's wedding.	**F** You want someone to lend you some money till the end of the month.

5 Work with a partner. Choose two of the mini-situations in 4 and write a short phone conversation for each one. Include an offer and a request in each conversation.

Language reference: offers & requests

Offers

Here are two common ways of asking someone if you can do something for them.
Shall I give you a lift?
Would you like me to help you?

Requests

There are many ways of asking someone if they can do something for you. Usually, the more words you use, the more polite or formal you sound.

I was wondering if you could ...? ↑ more polite / formal
Would you mind ...?
Could you ...? ↓ more direct / formal

Here are some ways you can request permission – ask someone if it is okay for you to do something.
Can I use your phone, please?
Is it okay if I bring my friend?

Telephone talk

1 Lorna finally tries to get in touch with her husband at work. He works for a company called Butler and Crowmarch. Complete her conversation with the receptionist using the most appropriate expressions.

> R: (1) **Yes / Good morning**. Butler and Crowmarch.
> L: (2) **Could I / I want to** speak to Mr Carr, please?
> R: Certainly. (3) **Who's speaking? / Who are you?**
> L: Mrs Carr.
> R: (4) **Wait / Hold on, please** and I'll try to put you through.
> Hello. (5) **He's not there. / I'm afraid Mr Carr is not at his desk at the moment.**
> L: Oh. (6) **Do you know when he'll / When will he** be back?
> R: I'm not sure. (7) **Would you like / Do you want** me to ask his assistant?
> L: Yes, please.
> R: Right. Hold on a moment then, please. (8) **He's busy till five. / I'm afraid Mr Carr is in a meeting until five o'clock.**
> L: Oh, okay. (9) **Can I / Let me** leave a message.
> R: Certainly.
> L: (10) **Tell him / Could you tell him** to phone me before he leaves the office? I want him to do some shopping.
> R: No problem, Mrs Carr. I'll pass on the message.
> L: Thank you. Goodbye.

2 🔊 **62** Listen and compare your version with the version on the recording.

3 Work with a partner. Practise the conversation. Take it in turns to be Lorna and the receptionist.

1 🔊 **63** The following telephone numbers have been copied down incorrectly. Listen to the recording and correct the numbers.

a) Heathrow airport flights: 0870 111 0123
b) Train times and fares: 0845 748 4952
c) Buses and coaches: 0875 580 8080
d) Car breakdowns: 0500 887766
e) British Tourist Authority: 020 7746 9000
f) Directory Enquiries: 190

2 Explain your answers in 1 to a partner. Take it in turns to identify the mistake and say what the correct number is. Do not show each other any numbers you have written down.

For example: *For Heathrow airport it's not one, double one. It's 0, double 0. Do you agree?*

3 Work with a partner and complete the following task.

a) Write down five telephone numbers that are important to you.
b) Take it in turns to dictate the numbers to each other.
c) Check that you wrote down your partner's numbers correctly.
d) Explain to each other why the numbers are important.

The 'latest thing'

(Adapted from *The Guardian*)

Reading **1** You are going to read an article about a father who doesn't want to buy a mobile phone for his twelve-year-old son. Why do you think he does not want his son to have a phone? Discuss with a partner. Read the article. Are any of your ideas mentioned?

Why I bought my child a gun

Every five minutes my children ask me for the 'latest thing'. They tell me that all their friends have it already and they can't live without it. Our house is full of Game Boys, Play
5 Station CDs and a million other 'latest things'.

But, the one 'latest thing' we have refused to buy is a mobile phone. Our twelve-year-old wants one, and we've said 'no'. He says he'll only use it for texting and he really needs it for emergencies.
10 We don't want him to have a mobile phone, because they may be bad for children's health. Unfortunately, when I say, 'I don't want you to have a mobile phone, because you might get a brain tumour,' he tells me that he doesn't mind.

15 Why do twelve-year-old boys only want things that are bad for them? We've already told him that he can't listen to Rap music – the words are disgusting. And I've said no to beer with his meals. Right now, I'm saying no to everything.
20 Then a few weeks ago he asked for something called a BB gun. He says everybody's got one. Of course they have. He shows me a website full of them and tells me it only fires plastic pellets. Finally, I say yes. I can't believe I've said no to
25 phones and yes to guns.

In October our son becomes a teenager, and I pray that research will find that mobile phones
30 are safe … even better, that they make young people less moody – and more interested in personal hygiene.

Until then, I'm saying no.

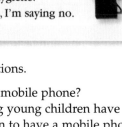

2 Work in small groups. Discuss the following questions.

- Who is the youngest person you know with a mobile phone?
- What are the arguments for and against letting young children have mobile phones?
- At what age do you think it's okay for children to have a mobile phone?

Lexis: *say,* *tell, ask* **1** Complete this summary of the article by choosing the most appropriate alternative.

a) The father's twelve-year-old son always **says / tells / asks** him for the 'latest thing'.
b) He **says / tells / asks** him that he wants a mobile phone.
c) He **says / tells / asks** that he'll only uses it for texting.
d) He **says / tells / asks** him that he doesn't mind getting a brain tumour.
e) The son then **says / tells / asks** for a BB gun.
f) He **says / tells / asks** everybody's got one.
g) He **says / tells / asks** him it only fires plastic pellets.
h) The father **says / tells / asks** 'no' to the mobile phone and 'yes' to the gun.

2 Complete the following rules with *say, tell* or *ask*.

a) You ____ (somebody) for something.
b) You ____ somebody something.
c) You ____ something.

'I can't talk now.'

Who? What? Where?

Listening **1** 🔲 64 You are going to listen to six short conversations. Listen and answer these questions: Who is speaking? What is the situation? Where are they? Choose from the places in the box.

> in a car park   at a club   at a bus stop   at home   at the zoo   at home

2 Which of the situations in 1 have you been in? Tell your partner.

Close up

Indirect questions

1 Work with a partner. Look at the position of subject and verb in these sentences and discuss the questions below.

Direct questions

be

question word	verb	subject
Where	*are*	*the toilets*

? →

Indirect questions

question frame	subject	verb
Do you know where	*the toilets*	*are*

?

Other verbs

question word	auxiliary	subject	verb
–	**Has**	*the last bus*	*gone*

? →

question frame	subject	verb
Do you know if	*the last bus*	*has gone*

?

a) Where does the subject go in direct questions with *be*?
b) Where does the subject go in direct questions with other verbs?
c) Where does the subject go in indirect questions?

2 Put the subjects in the correct position in these direct and indirect questions. Listen again to the six conversations and check your answers.

Subjects	Direct questions	Indirect questions
a) the cloakroom	Where is *the cloakroom*?	Could you tell me where *the cloakroom* is?
b) the time	What is?	Have you any idea what is?
c) the lions	Where are?	Do you know where are?
d) I	Could have a Zoomatron?	Do you think could have a Zoomatron?
e) I	Where can get a taxi?	Do you know where can get a taxi?
f) we	Where did leave it?	Can you remember where left it?

3 Work with a partner. Re-write the ends of these indirect questions in the correct order.

a) Do you know what   is address my ?
b) Can you remember who   was English teacher first your ?
c) Do you know what   is star sign your ?
d) Do you know if   parents born in were city this your ?
e) Do you think   is my improving English ?
f) Could you tell me how long city you in living this been have ?

4 Ask each other the questions in 3.

Language reference: indirect questions

The word order in indirect questions is different from the word order in direct questions. It is the same as in normal statements: *subject + verb (+ object)*. You do not use the auxiliaries *do/does/did*.

Question frame	Subject	Verb	(Object)
Do you think	*I*	*could have*	*a Zoomatron?*
Do you know if	*the last bus*	*has gone?*	
Can you remember who	*your first English teacher*	*was?*	
Could you tell me where	*you*	*live?*	

15

Review 3

The waiting game

Language reviewed: describing people (Unit 11); *for* & *since* (Unit 13); present perfect simple & present perfect continuous (Unit 13); indirect questions (Unit 14); noun phrases with *at* & *on* (Unit 13)

Listening **1** 🔲 65 You are going to listen to a radio reporter do three interviews with people in a queue to get tickets for the Wimbledon tennis championships. Look at the picture while you are listening and answer the questions.

a) Who thinks they will get into Wimbledon?
b) Who doesn't think they will get in?

Hyacinth | Derek | Kati | Oona | Maggy

2 Rearrange the words to make the questions that the reporter asked in the first interview.

a) Could you tell me   come from where you ?
b) Could you tell me   been have how long waiting you ?
c) Do you think   get in you will ?
d) Do you know   are how in many front people of there you ?

3 Listen to the first interview again and check the word order of the questions in 2. How does the woman answer the questions?

4 Complete the sentences from the interviews. Put the verbs into the present perfect simple or the present perfect continuous and choose *for* or *since*.

a) You (**look**) at her **for/since** hours.   *You've been looking at her for hours.*
b) I (**wait**) here **for/since** a quarter past eight this morning.
c) I (**be**) in London **for/since** four weeks.
d) It (**rain**) **for/since** half past one.
e) We (**be**) here **for/since** about eight.
f) We (**chat**) **for/since** ages.

5 Listen to the interviews again to check your answers to 4.

6 Work in small groups. Which do you prefer:

a) watching big sporting events live?
b) watching big sporting events on TV?
c) not watching big sporting events?

Discuss your answers and give examples from your own experience.

Lexis: describing people

1 Complete the descriptions with words from the box. Match each description to a person in the picture of the queue for Wimbledon on page 88.

| bags | cheeks | hard-working | humour | irritating | miserable | outfits | teeth |
| wavy | wrinkled |

A She's got pale skin and a few freckles, but the most noticeable thing about her is her eyelashes. She doesn't have any! She always looks _____ , but, in reality, she is not unhappy. She is serious and _____ – and always extremely polite.

B She's got short, grey _____ hair and always wears green to match her green eyes. Her _____ are always red – is it because she is embarrassed or does she suffer from the cold? Certainly, she is very shy, but she is a loyal friend and can be good fun to be with.

C She's an elderly lady with a warm personality and a friendly face. Sociable and easy-going, she has a wonderful sense of _____ and seems to be smiling all the time. Even with her tanned, _____ face, she is still good-looking.

D He's fifty-two but looks older. With untidy hair, big, bushy eyebrows and a moustache that seems to have some of his dinner still in it, he usually looks a mess. In fact, you could say that personal hygiene was not his strong point. He has _____ under his eyes because he doesn't sleep enough. He wears an old-fashioned suit (does he sleep in it?) and has an _____ habit of looking the other way when you talk to him.

E She's fifty and she always likes to look her best when she goes out. She wears smart _____ and chooses lipsticks to match. Red is her favourite colour because this shows off her row of beautiful pearly _____ . She has recently dyed her hair pink. She is very sure of herself and some people think she is rather bossy.

2 On a piece of paper write a short description of another student in your class. Fold your piece of paper and give it to your teacher. Then take a piece of paper with a description written by another student and guess who is being described.

Lexis: *at* & *on*   **1** Complete the sentences in the questionnaire with *at* or *on*.

HOW PATIENT ARE YOU?

1 You're _____ the internet and downloading an interesting programme, but it's very, very slow. How long will you wait before giving up?   _____ **minutes**

2 You are _____ a party _____ a friend's house. It's extremely boring, and you only know one person – your friend. How long will you wait before going home? _____ **minutes**

3 You are going _____ a business trip tomorrow and you decide to have your hair cut before you go. It is very, very busy _____ the hairdresser's. How long will you wait before giving up?   _____ **minutes**

4 You're sitting _____ a plane, and the person _____ your right is listening to loud music _____ his personal stereo. How long will you wait before asking him to turn it down?   _____ **minutes**

5 You are going out _____ a date. Your friend is waiting for you _____ the cinema. You are _____ the bus stop, but your bus does not arrive. How long will you wait before calling a taxi _____ your mobile phone?   _____ **minutes**

Total number of minutes: _____

2 Answer the questions in the questionnaire. For each question, write the maximum number of minutes that you will wait. When you have finished, add up the minutes for all the questions. Write your total.

3 Compare your answers with other people. Who is the most patient/impatient person in the class?

National sport

> **Language reviewed:** passives (Unit 12); dynamic & stative meanings (Unit 12); verb patterns (Unit 11); imperatives (Unit 11); *say, tell & ask* (Unit 14); offers & requests (Unit 14); phrasal verbs (Unit 11)

Passives

1 Complete the following statements with an appropriate passive form of the verb. Then decide if the statements are true or false. Check your answers on page 127.

    a) The 1992 Olympic games (**hold**) in Atlanta, USA. True or false?
    b) Cricket (**play**) by two teams of thirteen players. True or false?
    c) The game of rugby (**invent**) at Rugby School, England in 1823. True or false?
    d) Mount Everest (**climb**) for the first time in 1953. True or false?
    e) Bob Beamon's 1968 long jump world record of 8.9 metres (**never break**). True or false?
    f) France (**beat**) 3–1 by Brazil in the 1998 football World Cup final. True or false?

2 Make up three more true/false statements about trivia using passive verb structures. Exchange your statements with your partner. Are they true or false?

Dynamic & stative meanings

1 You are going to look at some pictures of a London street. Before you look at the pictures, choose the best verb forms in the questions below.

    a) What **happens / is happening** in your picture?
    b) How **do the people stand / are the people standing**?
    c) What **do they wear / are they wearing**?
    d) What **do they have / are they having** in their hands?
    e) Where **do you think / are you thinking** the people **come / are coming** from? Why?

2 Work with a partner. Student A, look at the picture on page 127. Student B, look at the picture on page 128. Discuss the questions in 1. How many similarities and differences can you find between the pictures?

Reading

1 Read the article below about queuing in Britain. Choose either the *to*-infinitive or the *-ing* form for the verbs in brackets. How useful is the advice in the article?

The noble art of queuing

There is one sport at which the British are always the world champions. Nobody can beat them at the noble art of queuing. The British actually look forward to (1 **spend**) their weekends in a queue, waiting for a shop to open or waiting for a parking space at the furniture superstore.

If you ever decide (2 **visit**) Britain, you will need (3 **know**) some of the basic rules of the sport.

First of all, remember that you only need one person to make a queue. If you are alone at a bus stop, for example, don't look too relaxed. Make sure that you are in the queue and look optimistically to your right.

If you want (4 **keep**) your place in the queue, never leave a space between you and the person in front, otherwise the person behind you will ask, 'Are you in the queue?' (meaning 'Don't you know how to queue properly?').

Conversation is generally not a good idea, and only two topics are acceptable: the weather and the bus timetable. Anything more and you will end up with a complete stranger sitting next to you, telling you their life story.

Unfortunately, the bus does not always stop in the correct place. Try (5 **stay**) calm and, whatever you do, don't jump the queue. You can be sure that every single person in the queue knows exactly who is in front of them, and who is behind.

Follow these simple rules and you, too, can enjoy (6 **visit**) the home of the noble art of queuing. But if you decide not to follow the rules, be prepared for the worst.

2 🔲 66 Listen and check your answers.

3 Work with a partner. Complete the following task.

    a) <u>Underline</u> all the examples of imperatives you can find in the article.
    b) Prepare a list of useful 'dos' and 'don'ts' for foreign visitors to your country (eg driving; using public transport; eating out; visiting someone's home).
    c) Compare your list with other people in the class.

1 Have you ever been late for work, a meeting, an appointment or a lesson? What did you say? Tell your partner.

2 Look at the outline of a telephone conversation. Choose the correct word in each sentence.

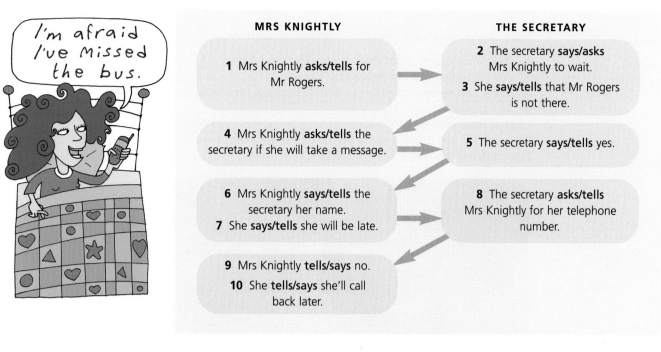

MRS KNIGHTLY

1 Mrs Knightly **asks/tells** for Mr Rogers.

THE SECRETARY

2 The secretary **says/asks** Mrs Knightly to wait.

3 She **says/tells** that Mr Rogers is not there.

4 Mrs Knightly **asks/tells** the secretary if she will take a message.

5 The secretary **says/tells** yes.

6 Mrs Knightly **says/tells** the secretary her name.
7 She **says/tells** she will be late.

8 The secretary **asks/tells** Mrs Knightly for her telephone number.

9 Mrs Knightly **tells/says** no.
10 She **tells/says** she'll call back later.

3 Match the stages (*1–10*) in the telephone conversation in 2 with the speeches (*a–j*) below.

a) Ah, would you mind taking a message?
b) Certainly. Could you hold the line, please?
c) Certainly.
d) I'll call back later.
e) Erm, well, it's Joanna Knightly here.
f) I'm afraid Mr Rogers is not in yet, madam.
g) I've got an appointment with Mr Rogers at 9.15 and I'm afraid I've missed the bus …
h) Oh, hello. Can I speak to Mr Rogers, please?
i) That's all right, thanks.
j) Would you like to give me your telephone number, and I'll ask Mr Rogers to call you when he gets in.

4 ▣ **67** Listen to the conversation to check your answers. Practise the conversation with a partner.

1 Complete the sentences with words from the box.

down   out   out   over   through   up   up

a) My car has broken ____ .
b) I tried to telephone earlier but I couldn't get ____ .
c) I went ____ with some friends last night, so I went to bed very late and overslept this morning.
d) The bus has run ____ of petrol, and we're waiting for another one to arrive.
e) A friend said that she would pick me ____ in her car but she hasn't arrived yet.
f) I split ____ with my boy/girlfriend last night and I need a bit of time to get ____ it.

2 Work with a partner. Discuss these questions.

• Which sentence in 1 is the best excuse for being late?
• Which is the worst excuse?
• What other excuses can you think of?

3 Work with a partner. Write and practise a telephone conversation between a person who is late for work and their boss.

Night clubs

Language reviewed: informal language (Unit 13); modals of obligation & permission (Unit 9); clothes & accessories (Unit 6)

1 Work in groups of four. Discuss the following questions.

- How many good night clubs are there in your city?
- Which is the most expensive club to get in to?
- Have you or your friends ever had difficulty getting in to a club? Why?

2 Look at these pictures of the scene and the characters in a sketch called *The Door*. Compare the pictures to your favourite night club and the sort of people who go there. How different are they? Tell your partner.

3 ▣ 68 You are going to listen to and read the sketch. What do the bouncers do so that they can go home early?

4 Work in groups of four. You are going to perform the sketch.

- a) Decide who is going to play each character. (The first man, second man and third man can be played by the same person. The first woman and second woman can be played by the same person.)
- b) Practise your parts individually. Think about what voice your character will have, what they will look like and how they will act.
- c) Perform the sketch for the rest of the class.

The Door

Scene   Outside a night club. Two bouncers, B1
and B2, one on either side of the door.
Music coming out of the club.

Characters   **B1** (Bouncer 1)
5   **B2** (Bouncer 2)
               M1 (First man)
               W1 (First woman)
               M2 (Second man)
               W2 (Second woman)
10   **M3** (Third man)

B1   All right, mate?
B2   All right.
B1   You look completely knackered – what have you
been up to?
15 **B2**   I *am* knackered – I've worked every night this
week.
B1   What? You're mad.
B2   Yeah, but I'm skint, mate. I need the cash. I'm
looking forward to getting home tonight though –
20   know what I mean?
B1   Cheer up – it's midnight, and there's hardly
anybody here. I reckon we can finish early tonight.
B2   No – look, people are starting to arrive now.
B1   Don't worry – we'll soon get rid of them.

25 *First man approaches.*

B1   Sorry mate, you can't come in.
M1   What do you mean I can't come in?
B1   Sorry mate, we have a very strict dress code here,
and you can't come in.
30 **M1**   Why not?
B1   Because you're wearing trainers.
M1   But I was here last night and I was wearing exactly
the same clothes.
B1   Last night was 'casual night'. Tonight is 'smart
35   casual' night.
M1   Smart casual night? What are you talking about?
B1   On smart casual night, you have to wear smart
casual clothes. You can't wear jeans, trainers or
baseball caps.
40 **M1**   Well, I'm not coming here again.

First woman approaches.

B1   Sorry love, you can't come in.
W1   What?
B2   Sorry love, we have a very strict dress code here,
45   and you can't come in.
W1   But I'm a model. You have to let me in.
B1   Sorry love, we can't let you in. You're wearing
jeans.
W1   But they're designer jeans. I paid a lot of money for
50   them. Everybody wears jeans.
B2   Sorry love, the rules are the rules. You can't
come in.
W1   I'm going to tell all my friends about this.

Second man approaches.

55 **B2**   Sorry mate, you can't come in.
M2   What?
B1   Sorry mate, we have a very strict dress code here,
and you can't come in.
M2   But I'm wearing a suit.
60 **B2**   That's right. It's smart casual night, and you're
wearing a suit, so you can't come in.
M2   But I came here on Monday night and I was
wearing exactly the same clothes.
B1   Monday night was formal night, sir. On formal
65   night you have to wear a suit.
B2   Yeah, tonight is smart casual night, and you have to
wear smart casual clothes.
M2   How ridiculous. I'm not coming here again.

Second woman approaches.

70 **B1**   Sorry love, you can't come in.
W2   Why not? I'm twenty-one.
B2   Sorry love, we have a very strict dress code, and
you can't come in.
W2   But I'm not wearing trainers or jeans or a baseball
75   cap.
B1   No, but your skirt's too short. You can't wear a
mini-skirt on smart casual night.
W2   Look, I'm the DJ's girlfriend. You have to let me in.
B2   Yeah, and I'm the DJ's brother-in-law. Now get
80   lost!
W2   Ah, right. I'll see you later.

Third man approaches.

B1   Evening, sir.
M3   Evening.
85 **B2**   All right, you can go in.

Almost immediately the third man comes out.

B1   That was quick, sir.
M3   It's too boring – there's nobody in there!
B1   Right, let's go home.
90 **B2**   All right mate. See you tomorrow.

16 Lifestyle

Reading

1 Work with a partner. Choose an appropriate alternative to give somebody advice on how to live longer. Decide on the top three tips for a healthy and longer life.

You'll live longer if you …
a) eat a low-**calorie** / -**vitamin** / -**protein** diet.
b) eat three quarters **junk** / **frozen** / **plant** food and one quarter **animal** / **tinned** / **baby** food.
c) eat seven servings of **jam** / **fruit and vegetables** / **chocolate** every day.
d) stop eating when you are **50%** / **80%** / **100%** full.
e) do the things you **enjoy** / **hate** / **can**.
f) have a strong network of **advisers** / **friends** / **doctors**.

2 Read this article about the lifestyle on the island of Okinawa in Japan. Which tips from 1 are mentioned?

How not to die before you get old

Chiako is active and healthy. She gets up at 7am every day, takes a brisk 30-minute walk and plays gate-ball with her friends three times a week. There is nothing unusual about this, except that Chiako is 102 years old. She is not alone – there are hundreds of healthy
5 centenarians who lead similar lives in Okinawa.

Okinawa is a group of islands between Japan and Taiwan. Near a beach, there is a large stone with the following words on it: 'At 70 you are still a child, at 80 you are just a youth, and at 90, if the ancestors invite you into heaven, ask them to wait until you are 100, and then
10 you might consider it.'

Okinawans manage to stay slim in old age by eating a low-calorie diet which consists of three quarters plant food and one quarter animal food. They eat seven servings of fruit and vegetables every day and they stop eating when they are 80% full.

15 They also keep active by dancing, walking and gardening. In other words, they do the things they enjoy.

Okinawans have developed a stress-resistant personality. Nobody is in a hurry, timetables are non-existent and there is always tomorrow. Hundreds of people, both young and old, go to the beach every day
20 to watch the spectacular sunsets. In Okinawa there is always time to watch the sun set.

As well as large extended families, Okinawans have strong networks of friends. 'When someone is ill and doesn't come to work, a neighbour will always knock on their door to find out how they are.'
25 There's no magic pill. If you have good friends, a healthy diet and a stress-free lifestyle, you will live longer. It's as simple as that!

3 How different is your lifestyle from the one described on Okinawa? Compare with your partner.

1 Complete these collocations with words from the article on Okinawa.

a) How often do you go for a b_____ walk?
b) Do you think you l_____ a healthy lifestyle?
c) Do you feel that you are always i_____ a hurry?
d) Do you have a large e_____ family?
e) Do you have strong n_____ of friends?

2 Work with a partner. Ask each other the questions in 1.

Anecdote Think about the healthiest or fittest person you know. You are going to tell your partner about them. Choose from the list the things you want to talk about. Think about what you will say and what language you will need.

☐ Is it a man or a woman?   ☐ What do they do for a living?
☐ How old are they?   ☐ What do they do to stay healthy and fit?
☐ How do you know this person?   ☐ Have they ever been unhealthy or unfit?
☐ What do they look like?   ☐ How is their lifestyle different from yours?

Health farms

Listening **1** ▭ **69** You are going to listen to a woman asking for information about a health farm.

a) What's the name of the health farm?
b) Why does she want the information?
c) What do you think her husband will think about her idea?

2 Complete the sentences by choosing the correct alternatives and then listen to the conversation again. Tick (✓) the activities which her husband will do at the health farm.

a) He'll **pass / take** a fitness test.   d) He'll **do / make** two hours of yoga.
b) He'll **make / go on** a diet.   e) He'll **do / have** a sauna.
c) He'll **take / have** a cigarette.   f) He'll **make / go for** a four-hour hike.

3 Work with a partner. Discuss these questions.

• Are there any health farms in your country like the one in the recording?
• What sort of people go to health farms?
• Would you like to go to one?

Close up

Future time clauses

Language reference p97

Verb structures p130

1 Work with a partner. Look at the following sentences from the listening in the previous section and answer the questions.

Conjunction	+	Subordinate clause	+	Main clause
As soon as	+	*he arrives*	+	*he'll take a fitness test.*
If	+	*he has a cigarette*	+	*he'll be in big trouble.*
When	+	*he finishes the week*	+	*he'll feel like a new man.*

a) Do these sentences refer to past, present or future time?
b) Which verb structure is used in the main clause?
c) Which verb structure is used in the subordinate clause?

2 Which of the conjunctions in 1 suggests:

a) something will *possibly* happen?
b) something will *certainly* happen at a particular time?
c) something will happen *immediately*?

3 Look at how the sentences in 1 are formed. Is the following sentence structure also possible?

main clause + conjunction + subordinate clause (*He'll take a fitness test as soon as he arrives.*)

4 Complete these sentences with the correct verb structure.

a) If there's nothing good on TV this evening, I **go / 'll go** out.
b) When I **'ll go / go** on holiday next summer I'll send you a postcard.
c) I'm going straight home as soon as the lesson **will finish / finishes.**
d) When I **'ll have / have** enough money I'm going to buy a new jacket.
e) If I get up early tomorrow I think I **go / 'll go** for a run.

5 How many sentences in 4 are true for you? Re-write the sentences as necessary so that they are all true for you. Compare your sentences with a partner.

will for prediction

1 Complete each of these quotes by inserting *will* in the correct position. Match each quote with the person who you think made the prediction.

a) 'Man *will* not fly for fifty years.'	1 Bob Metcalf, founder of 3Com Corporation, in 1995. (A year later, he took his magazine article, liquefied it in a blender, and ate it with a spoon.)
b) 'No woman in my time be Prime Minister.'	2 Wilbur Wright to his brother Orville in 1901. (In 1903, the Wright brothers made the first flight)
c) 'The internet collapse within a year.'	3 Conservative politician Margaret Thatcher in 1969. (She became British Prime Minister in 1979.)

2 Work in small groups. You are going to consult the *Oracle* to find out things about your future. Turn to page 128 and follow the instructions. Compare your answers.

3 Think about the topics in the box and use the sentence beginnings to write about your life in the future. Compare with your partner.

| family   children   relationships   health and fitness   house   job   travel |
| possessions   money   free-time   hair   English |

I'll definitely … / I definitely won't …   I hope I'll … / I hope I won't …
I'll probably … / I probably won't …   I think I'll … / I don't think I'll …

Language reference: future forms

Future time clauses

When you are talking about the future you use a future form in the main clause but you use the simple present in the subordinate clauses after *when, if, as soon as, before, after*, etc.

conjunction	subordinate clause	main clause
When	he **finishes** the week	he'll feel like a new man.
If	he **has** a cigarette here	he'll be in big trouble.

Note: Main clause + conjunction + subordinate clause (*He'll feel like a new man when he finishes the week.*) is an alternative order.

will for prediction

You use *will* + infinitive to make predictions about the future. You can grade or qualify your predictions by using the following structures.

I'll definitely / I definitely won't go to England next summer.
My father will probably / My father probably won't retire when he's sixty-five.
I hope I'll / I hope I won't have more than two children.
I think I'll / I don't think I'll be rich and famous. NOT ~~I think I won't ...~~

Food glorious food

Lexis: food

1 Work with a partner. Look at the shopping list and tick (✓) the items this person has bought. Which six items have they forgotten?

Fruit and vegetables
oranges, lemons, bananas,
apples, grapes, peaches,
potatoes, tomatoes, lettuce,
spinach, carrots, cauliflower,
aubergine, mushrooms,
red peppers, green beans,
cucumber, onions, garlic
Meat and fish
a chicken, sausages, trout,
sardines
Other
prawns, tea, soup, nuts

2 Place the items on the lines in these two diagrams. Compare with your partner.

have had recently		couldn't live without
haven't had recently		could live without

3 Which of the items in 1 are never/always on your own shopping list? Add other things that are always on your shopping list. Compare with your partner.

Sounds & spelling

1 ▭ **70** The relationship between vowel sounds and spelling isn't always obvious. Listen and repeat the words in column A and column B.

A		B	
a)	lettuce	1	nut
b)	onion	2	tomato
c)	banana	3	spinach
d)	sardines	4	beans
e)	orange	5	lemon
f)	aubergine	6	cauliflower

2 ▭ **71** Match a word from column A with a word from column B according to the highlighted vowel sounds. Listen and check your answers. Which word do you find most difficult to say?

Lexis: food idioms

1 Work with a partner. Look at the conversations and discuss.

a) Who do you think is speaking?

b) What do you think the conversations are about?

A

A: Is he tired?
B: No, he's full of **beans** / **spinach** / **mushrooms**.
A: Oh no – he'll never want to go to bed.

B

A: Hey, what do you think of the guy over there with the blue shirt on?
B: Um – he's okay, but he's not my cup of **hot chocolate** / **soup** / **tea**.
A: Good – he is mine.

C

A: Why can't I go out?
B: Look, I've told you a hundred times. It's raining. Now stop going on about it. You're driving me **sausages** / **nuts** / **onions**.
A: But why can't I?

D

A: No, I can't. It's too difficult.
B: No, it isn't. It's a piece of **toast** / **pizza** / **cake**. Come on.
A: No, no. Stop it. I'm going to fall over.

E

A: What have you done today? Nothing!
B: That's not true. I've read the paper.
A: And watched television for two hours. You're nothing but a lazy couch **potato** / **cucumber** / **tomato**.

F

A: What was it like?
B: Awful, it was so crowded. We were packed in like **grapes** / **sardines** / **garlic**.
A: Oh dear. You won't go there again then, will you?

2 Complete the idioms by choosing the correct alternatives.

3 ▭ **72** Listen to the conversations and check your answers to 2. Do you have any idioms like these in your language?

4 Replace the underlined phrases with an idiom from 1.

a) I am always very energetic late at night. I never want to go to bed.

b) I could never be friends with someone who watches TV all the time.

c) I hate places where you are with lots of other people.

d) I think that learning English is really easy.

e) I was a naughty child and drove my parents crazy.

f) Going clubbing isn't something I enjoy.

5 Are the sentences in 4 true or false for you? Compare with a partner.

How to eat a banana

Lexis: food preparation

1 You are going to read an extract from a website about recipes for dishes made with bananas. Tick (✓) the dishes you would like to try and put a cross (✗) next to the ones you wouldn't like to try.

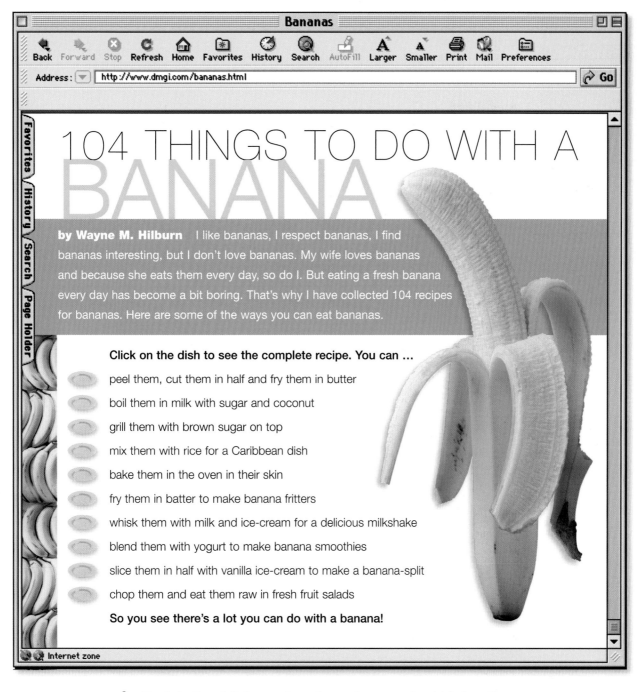

Bananas

Back Forward Stop Refresh Home Favorites History Search AutoFill Larger Smaller Print Mail Preferences

Address: http://www.dmgi.com/bananas.html   Go

104 THINGS TO DO WITH A BANANA

by Wayne M. Hilburn   I like bananas, I respect bananas, I find bananas interesting, but I don't love bananas. My wife loves bananas and because she eats them every day, so do I. But eating a fresh banana every day has become a bit boring. That's why I have collected 104 recipes for bananas. Here are some of the ways you can eat bananas.

Click on the dish to see the complete recipe. You can ...

- peel them, cut them in half and fry them in butter
- boil them in milk with sugar and coconut
- grill them with brown sugar on top
- mix them with rice for a Caribbean dish
- bake them in the oven in their skin
- fry them in batter to make banana fritters
- whisk them with milk and ice-cream for a delicious milkshake
- blend them with yogurt to make banana smoothies
- slice them in half with vanilla ice-cream to make a banana-split
- chop them and eat them raw in fresh fruit salads

So you see there's a lot you can do with a banana!

Internet zone

2 Read the list of dishes again and note down words which describe:
   a) different ways of preparing food (For example: *peel*)
   b) different ways of cooking food (For example: *fry*)
   c) one word meaning *not cooked*

3 Think of lots of different items of food which you can prepare and cook in the ways described in 2.

For example: *peel an apple, an orange, a potato*, etc.   *fry an egg, fish, onions*, etc.

4 Think about a meal you have eaten recently. Note down exactly what you ate. How did the cook prepare the food? How did they cook the food? Describe the meal in detail to your partner.

17 *Animals*

Lexis: animals

Test your knowledge of animals! Work with a partner and match the definitions (*a–f*) with the words (*1–6*). The answers are on page 124.

Animal facts

a) An animal that can last longer without water than a camel.
b) A person who treats sick animals.
c) An insect that can lift fifty times its own weight.
d) An animal that can run at 100 kph.
e) An animal that can live to seventy years old.
f) An animal that can recognise its own image in a mirror.

1 A cheetah.
2 A dolphin
3 A vet.
4 A giraffe.
5 An ant.
6 A tortoise.

Homophones

1 There are some words in English that sound exactly the same but have different spellings and different meanings. Complete the table by matching each of the words in the box with one of the clues below.

tail	weight	bear	right	deer	wait	Dear	tale	write	bare

Word A		Sound	Word B
1	*tail* – a cat has a long one.	/teɪl/	_____ – an imaginative story
2	_____ – brown animal with long legs / Bambi	/dɪə/	_____ – . . . sir or madam, . . .
3	_____ – a large animal with thick fur.	/beə/	_____ – empty / nude
4	_____ – correct / not wrong.	/raɪt/	_____ – use a pen to do this.
5	_____ – don't go / stay in one place	/weɪt/	_____ – in kilos, for example.

2 🔲 **73** Listen, repeat and check your answers. In your language do you have words that sound the same but have different spellings?

Close up

Relative clauses **1** Combine each of the following sentences with *that* to make one new sentence.

    a) I've got a friend. He lives in London.   For example: *I've got a friend that lives in London.*
    b) I've got a car. It isn't very easy to park.
    c) I know a woman. She's got a beautiful singing voice.
    d) I went to a private school. It was a long way from my house.
    e) My parents have got two dogs. They like going for long walks.
    f) I've got a sister. She works in a shop.
    g) Last week I watched a very sad film. It made me cry.

2 Work with a partner. Look at the new sentences you have written in 1. <u>Underline</u> the relative clauses in the new sentences. What is the subject of the verb in each relative clause?

    For example: *I've got a friend* | that | | lives | *in London.*
                                  subject   verb

3 In which sentences in 1 can you replace *that* with *which*? In which sentences can you replace *that* with *who*? What is the rule for using the relative pronouns *which*, *who* and *that*?

4 How many of the sentences in 1 are true for you? Compare your answers with a partner.

5 The definitions in column A are ungrammatical. Correct each one by ~~crossing out~~ one unnecessary word. Then match the definitions with a word from column B.

A	B
a) An animal that ~~it~~ can smell water five kilometres away.	1 A saddle.
b) A person who he studies birds.	2 A kangaroo.
c) An animal that it sleeps standing up.	3 A mosquito.
d) The only animal – apart from humans – which it gets sunburn.	4 An elephant.
e) A name for people who they are afraid of spiders.	5 An ornithologist
f) The thing that you sit on it when you ride a horse.	6 A pig.
g) An insect that you get malaria from it.	7 A horse.
h) An animal whose name it means 'I don't understand.'	8 Arachnophobic.

6 Use the ideas in the boxes (and your own) to write down three true statements about your feelings or the feelings of people you know well. Compare your statements with a partner.

I My mother My father My friend etc.	+	love(s) hate(s)	+	people men women children animals bars shops rooms etc.	+	who which that	+	are funny / serious. talk too quietly / loudly. are very cheap / expensive. drive too slowly / fast. are very big / small etc.

Language reference: relative clauses

A *relative clause* gives additional information about a person or a thing introduced in the main clause. It comes immediately after the <u>person</u> or <u>thing</u> it is describing.

*A <u>person</u> **who treats sick animals** is called a vet.*
*I've got a <u>car</u> **that isn't very easy to park**.*

You usually introduce a relative clause with a relative pronoun: **who** for people, **which** for things and **that** for people or things. The relative pronoun becomes the subject (or the object) of the verb in the relative clause so you don't need to use *she, him, it* etc.

*An ornithologist is a person **who studies birds**.* NOT ... ~~who he studies birds~~
*A mosquito is an insect **that you get malaria from**.* NOT ... ~~that you get malaria from it~~

Animal tales

1 Work in groups of three. You are going to read some true stories about the six animals in the pictures. Which animal do you think goes best with descriptions *A–F*?

A An animal that healed someone who was depressed.
B An animal that died of a broken heart.
C An animal that refused to be separated from another animal in the same house.
D An animal that knew when its owner was coming home.
E An animal that loved classical music.
F An animal that accidentally deleted some valuable files on a computer.

2 Work in groups of three. Student A, Student B and Student C read your two animal stories and match a description in 1 to each story.

Student A

STORY 1

Mr and Mrs Roper live near London with their son, Robert, and a mynah bird called Sammy. Robert travels a lot in his work and he is sometimes away for weeks or even months. He doesn't always tell his parents when he is coming home, but he doesn't need to. Mr and Mrs Roper always know when their son is going to arrive because Sammy starts calling 'Robbie' a few hours before Robert walks through the door.

STORY 2

Bill Bowell, a retired manager, was suffering from depression. The doctor gave him antidepressants, but they didn't help, and he was unable to work for twelve years.

Then he decided to swim with the dolphins.

'My life changed forever,' says Bowell. 'A dolphin called Simo looked into my eyes for a few minutes and I started to cry. All my emotions erupted like a volcano. As I cried, Simo put his head on my chest and stayed very still.' After swimming with dolphins Bowell says he has fully recovered.

Student B

STORY 1

In France, a man had to move to a new job two hundred kilometres away. He owned a dog and a cat and he loved them both. But he thought that the cat would prefer to stay in the same house with new owners.

So he moved house and only took the dog.

About three weeks later, the dog suddenly disappeared. For several days, the man looked for his dog, but didn't find him.

Then, seven weeks later, the dog turned up ... but he was not alone. By his side was the cat. They were tired and hungry after their long journey, and the cat's paws were bleeding. But they recovered quickly and were never separated again.

STORY 2

A bank worker in San Francisco decided to take his Siamese cat, Morris, into work with him one day. While the man was speaking on the telephone, Morris walked across the keyboard of his computer and accidentally keyed in a secret code that deleted files worth $100,000. As you can imagine, the man's employers were not amused.

Student C

STORY 1

People say that fish are cold, but this story proves that they have feelings too.

A friend was moving to another country, so we took her pet goldfish and put it in a bowl with our goldfish. They lived together for six months, and when the friend came back, we separated them again, and she took her goldfish home.

I immediately noticed that my goldfish was behaving strangely, banging against the side of the bowl. The next morning he was floating on the surface, dead.

Later that day, my friend phoned to say that her goldfish was also dead.

I believe they died of a broken heart.

STORY 2

While travelling in the north of England some years ago, my husband and I stopped in a quiet place for a picnic and played some Mozart on a CD player. After a few minutes we looked up and realised that we were surrounded by cows who were listening to the music. When the Mozart was finished, we put on a CD of modern music. The cows immediately turned round and walked off.

3 Work in groups of three. Without looking at the book, take it in turns to retell your stories to the other people in your group. Explain which descriptions from 1 you have matched to your stories. Which story do you like best?

Lexis **1** The words and expressions in the box are from the stories in the previous section. Use them to complete this joke about a clever dog.

> turned up   turned round   paw   decided to   stayed very still   walked off
> looked into his eyes

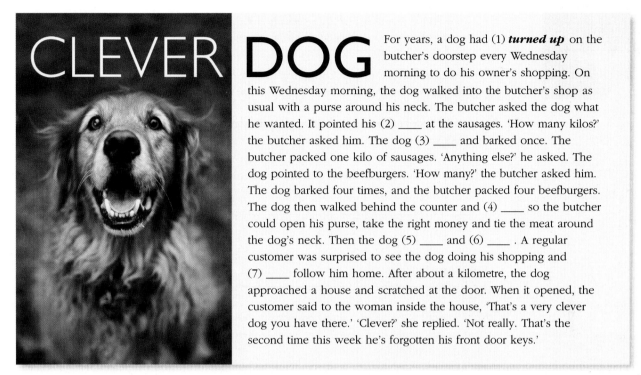

CLEVER DOG

For years, a dog had (1) ***turned up*** on the butcher's doorstep every Wednesday morning to do his owner's shopping. On this Wednesday morning, the dog walked into the butcher's shop as usual with a purse around his neck. The butcher asked the dog what he wanted. It pointed his (2) ____ at the sausages. 'How many kilos?' the butcher asked him. The dog (3) ____ and barked once. The butcher packed one kilo of sausages. 'Anything else?' he asked. The dog pointed to the beefburgers. 'How many?' the butcher asked him. The dog barked four times, and the butcher packed four beefburgers. The dog then walked behind the counter and (4) ____ so the butcher could open his purse, take the right money and tie the meat around the dog's neck. Then the dog (5) ____ and (6) ____ . A regular customer was surprised to see the dog doing his shopping and (7) ____ follow him home. After about a kilometre, the dog approached a house and scratched at the door. When it opened, the customer said to the woman inside the house, 'That's a very clever dog you have there.' 'Clever?' she replied. 'Not really. That's the second time this week he's forgotten his front door keys.'

2 🔲 74 Listen and check your answers to 1. Do you know any jokes or stories about animals? Tell your partner one of your jokes or stories.

Special friends

Listening **1** 🔲 75 Listen to Tim, Gus and Maxine being interviewed about their pets. Guess what their pets are from the words in the box. Compare your guesses with a partner. The answers are on page 127.

> a cat   a rat   a pig   a dog   a hamster   a parrot   a spider   a snake

Tim

Gus

Maxine

2 Work with a partner. Look at the following list of pet characteristics. Tick (✓) the ones that you think were mentioned in the interviews.

a) He/She's a good companion.
b) He/She listens to my problems.
c) He/She makes me laugh when he/she does silly things.
d) We have a special bond.
e) He/She helps me make friends with other people with pets.
f) He/She frightens people away.
g) He/She keeps me fit because I have to take him/her out for walks.
h) He/She looks cool.
i) He/She parties all night long.
j) He/She gives me unconditional love.

3 Listen to the interviews again and check your answers to 2. Put *T* for Tim, *G* for Gus or *M* for Maxine if they mention that their pet has one of the characteristics.

4 Which of the characteristics in 2 would you look for in a pet? Which of these characteristics would you look for in a person? Discuss with a partner.

Close up

Yasmina would like to be a tiger.

1 Work with a partner. The diagram shows the last question from the interview in the previous section. Discuss the questions.

If-clause	Main clause
If + past tense *If you were an animal*	*would + infinitive* *what animal would you like to be?*

a) Is the question about a real situation or an unreal situation?
b) Is the question about now or the past? What tense is used in the *If*-clause?

2 Replace the word *animal* in the table in 1 with words from the box and/or your own ideas. Ask your partner the questions. Discuss your answers.

> a famous person   a fictional character   a colour   a car   a month

3 Complete the *Unreal situation* column with conditional sentences so that they are true for you. Compare your sentences with your partner.

Real situation	Unreal situation
a) I'm not a member of the opposite sex.	➔ *If I was a member of the opposite sex, I'd / I wouldn't ____ .*
b) I'm not the president of my country.	➔ If ____ , I'd / I wouldn't ____ .
c) I haven't got $1 million.	➔ If ____ , I'd / I wouldn't ____ .
d) I don't speak English fluently.	➔ If ____ , I'd / I wouldn't ____ .
e) I can't fly a plane.	➔ If ____ , I'd / I wouldn't ____ .

4 Work in small groups. Look at these 'moral dilemmas'. Complete them with the correct verb form and then discuss your answers to each one.

a) If you (**find**) a wallet in the street with £20, would you give the wallet in to the police – but keep the cash?
b) If you saw your friend's partner kissing someone else, (**you tell**) your friend?
c) If a shop assistant (**give**) you too much change, would you keep the money and say nothing?
d) If a friend left their bag at your house by mistake, (**you look**) through it?
e) If you (**see**) some children stealing some chocolate from a shop, would you tell the shop owner?

5 Write down two more 'moral dilemmas' beginning with *If* + past tense and pass them on to another group. Discuss the answers.

Language reference: conditionals

You can use a conditional sentence to talk about a present situation that is unreal or not probable. Conditional sentences have two clauses: an *If*-clause and a main clause.

If-clause	**Main clause**
To show that a present situation is unreal, you use a past tense.	You usually use *would* + infinitive in the main clause.

Real situation	Unreal situation	If-clause	Main clause
time (now) = present simple	➔ time (now) = past simple	If I had $1 million,	I'd travel round the world.
I am not an animal.	➔ If I was/were an animal, ...*	If I could fly a plane,	I'd sell my car.
I live in an apartment.	➔ If I lived in an igloo, ...		

*Note: *If I / he / she / it* **were** is more formal than *If I / he / she / it* **was**.

Reptiles

1 Read the article about a pet snake and explain the links between the following.

    a) 2 years old – 5 years old   b) 20 centimetres – 1 metre   c) 2 minutes – 3 months

(Based on an article in The Guardian Weekend)

KING JIM

My son has been interested in having a snake
as a pet since he was two. I think he's fascinated by their power to make people like
me run away in horror. I've never been keen on the idea of having a snake in the
house and I was hoping he would get tired of asking for one in the end, but his
5 stepfather went ahead and bought a little surprise snake for Louis' fifth birthday.

    It was quite sweet: about twenty centimetres long and the width of a pencil –
a non-venomous Californian King snake which Louis called King Jim. But then
it grew and grew and grew. A year and a half later, it was about a metre long
and as thick as a sausage. Some people objected to it so much that they
10 stopped coming to our house.

    Personally I disapprove of keeping a wild animal as a pet. It must get so
bored of going round and round in its cage. I know he's unhappy because
once, when Louis left the cage door open for a couple of minutes, King Jim
escaped in a flash. We worried about him dying of cold or hunger, but to our
15 surprise he turned up in the kitchen downstairs three months later.

    When I think about it now, I can't believe we didn't tell our friends that we had
an escaped snake in the house.

2 Would you have a pet snake? What's the most unusual pet you know? Tell your partner.

**Lexis:
prepositions
after verbs &
adjectives**

1 Study the examples from the article above. Then complete the sentences to make
some true and some false statements about yourself.

verb or adjective	preposition	*-ing* form or noun or pronoun
My son has been interested	*in*	*having a snake.* (line 1)
Some people objected	*to*	*it.* (line 9)

    a) At school, I was fascinated *by* ... (line 2)   e) I'll never get bored ____ ... (line 12)
    b) I've never been keen ____ ... (line 3)   f) I often worry ____ (line 14)
    c) As a child, I never got tired ____ ... (line 4)   g) I feel happy when I think ____ ...
    d) My parents disapprove ____ ... (line 11)   (line 16)

2 Work with a partner. Read your partner's statements from 1 and guess which statements
are true and which are false.

Anecdote **1** 🔊 **76** Listen to Mandy talking about her friend's pet iguana. Which of the following
topics does she talk about?

    ☐ What kind of animal is it?   ☐ What sort of personality does it have?
    ☐ Who is its owner?   ☐ Where does it sleep?
    ☐ What's its name?   ☐ What does it eat?
    ☐ How old is it?   ☐ Does it need much exercise?
    ☐ What does it look like?   ☐ Can it do any tricks?

2 Work with a partner. Note down as much information as you can remember about the
topics Mandy talks about. Listen again and check your answers.

3 Think about a pet that you know: yours or somebody else's. You are going to tell your
partner about it. Choose from the list in 1 the things you want to talk about. Think about
what you will say and what language you will need.

18 Weird

Work in small groups. Look at the photograph below and discuss the questions.

- What do you know about crop circles?
- Who or what do you think made them?
- How do you think they are made?

> **crop circles** Patterns that began mysteriously appearing in fields in England and some other European countries in the 1980s.

Reading

Many theories have been put forward about who or what causes crop circles. Read this list of possible explanations and decide which is most and least believable. Discuss your answers with your partner.

LANGUAGE TOOLBOX

Who / What do you think ...?
I think ...
I don't think ...
Maybe it's ...
I've no idea.
I haven't a clue.

THE CREAM OF THE

CROP CIRCLE
THEORIES

•

WIND Strong winds blow the corn into spiral patterns.

ALIENS The circles are landing sites for alien spacecraft or messages from other planets. People say they have seen bright flashing lights on the nights when crop circles have appeared.

MAGNETIC FORCES The crop circles are produced by magnetic forces under the earth.

WEAPONS TESTING The crop circles are caused by military tests which the army want to keep secret.

HELICOPTERS The patterns are caused by the wind produced by helicopter rotor blades.

HOAXERS Groups of people create the crop circles at night. They say that they have made most, but not all, of the crop circles over the years.

The mother of all circles

Listening   **1** 📼 **77** One night in August 2001 the crop circle in this photograph appeared in southern England. You are going to listen to a crop circle expert being interviewed about it. Listen and complete each question with the correct word.

a) How ____ have you been interested in crop circles?
b) How ____ is it exactly?
c) How ____ circles are there altogether?
d) How ____ does it take to make a crop circle?
e) How ____ have crop circles existed?

Alton Barnes, Hampshire, England

2 Work with a partner. Match the questions in 1 to the answers below. Listen to the interview again and check your ideas.

1   Almost one kilometre wide.
2   Since 1980.
3   For about eleven years.
4   More than 400.
5   A few hours or several days.

3 What information in the interview did you find most surprising? How do *you* think the Alton Barnes crop circle was formed? Discuss with your partner.

Lexis: *How* + adjective / adverb ...?   **1** All of the questions in 1 above use the construction *How* + adjective/adverb. Make eight more questions by combining the question beginnings (*a–h*) with the most appropriate question ends (*1–8*). In some cases more than one combination is possible.

a) How long
b) How often
c) How many
d) How much
e) How far
f) How fast
g) How old
h) How well

1   cousins have you got?
2   does your car go?
3   do you travel by train?
4   is the oldest living person in your family?
5   does it take you to get to work/school?
6   is it from your house to the nearest beach?
7   do you know your neighbours?
8   cash do you have on you at the moment?

2 Use the questions in 1 and your own ideas to interview your partner.

3 Complete the table by writing down how long it takes you to do each activity. Guess the time it takes your partner to do the same things and then ask questions to check your ideas.

For example: *How long does it take you to get up in the morning?*

	Activity	You	Your partner
How long ...?	• get up in the morning • eat lunch during a working day • buy presents for people you love • choose from a menu in a restaurant • decide whether you like someone or not • get ready to go out for the evening • get to sleep at night		

Incredible but true

Reading **1** You are going to read three true stories. In each case a sentence is missing from the story. Match each of the sentences with a story and then re-insert the sentence in the appropriate position *1*, *2*, or *3*.

a) She was now nearly 22 and hadn't met the love of her life yet.
b) At that time Amy didn't know that Ian had just started his journey from Sydney to London.
c) It was a reply from another Laura Buxton, who had found the balloon in her garden 225 kilometres away.

A Two Lauras

Laura Buxton, 10, was celebrating her grandparents' golden wedding anniversary, when she had an idea. **1** She decided to release a gold and white helium-filled balloon with her name and address and a note attached. In the note she asked the person who found the balloon to write back. Ten days later a letter arrived at her home. **2** Both Lauras were aged 10 and both have three-year-old black Labradors, a guinea pig and a rabbit. **3** 'I chatted to Laura on the phone,' said the first Laura. 'I hope we can become best friends. We have lots in common.'

B Worlds apart

Amy Dolby took her seat on the flight from London to Sydney, Australia. She was going to Australia to surprise her boyfriend, Ian Johnstone. **1** He wanted to propose to Amy on 1 July because this was the fifth anniversary of their relationship. **2** They both stopped in Singapore to wait for connecting flights, but they didn't know that they were sitting a few metres away from one another. **3** Ian arrived in Amy's hometown just as she knocked on his door in Sydney. When they found out what had happened, Ian proposed over the phone, and Amy accepted.

C Text before marriage

A clairvoyant had once told Emily Brown that she would meet her husband when she was 21. **1** One day, she tapped the text message, 'Do you want to talk?' into her mobile. She then invented a number and sent the message. She didn't know that the number belonged to her future husband. **2** Peter Baldwin was at work 140 miles away when he got the message. He phoned Emily, and they chatted for about an hour. **3** They found that they had lots in common and made arrangements to meet. They got married six months later.

2 📼 78 Listen and check your answers to 1.

3 Work in small groups. Discuss these questions.

- Have you ever read or heard about 'incredible but true' stories like the stories in 1?
- Do you know any people (couples, friends, colleagues) who have met in a strange way?
- Have any strange coincidences or 'small world' incidents ever happened to you?

1 Refer to the stories in the previous section and answer these questions.

a) Who <u>had an idea</u>?
b) Who <u>made arrangements</u> to meet someone?
c) Who <u>took her seat</u> on her flight to Australia?

2 Work with a partner. Look at the following statements and choose the appropriate verb in each case.

a) If you don't **have / make / take** risks, you won't succeed in life.
b) You should never **have / make / take** a promise if you can't keep it.
c) Everybody should **have / make / take** a go at doing something dangerous once in their life.
d) All parents should **have / make / take** a course in parenting skills.
e) The press should not **have / make / take** photographs of famous people without their permission.
f) **Having / Making / Taking** mistakes is part of the process of learning a language.
g) The most important thing in life is to get a job where you can **have / make / take** lots of money.

3 Work with a partner. Decide if you agree or disagree with the statements in 2.

Close up

Past perfect

Language reference p110

Verb structures p129

1 Work with a partner. Look at the sentence from one of the stories in the previous section and discuss the following questions.

At that time Amy <u>didn't know</u> that Ian <u>had just started</u> his journey from Sydney to London.

a) Both <u>underlined</u> verb structures describe past events. What is the name of each tense?
b) Which tense shows clearly that one past event happened before the other past event?
c) How do you form these tenses? Complete the table.

	Affirmative	Negative	Question
Past simple	1 _____	She didn't know	2 _____ ?
Past perfect	He'd (had) started	3 _____	4 _____ ?

2 You are going to read two extracts from a story entitled *Reincarnation*. Read the first extract. Why did Jenny Cockell decide to travel to Ireland?

Reincarnation

Jenny Cockell was sure that she (1) **lived / had lived** before. As a child, she remembered her past life in her dreams. In particular, she often dreamt about Mary Sutton, a young Irish woman who (2) **died / had died** more than twenty years before Jenny was born. Over the years, Jenny became convinced that her dreams (3) **were / had been** real memories and that she (4) **was / had been** Mary in a previous life.

In her dreams she saw the house in Ireland where Mary and her family (5) **lived / had lived**. As her visions continued and became more detailed, Jenny (6) **realised / had realised** that Mary (7) **died / had died** in 1930 and that her children could still be alive. She (8) **wanted / had wanted** to find out and decided to travel to Ireland.

3 79 Work with a partner. Complete the first extract by choosing the most appropriate tense (past simple or past perfect) for the numbered verbs. Listen and check your answers.

4 Read the second extract. Who did Sonny think Jenny was? What do you think?

> In Ireland, Jenny quickly (1 **find**) the house that she (2 **see**) in her dreams. She then found out that Mary Sutton (3 **die**) in the early 1930s after giving birth to the last of eight children. After their mother's death, the children had all been sent to orphanages, but she finally contacted the eldest son, Sonny. It was an emotional day when Jenny (4 **meet**) the son she (5 **not see**) for fifty years. 'I talked to him about our family life together. I (6 **remind**) him of the day when he (7 **catch**) a rabbit. There were lots of other memories, and they convinced him that I (8 **be**) his mother in a previous life.'
>
> Jenny Cockell has written the story of her extraordinary past life experiences in a book entitled *Yesterday's Children*.

5 ▭ 80 Work with a partner. Complete the second extract by re-writing the numbered verbs in the most appropriate tense. Listen and check your answers.

6 Work with a partner. Discuss times you have felt some of the emotions in the box. Explain what had happened to make you feel that way.

When was the last time you	felt were	exhausted sad proud on top of the world frightened embarrassed jealous in a bad mood	?	What had happened? What had you done?

For example: *The last time I felt exhausted was on Friday. I'd been out till 3.00 am ...*

Language reference: past perfect

You use the past perfect when you are talking about the past and you want to refer to an earlier past time. The past perfect clearly shows that one past event happened earlier than other past events.

*As her visions **continued** and **became** more detailed, Jenny **realised** that Mary **had died** in 1930.*

Earlier past	Past	Now

Anecdote

Des and Lidia

1 ▭ 81 You are going to listen to Des and then Lidia talking about strange experiences they have had. Which of the following topics do they talk about?

Des Lidia

☐ ☐ Who had the strange experience? You, a member of your family, ... ?
☐ ☐ Where was the person when it happened?
☐ ☐ Were they alone?
☐ ☐ Did they see or hear something strange?
☐ ☐ Did they meet somebody in a strange situation?
☐ ☐ What exactly was strange about the experience?
☐ ☐ How did you or the person feel?
☐ ☐ What happened after the experience?
☐ ☐ What do you think about the experience? Can you explain it?

2 Work with a partner. Note down as much information as you can remember about each story. Listen again and check your answers. Which story do you think is the strangest?

3 Think of a strange experience you or somebody you know has had. You are going to tell a partner about it. Choose from the list in 1 the things you want to talk about. Think about what you will say and what language you will need.

We are not alone

1 You are going to read a short account of a famous UFO incident – a mysterious crash in Roswell, New Mexico in 1947. How many different explanations are there for the crash? Do you believe any of the explanations?

Roswell, New Mexico

On 8 July 1947 the US Air Force told the public that a flying disk had crashed in Roswell, New Mexico and that they had found bodies of aliens. Later the same day, the US Air Force changed their story and told reporters that the disk was in fact a weather balloon.

The story became famous when people said that the government had covered up the real story. Thirty years later, witnesses told newspapers that they had seen the aliens. They described the aliens in detail, and models were made according to their descriptions.

In 1994 the US Air Force changed the story again. Now they said that the crash at Roswell in 1947 had been a top secret radar balloon used for spying on the USSR. When Government officials investigated, they found that all documents recorded at Roswell from 1945 to 1949 had been destroyed more than forty years ago.

2 Work in small groups. Discuss these questions.

- Do you think there are forms of life on other planets?
- Do you think aliens have visited the Earth?
- What do you think aliens might look like?
- If you saw a UFO, what would you do?
- If you met an alien, what would you ask?
- If you had to elect someone to meet the alien leader, who would you choose? Why?
- If you could travel in a time machine would you choose to go forward or backward in time? Why?

Writing

1 Work with a partner. Discuss ways of completing *The night I met an alien* by answering the questions. Make notes and add as much detail as possible.

2 Write up your story from the notes you made in 1. Compare your stories with other people in the class.

THE NIGHT I MET AN ALIEN

It was an ordinary evening.
What time was it?
What was the weather like?
What were you doing?

For some reason, I looked up at the sky and I saw a strange object.
What did the object look like?

To my surprise, it landed and an alien got out.
What did the alien look like?
How did you feel?

Then it spoke to me in perfect English.
What did it say?
What was its voice like?

I asked it what I'd always wanted to ask an alien.
What did you ask?

It answered my question.
What did it say?

Eventually, it got back in the object and flew away. I stood still for a while, and when I turned round, I noticed that something had changed.
What had changed?

My life would never be the same again.

19 Wheels

Reading

1 You are going to read three descriptions of people's first cars. Match each description (*A–C*) with one of the pictures (*1–3*) below. Which car caused its owner the most problems?

MY FIRST CAR

A My first car was a Citroën 2CV. I think someone gave it to me – it was very old. It used to break down almost every time I went out in it.

Once I was driving along a country road, and the bonnet blew up against the windscreen, and blocked my view of the road. It was really dangerous because I couldn't see anything.

Another time, it was raining heavily, and one of the windscreen wipers fell off. I had to stop and wait for the rain to stop.

I used to have a love/hate relationship with that car – I loved it when it worked, but I hated it when it broke down.

B It wasn't my car: it was my boyfriend's. It was a blue VW Beetle with a sunroof and white-walled tyres.

Every weekend we used to drive out of town with our tent in the back and drive until we felt like stopping. Sometimes we took friends.

It wasn't a big car, but I remember one weekend we went to Paris with four friends. There were six of us in this little car! I don't think we took any luggage, because there wasn't any space for suitcases. The engine was in the back, and there was only a tiny boot in the front. But we didn't use to worry about that sort of thing when we were younger.

C Daddy gave me my first car when I was 17. I didn't even have my driving licence. It was a sweet little red Porsche with a blue steering wheel and blue seats. It was cute, but I didn't use it much because I used to prefer motorbikes. All my boyfriends had big motorbikes. My daddy used to introduce me to all these nice guys – lawyers and businessmen – but I wasn't interested in them. I was a rebel and I used to enjoy the danger of going on fast motorbikes.

My poor daddy – I used to drive him crazy.

2 What was the first car you drove? Or what was the first car you remember going in as a child? Describe it to your partner.

Lexis: cars　**1**　Find nine words and expressions in the texts in the previous section that describe parts of a car.

2　Work in small groups. Imagine you are going to buy a new car. Divide the following features into 'important' and 'not important'. What other features are important in a car?

> Air-conditioning　Easy to park　Economical to run　Electric sunroof
> Good stereo　Large boot　Leather seats　Looks good　Power steering
> Powerful engine　Spacious interior　Sporty wheels

Anecdote　Imagine your dream car. You are going to tell your partner about it. Choose from the list below the things you want to talk about. Think about what you are going to say and how you are going to say it.

☐　What kind of car is it?

☐　Is it a modern car, or is it an old model?

☐　What colour is it?

☐　What's it like inside?

☐　What kind of seats has it got?

☐　What special features has it got?

☐　What's the top speed?

☐　What CDs have you got in your car?

☐　Where would you like to go in your car?

☐　Who would you take with you?

Close up

Past time:
used to +
infinitive

Language reference p114

1　Work with a partner. Look at these extracts from the article in the previous section. Match each <u>underlined</u> verb structure with a description (1–3). In which case is it *not* possible to use *used to* + infinitive to talk about the past?

a)　'Every weekend <u>we used to drive</u> out of town …'　　1　A single action in the past

b)　'… one weekend <u>we went</u> to Paris …'　　2　A repeated action in the past

c)　'<u>I used to have</u> a love/hate relationship with that car …'　　3　A state in the past

2　Work with a partner. Look at the following sentences. Where it is possible, replace the past simple with *used to / didn't use to* + infinitive.

When I was a child …

a)　My parents <u>had</u> a big old Citroën. *My parents used to have a big old Citroën.*

b)　My mother <u>drove</u> me to school every day.

c)　I <u>didn't like</u> going on long journeys. I <u>was</u> car sick.

d)　One summer we <u>went</u> to France on a camping holiday.

e)　My parents <u>never cleaned</u> the car. It <u>smelled</u> awful.

f)　Eventually my parents <u>sold</u> the car and <u>bought</u> a smaller one.

3　Change the sentences in 2 so that they are true for you. Compare with a partner.

4　Work with a partner. Use the topics in the box and your own ideas to talk about and compare your life now with your life ten years ago.

> the holidays you go on　the car you have　the people you go out with
> the TV programmes you watch　the amount you sleep　the hairstyle you have
> the things you do at weekends　the music you listen to

For example: *I used to spend every summer holiday in my grandparent's house in a tiny village. These days I usually go abroad. I love travelling …*

Language reference: *used to*

You can use *used to* + infinitive to talk about past habits (repeated actions in the past) or past states. It describes things that were true in the past, but are not true now.
Every weekend **we used to drive** out of town.
We didn't use to worry about that sort of thing.
What sort of car **did you use to have?**

For and against cars

1 Work in small groups. Discuss the advantages and disadvantages of owning a car. Note down as many points as you can.

2 📼 **82** You are going to listen to three friends discussing the same thing. Listen to their conversation. How many of the points you noted down in 1 do they mention?

3 Work with a partner. Complete the conversation with Karen, Ron and Jill with one word in each space. Then listen and check your answers.

K: You're late!

R: Yes, I'm really sorry – I had to wait ages for a bus.

J: Why didn't you drive?

R: Ah, well. I've sold my car.

K: Oh, are you getting a new one?

R: No, I'm not getting another car. I've decided to live without one.

J: Wow – what made you do that?

R: I (1) *think* there are too many cars, and this town is far too polluted.

J: Well, that's true, (2) ___ a car is useful.

R: I don't think (3) ___ . Not in the city centre, anyway. I can never find anywhere to park, and you spend most of the time sitting in traffic jams.

K: But how are you going to get to work?

R: By bicycle.

K: (4) ___ you think bicycles are dangerous?

R: Not really. I don't think they're as dangerous as cars.

J: Well, I couldn't do without my car. I have to take the children to school every day.

R: I don't (5) ___ children get enough exercise these days – they should walk to school.

K: Well, I haven't got children, but I (6) ___ with Jill – I couldn't live without my car. I sometimes have to come home late from the office.

R: Why don't you get the bus? Public transport is very good.

K: That's not (7) ___ . The buses are not very regular where I work and anyway, as a woman, I don't feel safe waiting for a bus late at night.

R: Okay, I see what you (8) ___ , but aren't you worried about pollution?

J: Of course, but you don't understand – it's easy for you to worry about the environment. I have to worry about carrying the shopping and children and …

R: Okay, okay, you're (9) ___ ! Come on. Let's get another drink. Hey, (10) ___ do you think of my new haircut?

4 📼 **83** Listen and repeat the highlighted expressions. Copy the stress and intonation exactly.

5 Whose opinion do you agree with most?

Close up

Opinions

1 Look at the highlighted expressions in the conversation in the previous section. Complete the following categorisation to show the function of each expression.

a) Ask for an opinion: (1) *Don't you think …* (2) ____
b) Give an opinion: (1) *I think …* (2) ____
c) Agree partly with an opinion: (1) *Well, that's true, but …* (2) ____
d) Agree completely with an opinion: (1) *I agree with …* (2) ____
e) Disagree with an opinion: (1) *I don't think so.* (2) ____

2 Work in groups of three. Complete the following task.

a) Choose one of the topics in the box (or your own idea) and note down all the advantages and disadvantages that you can think of.
b) Write a short conversation between three friends with your ideas from *a*. Use expressions from 1.
c) Act out your conversation in front of the class. Vote for the best conversation.

> Fast food   Living abroad   Being a woman or a man   Being rich or famous
> Public transport   Marriage   Cloning   Capital punishment
> Living with your parents   Private education   Private health care

Advice & suggestions

1 84 You are going to listen to a radio programme called *Road Rage*. Listeners phone the radio station with travel questions and problems, and the presenter, Dave Darby, gives them advice. Listen and tick (✓) which of the following problems are mentioned.

a) I want to go somewhere nice on holiday but I hate flying.
b) I'm sick of wasting time in traffic jams.
c) I'm a bus driver and I don't get enough exercise.
d) My husband, who is normally kind and considerate, gets very aggressive when he is driving. It frightens me.
e) I can drive but I can't pass my test.
f) I don't want to contribute to the pollution of the environment.

2 Work with a partner. Dave gives Mark three pieces of advice. Listen again and match the beginnings with the ends of each sentence. Do you think this is good advice?

a) Why don't you …   1 use public transport.
b) You could …   2 learn a new language.
c) If I were you I'd …   3 work at home.

3 Work with a partner. If you were Dave Darby, what advice would you give to the second caller, Sharon? Use the sentence beginnings in 2 and make some suggestions.

4 Work with a partner. Invent and act out short conversations where Student A has a problem and Student B gives some advice. Use the other travel problems in 1 as your starting point or your own ideas.

Language reference: opinions, advice & suggestions

There are many ways to ask for, give, agree with or disagree with opinions.

Ask for an opinion: ***What do you think*** of my new jacket?
Give an opinion: ***I think*** it's great.   ***I don't think*** it's very nice.
Agree with an opinion: Partly: ***That's true, but*** …   ***I see what you mean, but*** …
            Completely: ***I agree with you.   You're right.***
Disagree with an opinion: ***I don't think so.   That's not true.***

There are many ways of giving advice or making suggestions.

Why don't you work at home.   ***You could*** use public transport.
If I were you I'd learn a new language.

A family holiday

Reading & listening

Bill Bryson

Bill Bryson was born in America but lived for many years in England. He's the best-selling author of many humorous travel books.

1 85 Read and listen to this extract from a book called *The Lost Continent* by Bill Bryson. He is describing the holiday journeys he used to make with his family. Are the following statements true or false? Compare your answers with a partner.

a) The writer used to go on holiday with his parents and his cousins.
b) The children used to make a 'bomb' that looked like a porcupine.
c) The 'bombs' used to make other cars crash.
d) The parents never used to understand why other drivers got angry.
e) Most of the time, the mother used to keep quiet.

(From *The Lost Continent*, by Bill Bryson)

In my memory, our vacations were always taken in a big blue Rambler station-wagon. It was a cruddy car – my dad always bought cruddy cars, until he got to the male menopause and started buying zippy red
5 convertibles – but it had space. My brother, sister and I in the back were miles away from my parents up front. We <u>quickly</u> discovered that if you stuck matches into an apple or hard-boiled egg, so that it resembled a porcupine, and <u>casually</u> dropped it out the window it was like a bomb. It would
10 explode with a small bang and a surprisingly big flash of blue flame, causing cars following behind to veer in an amusing fashion.
   My dad, miles away up front, never knew what was going on and could not understand why all day long cars would zoom up alongside him with the driver gesticulating <u>furiously</u>, before tearing off into the distance. 'What was that all
15 about?' he would say to my mother.
   'I don't know, dear,' my mother would answer <u>mildly</u>. My mother only ever said two things. She said, 'I don't know, dear.' And she said, 'Can I get you a sandwich, honey?'
   Occasionally on our trips she would volunteer other pieces of intelligence
20 like, 'I think you hit that dog/man/blind person back there, honey,' but mostly she <u>wisely</u> kept quiet.

2 Match adverbs <u>underlined</u> in the text in 1 with adverbs from the box below to get pairs with similar meanings.

> angrily   in a relaxed way   intelligently   gently   rapidly

3 Find the following words in the text and choose the most appropriate meaning from the alternatives.

a) a station-wagon (line 2): (1) *a big car with a long body*; (2) *a small sports car*
b) cruddy (line 2): (1) *lovely and new*; (2) *old and ugly*
c) zippy (line 4): (1) *fast*; (2) *slow*
d) to veer (line 11): (1) *to continue driving in a straight line*; (2) *to change direction suddenly*
e) zoom up (line 13): (1) *drive slowly*; (2) *drive fast*
f) tearing off (line 14): (1) *driving away fast*; (2) *driving away slowly*

4 What did you use to do to pass the time on long car journeys when you were a child? Tell your partner.

24 Hours From Tulsa

Song

1 Work with a partner. The pictures illustrate a song called *24 Hours From Tulsa*. Discuss which is the most logical order for the story.

2 🔲 86 Listen and read the lyrics of the song and check your ideas in 1.

Dearest Darling,
I had to write to say that I won't be home anymore.
'Cause something happened to me,
While I was driving (1) ____ and I'm not the same
    anymore.

Oh, I was only twenty-four hours from Tulsa,
Ah, only one day away from your arms,
I saw a welcoming (2) ____ ,
And stopped to rest for the night.

And that is when I saw her,
As I pulled (3) ____ outside of the small hotel
    she was there.
And so I walked up to her,
Asked where I could get (4) ____ to eat and
    she showed me where.

Oh, I was only twenty-four hours from Tulsa,
Ah, only one day away from your arms.
She took me to the café.
I asked her if she would stay.
She said okay.

Oh, I was only twenty-four hours from Tulsa,
Ah, only one day away from your arms.
The jukebox started to play
And nighttime (5) ____ into day.

As we were dancing (6) ____ ,
All of a sudden I lost (7) ____ as I held her charms
And I caressed her, kissed her,
Told her I'd die before I would let her out of my arms.

Oh, I was only twenty-four hours from Tulsa,
Ah, only one day away from your arms.
I hate to do (8) ____ to you,
But I love somebody new.
What can I do?

And I can never, never, never
Go home again.

3 Complete the lyrics with words from the box. Listen again and check your answers.

closely	control	home	in	light	something	this	turned

4 The song is the story of why a man has decided to break up with his partner. Work in small groups. Discuss these questions.

a) What do you think of the man in the song?
b) What do you think of the woman at the hotel in the song?
c) What do you think is the kindest or cruellest way to break up with a partner?

Review 4

Big Game Lottery

Language reviewed: past time – *used to* (Unit 19); prepositions after verbs and adjectives (Unit 17); *will* for prediction (Unit 16); future time clauses (Unit 16); conditionals (Unit 17)

Work with a partner. Look at the proverbs below. Do you have similar proverbs in your language? Which of these proverbs do you agree with?

'It is better to be born lucky than rich.'
'Great fortune brings great misfortune.'
'If something can go wrong, it will go wrong.'

Reading

1 Read the newspaper article about a lottery winner. If you were in Mrs Alvarado's position, would you feel the same as her? Why / Why not?

Colorado woman wins top prize

A 67-year-old woman has won $198 million in the Big Game Lottery, the biggest prize in US history. Eva Alvarado, who **moved** to the United States in 1984, lives in Colorado Springs, where she works as a cleaner in a home for mentally handicapped children.

Two years ago, Mrs Alvarado's husband **died** in an accident in the potato factory in Bingham County, Idaho, where they both **worked**. 'We **hated** that factory and we **did** the lottery every week because we **dreamed** of escaping to a better life,' Mrs Alvarado **said** yesterday. 'But when Ramón died, I moved here and I don't want to change my life now. This job is the luckiest thing that has ever happened to me. I don't want to leave the children.'

Mrs Alvarado **told** reporters that she wanted to spend some of the money on a new playroom for the children's home.

2 Work with a partner. Read the article again. Which four verbs in **bold** can you replace with the structure *used to* + infinitive? Why can't you replace the other verbs with the same structure?

Past time: *used to*

1 Look at the following statements. Where possible, replace the simple past verb forms with *used to* or *didn't use to*.

a) I was born in a hospital.
b) As a child, I lived in a small village.
c) I shared a bedroom with my brother/sister.
d) I watched the Cartoon Network on TV every day.
e) My parents gave me lots of pocket money.
f) We went to Disneyland once as a special treat.
g) I didn't enjoy English lessons at school.

2 How many of the statements in 1 were true for you as a child? Re-write the sentences so that they are all true for you. Compare your sentences with a partner.

Listening **1** ▭ **87** You are going to listen to a radio phone-in programme where callers comment on Mrs Alvarado's lottery win. Complete these comments with an appropriate preposition. Listen and check your answers.

a) Mrs Alvarado is obviously very fond ____ the children.
b) She will soon get tired ____ all the letters.
c) She needs to think ____ her future now.
d) She doesn't sound very excited ____ winning the lottery.
e) She's more interested ____ the children than the money.
f) She doesn't have to worry ____ the future anymore.

2 Look at some predictions about Mrs Alvarado's life. Listen again and tick (✓) the ones you hear on the programme.

a) She'll give up her job soon.
b) Life will be very difficult.
c) Everyone will ask her for money.
d) She'll buy a new house and a car.
e) She'll give most of the money away.

f) She'll need a financial adviser.
g) She'll take a long holiday.
h) She'll change her mind about giving money to the children's home.

3 Work with a partner. Which of the predictions in 2 would you make? Do you think it is possible to continue the same lifestyle if you win the lottery? What would you do if you won $198 million?

Future time clauses **1** Complete the sentences with the correct alternative.

a) As soon as the lesson **'ll finish / finishes**, Becky's going to buy a lottery ticket.
b) Terry will get married when he **'ll meet / meets** the right girl.
c) As soon as Ron **'ll get / gets** home this evening, he's going to do his homework.
d) If it **'ll rain / rains** tomorrow, Jenny will probably come in by car.
e) Sandy will probably retire when she **'ll be / is** fifty.
f) Tim will probably get a well-paid job when he **'ll finish / finishes** university.

2 Work with a partner. Replace the names in 1 with names of people in the class. How many true statements can you make?

Conditionals **1** Change the following 'facts' if necessary to make them all true for you. Then write conditional 'dream' sentences. Compare your sentences with your partner.

Facts	Dreams
a) I don't have $1 million.	→ *If I ... If I had $1 million, I'd buy a beautiful yacht.*
b) I don't speak perfect English.	→ *If I ...*
c) I'm not the mayor of this city.	→ *If I ...*
d) I can't travel in time.	→ *If I ...*
e) I'm a man/woman.	→ *If I ...*

2 Work with a partner. Choose a conditional sentence from 1 and take it in turns to continue a chain of conditions. Who can create the longest 'conditional chain'?

For example:

STUDENT A

If I had $1 million, I'd buy a beautiful yacht.

STUDENT B

If I bought a beautiful yacht, I'd sail around the Mediterranean.

If I sailed around the Mediterranean, I'd ... etc.

It's your lucky day!

Language reviewed: relative clauses and relative pronouns (Unit 17); *have/make/take* + noun structures (Unit 18); *how* + adjective/adverb (Unit 18); past perfect (Unit 18)

Relative clauses

1 Complete the questions by choosing the correct alternative.

a) Do you know anyone who **is / he is** really lucky or unlucky?
b) Are there any numbers that **are / they are** especially lucky for you?
c) Do you wear or carry an object which **brings / it brings** you luck?
d) Is there anything special that **do / you do** before an exam to bring you luck?
e) Have you ever received a letter or an e-mail that **promised / it promised** you good luck?

2 Work with a partner. Discuss the questions in 1.

Reading

1 If you received this e-mail message, what would you do? Discuss with a partner.

⬜   🔲 **Good luck!**   🗗🗐

📤 Send Now 📥 Send Later 🗒 Save as Draft 📎 Add Attachments ✒ Signature ▾ 📋 Options ▾ 📄 Rewrap

📧 To: Kay Jones
📧 Cc: Philip Riley
📧 Bcc:

Subject: | Good luck!

▷ Attachments: *none*

🔤   Geneva ▾   Medium ▾   **B** *I* <u>U</u> **T**   ▤ ▤ ▤   ⅓≣ ⅓≣ ⬅≣ ➡≣   **A** ▾ ◈ ▾   —

This message is from a friend who wishes you good luck. In less than five days, this message will bring you good luck if – and only if – you pass it on to other friends. This is not a joke. You will definitely receive good news in the mail if you send the message to friends who also need good luck. You must pass on this message in less than 120 hours.

Good luck, but remember: you must send 20 copies of this message in 120 hours.
DO NOT SIGN YOUR MESSAGES.

---

2 The e-mail continues below with stories about people who did or didn't pass on the e-mail message. Complete the text by choosing the appropriate verb.

- Ana Cuevas from Peru was (1) **making / taking** a course in web programming. She (2) **made / took** her final exam two days after receiving the message and got top marks.

- A New York stockbroker received the message on her first day in a new job. The next week, she (3) **had / made** $14 million for her company.

- 83-year-old, Piotr Wojdylo (4) **had / took** a serious illness and the doctors said he (5) **had / took** only six months to live. He was (6) **making / taking** arrangements for his funeral when he got the message. Five years later, he is alive and well.

- A businessman from Salt Lake City received the message but (7) **had / made** the mistake of asking his secretary to pass it on. She forgot. Four days later, he (8) **had / took** a terrible car crash, even though he was only driving at 15 mph.

- Photographer, Wesley Pratt, waited outside Madonna's home for six days. Finally, he (9) **made / took** the photos that he wanted, but when the film was developed, the pictures were black. He had completely forgotten to pass on the message.

- Regina Witte received good luck messages every Monday for three months, but did nothing. Finally, she decided to (10) **make / take** the risk of deleting the message from her computer. She (11) **had / made** the wrong decision! Her computer crashed one hour later.

---

3 Work with a partner. Complete each question with a word from the box.

> fast   long   long   much   often   old   well

a) How ____ did Ana Cuevas do in her examination?
b) How ____ money did the New York stockbroker make?
c) How ____ was the man with the serious illness?
d) How ____ did the doctors say he would live?
e) How ____ was the businessman from Salt Lake City driving?
f) How ____ did the photographer wait to take photos of Madonna?
g) How ____ did Regina Witte receive good luck messages?

4 Read the e-mail message in 2 again and answer the questions in 3.

Past perfect **1** Read the article below and explain the title.

A lucky escape

The day started badly. I woke up late because I (1 **forget**) about the alarm clock the night before. I got dressed in five minutes and called a taxi to go to the airport. Thirty minutes later the taxi had still not arrived. I called the taxi company, and they explained that the taxi (2 **break down**). So, I decided to take my own car to Heathrow, picked up my bag and left the house. But when I got in the car, the engine wouldn't start. I realised that I (3 **leave**) the headlights on last night. I decided to try the taxi company again, but when I put my hand in my pocket, my telephone wasn't there. I (4 **leave**) it in the kitchen so I went back inside to get it. I opened the door and could hear the radio, which I (5 **forget**) to switch off. 'This is the BBC News at eight o'clock on Sunday the seventh of April,' I heard. 'Eight o'clock,' I thought, 'but it's only seven o'clock,' and I looked at my watch to check. Suddenly, I remembered. It *was* eight o'clock! The clocks (6 **change**) that weekend! There was no point going to the airport now. The plane (7 **already take off**). But as I sat there listening to the news, I realised how lucky I had been. A plane (8 **crash**) just after take-off at Heathrow, and it was feared that all 217 people aboard (9 **die**).

This is the BBC News at eight o'clock...

2 Work with a partner. Complete the story by putting the verbs into the past perfect.

3 🔊 88 Listen and check your answers.

Anecdote Think about a lucky or an unlucky experience you have had. You are going to tell your partner about it. Choose from the list below the things you want to talk about. Think about what you will say and what language you will need.

☐ Was it a lucky or unlucky experience?   ☐ What were you doing?
☐ When did it happen?   ☐ What happened?
☐ Where were you?   ☐ Why was it lucky (or unlucky)?
☐ Who were you with?   ☐ How did you feel afterwards?

Let's talk about ...

START

1
... somebody with an unusual name

2
... somebody who is important to you

27
... the person you speak to most on the phone

28
... the most helpful person you know

29
.. a time you were late

30
... the healthiest person you know

26
... a foreign person you know

25
... the last time you went out and had a good time

24
... your favourite historical figure

23
... a time when you got into trouble

FINISH

38
... three good reasons for learning English

22
... something you feel strongly about

21
... how you relax

20
... things that make you happy or unhappy

19
... your favourite subject at school

18
... the qualities of your ideal partner

3 ... your favourite city

4 ... a place you don't like

5 ... your dream holiday

6 ... a couple you know

7 ... a romantic film

31 ... the sort of food you love or hate

32 ... a pet you know

8 ... how you keep fit

33 ... the sort of people you don't like

9 ... doing sports at school

34 ... the slowest person you know

10 ... an interesting character in a film

35 ... a strange experience

11 ... one of your neighbours

37 ... a terrible journey

36 ... your dream car

12 ... the best present you've ever received

13 ... the last present you bought someone

17 ... your plans for next weekend

16 ... a pop band you love or hate

15 ... a retired person you know

14 ... the best or worst job you can imagine

Play the game in small groups. You will need a dice and counters.

1 Place your counters on the square marked START and throw the dice.

2 The first player to throw a six starts the game.

3 The first player throws the dice and moves their counter along the board according to the number on the dice.

4 Players then play in turns moving around the board.

5 When a player lands on a purple square they have to talk about the subject for thirty seconds.

6 When a player lands on an orange square they have to talk about the subject for sixty seconds.

7 If a player has nothing to say or can't talk for the necessary time, they are allowed to pass and miss a turn.

8 The game continues until the first player reaches the square marked FINISH.

Additional material

1 Me

I never forget a face, 1

Try to put the right names under each photograph.

a) _____   b) _____   c) _____   d) _____   e) _____   f) _____

How many did you remember? (The average score is three or four correct answers.)
Go back to page 6 to find out how you can improve your memory.

1 Me

Close up. Subject questions, 2

Student A

Try to complete these general knowledge facts. Ask your partner appropriate questions to check your answers.

a) _____ created Sherlock Holmes. ➔ *Who created Sherlock Holmes?*
b) J.K. Rowling created _____ . ➔ *Who did J.K. Rowling create?*
c) _____ created Tarzan.
d   Alexander Fleming discovered _____ .
e) _____ invented the telephone.
f) Elvis Presley lived in _____ .
g) _____ built the Taj Mahal.
h) The French football team won _____ in 1998.

2 Place

Dream holiday, 4

1 a) Portuguese
2 b) Turkey
3 a) China
4 c) Poland
5 b) Spain
6 c) Japan

17 Animals

Lexis: animals

Answers:
a 4   b 3   c 5   d 1   e 6   f 2

2 Place

Cities of the world, 1

Student A

The capitals are Tokyo, Seoul, Reykjavik, Berlin, Cairo and Prague.

You have ten country maps. Five cities are marked on maps *a–e*. Use the Language toolbox to describe to Student B exactly where these cities are. Student B will then describe the location of the other five cities (*f–j*) . Mark them on your map. Compare your maps with Student B.

LANGUAGE TOOLBOX

It's in the	south-west.
	south-east.
	north-west.
	north-east.
	centre.

| It's on the | _____ coast. |
| | river _____ . |

| a | JAPAN | b | FRANCE | c | SOUTH KOREA | d | ICELAND | e | GERMANY |

Tokyo
Nice
Seoul
Reykjavik
Berlin

| f | SPAIN | g | USA | h | EGYPT | i | AUSTRALIA | j | CZECH REPUBLIC |

3 Couples

True love. Reading, 3

Student A

1   These are the answers to some comprehension questions about the article, *Great love affairs*, on page 20. Write the questions.
    a) In 1998. ➔ *When ...?*   b) In the 17th century. ➔ *When ...?*   c) Twenty-two years. ➔ *How long ...?*
    d) At a polo match. ➔ *Where ...?*

2   Give your questions to your partner.

3   Check your partner's questions. Answer them and then discuss the questions and answers.

4 Fit

Lexis

Personality	Sport	Person	Place
A Cathy Freeman (*Picture 1*)	athletics	athlete	track
B Raúl (*Picture 4*)	a) *football*	football player	pitch
C Shaquille O'Neal (*Picture 2*)	basketball	d) *basketball player*	court
D *Michael Schumacher* (*Picture 3*)	motor racing	racing driver	race track
E Inge de Bruijn (*Picture 5*)	b) *swimming*	swimmer	f) *swimming pool*
F *Venus Williams* (*Picture 6*)	c) *tennis*	e) *tennis player*	court

4 Fit

Close up. Comparatives, 5

a)   London isn't as wet as Rome. (London annual average: 594 mm rainfall. Rome annual average: 749 mm rainfall.)

b)   The Maracana Municipa Stadium in Rio de Janeiro is much larger than the Stade de France in Paris. (Maracana capacity: 205,000. Stade de France capacity: 110,000.)

c)   The US Army is much smaller than the North Korean Army: (US Army: 524,900. North Korean Army: 1,000,000.)

d)   Heathrow Airport (London) is a bit busier than Los Angeles International Airport. (London Heathrow: 51,368,000 passengers per annum. Los Angeles International Airport: 51,050,000 passengers per annum.)

e)   Ireland isn't as big as Cuba. (Ireland: 83,050 square kilometres. Cuba: 114,530 square kilometres.)

f)   The Statue of Liberty isn't as tall as the Eiffel Tower. (The Statue of Liberty: 93 metres. The Eiffel Tower: 300 metres.)

4 Fit

Lexis: numbers, 6

Student A

You and Student B each have a set of questions. Student B has the answers to your questions. Ask Student B your questions and write down the answers. (You could try and answer them by yourself first.) In the box you have the answers to Student B's questions. When you have finished, compare your answers. Which piece of trivia is the most interesting?

a)   How fast can a dolphin swim?

b)   How much money did Tom Cruise earn in 2000?

c)   How many words does a woman speak in a normal day?

d)   What percentage of the body's energy does the brain use?

e)   What is the longest distance ever travelled in a wheelchair?

f)   What is the highest rugby score ever recorded? (A game in Denmark in 1973.)

2%   105 km/h   32–0 $38.5 m   4,203 km   2,175

11 Smile

Lexis: the face, 5

11 Smile

Lexis: describing character, 5

Your description of a dog is your own personality.

Your description of a cat is your partner's personality.

Your description of a rat is your enemy's personality.

Your description of coffee is how you see love.

Your description of an ocean is your own life.

1 Me

Close up. Subject questions, 2

Student B

Try to complete these general knowledge facts. Ask your partner appropriate questions to check your answers.

a) Arthur Conan Doyle created _____ . → *Who did Arthur Conan Doyle create?*
b) _____ created Harry Potter. → *Who created Harry Potter?*
c) Edgar Rice Burroughs created _____ .
d) _____ discovered penicillin.
e) Alexander Graham Bell invented _____ .
f) _____ lived in Graceland.
g) Shah Jahan built _____ .
h) _____ won the World Cup in 1998.

---

2 Place

Cities of the world, 1

Student B

The capitals are Tokyo, Seoul, Reykjavik, Berlin, Cairo and Prague.

You have ten country maps. Listen to Student A describe the location of five cities on maps *a–e*. Mark them on your map. Then use the Language toolbox to describe to Student A exactly where the five cities on maps *f–j* are located. Compare your map with Student A.

LANGUAGE TOOLBOX	
It's in the	south-west.
	south-east.
	north-west.
	north-east.
	centre.
It's on the	_____ coast.
	river _____ .

---

3 Couples

True love. Reading, 3

Student B

1 These are the answers to some comprehension questions about the article, *Great love affairs*, on page 20. Write the questions.
   a) In 1936. → *When ...?*
   b) In April 1970. → *When ...?*
   c) Ten months. → *How long ...?*
   d) Nineteen years. → *How long ...?*

2 Give your questions to your partner

3 Check your partner's questions. Answer them and then discuss the questions and answers.

---

4 Fit

Lexis: numbers, 6

Student B

You and Student A each have a set of questions. In the box you have the answers to Student A's questions. Student A has the answers to your questions.
Ask Student A your questions and write down the answers. (You could try and answer them by yourself first.)
When you have finished, compare your answers. Which piece of trivia is the most interesting?

7,120   194–0   30 km/h   20% $43.2 m   40,075.16 km

a) How fast can a cheetah run?
b) How much money did Britney Spears earn in 2000?
c) How many words does a man speak in a normal day?
d) What percentage of the body's weight is the brain?
e) What is the longest distance ever travelled on a windsurfer?
f) What is the highest international football score ever recorded? (Australia versus Samoa.)

5 Review 1

Sophie & Paul, 4

Read Sophie's answers and write out the questions

1	(*name*) *What's your name?*	Sophie Smith.
2	(*old*)	28.
3	(*do*)	Computer programmer.
4	(*star sign*)	Aquarius.
5	(*tall*)	1m 60.
6	(*like*)	Sociable, sensitive, reliable.
7	(*films*)	My favourite is 'Pulp Fiction' – but also all the films by Quentin Tarantino.
8	(*favourite*)	Nicholas Cage.
9	(*wear*)	Designer clothes.
10	(*free time*)	Restaurants, going to the gym, being with interesting people.
11	(*worst fault*)	Forgetting people's names – my memory is hopeless.
12	(*dream weekend*)	Staying in a five-star hotel in New York with the man of my dreams. Going shopping for designer clothes and then flying back home in first class.

11 Smile

What are you like? Reading, 1

If you scored 19–24, YOU'RE AN OPTIMIST!

You always try to see the positive side of life. You know how to enjoy yourself and you don't waste time worrying about things that may never happen. But be careful – your friends might find your optimism rather irritating at times.

If you scored 13–18, YOU'RE MR OR MS SENSIBLE!

You are a realist. You know life has ups and downs but you hope to have more good times than bad times in your life. But be careful – you can be too serious at times. You need to show your feelings a bit more.

If you scored 8–12, YOU'RE A PESSIMIST!

You must try to stop having negative thoughts. You need to learn how to enjoy the good things in life and stop worrying about things that may never happen. And remember, there are many people in worse situations than you.

13 Dance

Reading

What it means

If you scored 20–29

When you dance, you really express yourself. You may look like an octopus in a blender, but you don't care what other people think. Good for you! No party is complete without you.

If you scored 11–19

You enjoy dancing but you're too worried about your image. You should let yourself go. Be a bit less serious about life.

If you scored 10 or less

Hmm, what *do* you enjoy? Do you collect stamps? Hopefully you are an interesting person to talk to!

15 Review 3

National sport. Passives, 1

a) False – Barcelona.

b) False – eleven players.

c) True.

d) True.

e) False – but it wasn't broken till 1991 (twenty-three years later). His jump at the Mexico Olympics is considered by many to be the greatest athletic achievement of all time.

f) False – Brazil were beaten by France 3–0.

15 Review 3

National sport. Dynamic & stative meanings, 2

Student A

17 Animals

Special friends. Listening, 1

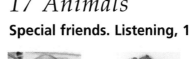

Tim's pig, Harriet,   Gus' spider, Hendrix   Maxine's hamster, Page

16 Lifestyle

Close up. *will* for prediction, 2

The Oracle

- Choose a question you want to ask.
- Take it in turns to roll the dice with the question in your mind.
- Find the letter corresponding to your question, and the number you threw on the dice. Find your answer where they meet. For example: you asked question *d* and you threw *4*, so the *Oracle* says 'One of each.'

a) What will the love of my life look like?
b) Will I be famous one day?
c) Will I travel the world?
d) How many children will I have?
e) Where will I be most happy?
f) What will I look like in ten years' time?

15 Review 3

National sport. Stative & dynamic meanings, 2

Student B

	1	2	3	4	5	6
a	Not as you expect.	Gorgeous.	Not classically good-looking, but you'll never look at anybody else.	Very fit.	He/She will have wonderful eyes.	He/She'll look like you.
b	No, you won't.	No, but you'll meet someone famous.	You'll be well-known in your profession.	You'll be in the news for doing something crazy.	You'll have your fifteen minutes of fame.	Yes, but you'll have to work very hard.
c	Yes, for pleasure.	Yes, for your job.	No, but you'll travel in your own country.	No, but you'll meet people from all over the world.	You'll have wonderful holidays abroad.	You'll travel when you're older.
d	More than you expect.	The same as your parents.	Your career will be more important.	One of each.	You'll have a big family.	Enough.
e	At home in bed.	In the mountains.	Abroad.	Near the sea.	Everywhere.	In a big city.
f	Completely different.	Like your mother.	Fabulous.	Younger than you are.	No different.	Like your father.

Verb structures

Basic structures

ASPECT	VOICE	TENSES	
		Present	Past
simple	active	He **writes** letters.	He **wrote** letters.
	passive	Letters **are written**.	Letters **were written**.
continuous	active	He **is writing** letters.	He **was writing** letters.
	passive	Letters **are being written**.	Letters **were being written**.
perfect	active	He **has written** letters.	He **had written** letters.
	passive	Letters **have been written**.	Letters **had been** written.
perfect continuous	active	He **has been writing** letters.	He **had been writing** letters.

Present simple

See Units 6 and 12.

Affirmative	Negative	Question
I/You/We/They **write**.	I/You/We/They **don't** (**do not**) **write**.	**Do** I/you/we/they **write**?
He/She/It **writes**.	He/She/It **doesn't** (**does not**) **write**.	**Does** he/she/it **write**?

Present continuous

See Units 8 and 12.

Affirmative	Negative	Question
I'm (**am**) writing	I'm **not** (**am not**) writing.	**Am** I writing?
You/We/They**'re** (**are**) writing.	You/We/They**'re not** (**are not**) writing.	**Are** you/we/they writing?
He/She/It**'s** (**is**) writing.	He/She/It **isn't** (**is not**) writing.	**Is** he/she/it writing?

Note: When a verb ends with a single vowel letter followed by a single consonant letter, you usually double the final consonant letter before -*ing*: *chat – chatting; jog – jogging; refer – referring; stop – stopping.*

Present perfect simple

See Units 7 and 13.

Affirmative	Negative	Question
I/You/We/They **'ve** (**have**) **written**.	I/You/We/They **haven't** (**have not**) **written**.	**Have** I/you/we/they **written**?
He/She/It**'s** (**has**) **written**.	He/She/It **hasn't** (**has not**) **written**.	**Has** he/she/it **written**?

Note: See list of irregular verbs on page 132.

Present perfect continuous

See Unit 13.

Affirmative	Negative	Question
I/You/We/They **'ve** (**have**) **been** writing.	I/You/We/They **haven't** (**have not**) **been** writing.	**Have** I/you/we/they **been** writing?
He/She/It**'s** (**has**) **been** writing.	He/She/It **hasn't** (**has not**) **been** writing.	**Has** he/she/it **been** writing?

Past simple

See Units 3, 6 and 7.

Affirmative	Negative	Question
I/You/He/She/It/We/They **wrote**.	I/You/He/She/It/We/They **didn't** (**did not**) **write**.	**Did** I/you/he/she/it/we/they **write**?

Note: See list of irregular verbs on page 132. When a verb ends with a single vowel letter followed by a single consonant letter, you usually double the final consonant letter before -*ed*: *chat – chatted; jog – jogged; refer – referred; stop – stopped.*

Past continuous

See Unit 3.

Affirmative	Negative	Question
I/He/She/It **was writing**.	I/He/She/It **wasn't** (**was not**) writing.	**Was** I/He/She/It writing?
You/We/They **were writing**.	You/We/They **weren't** (**were not**) writing.	Were you/we/they **writing**?

Past perfect

See Unit 18.

Affirmative	Negative	Question
I/You/He/She/It/We/They **'d** (**had**) **written**.	I/You/He/She/It/We/They **hadn't** (**had not**) **written**.	**Had** I/you/he/she/it/we/they **written**?

Note: See list of irregular verbs on page 132.

used to

See Unit 19.

Affirmative	Negative	Question
I/You/He/She/It/We/They **used to write**.	I/You/He/She/It/We/They **didn't use to write**.	**Did** I/you/he/she/it/we/they **use to write**?

(be) going to
See Unit 8.

Affirmative	Negative	Question
I'm (am) going to write.	I'm not (am not) going to write.	Am I going to write?
You/We/They're (are) going to write.	You/We/They're not (are not) going to write.	Are you/we/they going to write?
He/She/It's (is) going to write.	He/She/It isn't (is not) going to write.	Is he/she/it going to write?

Present continuous for future
See Unit 8 and page 129.

will
See Unit 16.

Affirmative	Negative	Question
I/You/He/She/It/We/They'll (will) write.	I/You/He/She/It/We/They won't (will not) write.	Will I/You/He/She/It/We/They write?

Modals

Affirmative	Negative	Question
can: see Units 9 and 14.		
I/You/He *etc.* can write.	I/You/He *etc.* can't (cannot) write.	Can I/you/he *etc.* write?
could: see Units 9 and 14.		
I/You/He *etc.* could write.	I/You/He *etc.* couldn't (could not) write.	Could I/you/he *etc.* write?
must: see Unit 9.		
I/You/He *etc.* must write.	I/You/He *etc.* mustn't (must not) write.	Must I/you/he *etc.* write?
may		
I/You/He *etc.* may write.	I/You/He *etc.* may not write.	May I/you/he *etc.* write?
might		
I/You/He *etc.* might write.	I/You/He *etc.* mightn't (might not) write.	Might I/you/he *etc.* write?
shall		
I/You/He *etc.* 'll (shall) write.	I/You/He *etc.* shan't (shall not) write.	Shall I/you/he *etc.* write?
Shall is usually only used with questions in the first person (*I* and *we*): *Shall I/we write?*		
should: see Units 9 and 19.		
I/You/He *etc.* should write.	I/You/He *etc.* shouldn't (should not) write.	Should I/you/he *etc.* write?
will: see Unit 16.		
I/You/He *etc.* 'll (will) write.	I/You/He *etc.* won't (will not) write.	Will I/you/he, *etc.* write?
would: see Unit 17.		
I/You/He *etc.* 'd (would) write.	I/You/He *etc.* wouldn't (would not) write.	Would I/you/he *etc.* write?

Future time clauses
See Unit 16.

Subordinate clause	Main clause
If he has a cigarette,	he'll be in big trouble.
When he finishes the week,	he'll feel like a new man.
As soon as he arrives,	he'll take a fitness test.

Note: The two clauses can usually be used in either order:
He'll be in big trouble if he has a cigarette.

Conditional clauses
See Unit 17.

If-clause	Main clause
If I had $1 million,	I'd travel round the world. I'd buy a big house.
If I was/were an animal	I'd be a lion. I'd be a bird so I could fly.
If I could live anywhere	I'd choose somewhere hot. I wouldn't stay here!

Note: The two clauses can usually be used in either order:
I'd travel round the world if I had $1 million.

Relative clauses
See Unit 17.

(The main clauses are in *italic*. The relative clauses are in bold.)
A cheetah is an animal **that can run at 100 kph.**
A person **who treats sick animals** *is called a vet.*
Miaow is a noise **cats make.**
The people **my brother works with** *are all mad.*

Grammar glossary

main verb · adjective · conjunction · modal auxiliary verb · adverb · article · pronoun · main verb

Learn these useful words and you can understand more about the language you are studying.

determiner · noun · pronoun · main verb · preposition · noun · auxiliary verb

Agents are people or things that perform an action in a passive sentence.
For example: *She was pardoned by **President Clinton** in 2001.*

Clauses are groups of words containing a verb.

main clause	subordinate clause
I waited	but he didn't come.

For example:

Note: Subordinate clauses are usually introduced by conjunctions.

Collocation refers to words that frequently occur together.
For example: *common sense   get on well   Merry Christmas*

Dynamic meaning is a way of referring to verbs when they describe actions. Verbs with dynamic meanings can be used in both simple and continuous verb forms.
For example: *People usually **chat** to each other on the bus.*
*Some people **are chatting** in the next room.*

Expressions are groups of words that belong together where the words and word order never or rarely change.
For example: ***black and white**   **That reminds me**, I must buy some toothpaste.*
How do you do?

Idioms are expressions with a meaning that cannot be understood by taking the meaning of each individual word.
For example: *It's **a piece of cake**. = It's really easy.   He's **full of beans**. = He's very energetic.*

If-clauses are used to introduce conditions where you can describe a real situation (possible) or an unreal situation (improbable or impossible).
For example: *If it's nice weather, we'll go for a picnic.* (real situation)
If I won the lottery, I'd quit my job and never work again. (unreal situation)

Intransitive verbs do not take an object.
For example: *He's **arrived**.   Is Marta still **sleeping**?   **Sit down**!*

Objects usually come after the verb and show who or what is affected by the verb.
For example: *She closed **the window**.   My neighbour hates **me**.   I've made **a cup of tea**.*
Note: Some common verbs take a direct object (DO) and an indirect object (IO).

IO	DO		IO	DO		IO	DO
him	a kiss		her	some flowers		students	English

For example: *She gave* him a kiss   *He sent* her some flowers   *I teach* students English

Particles are adverbs or prepositions that form part of a phrasal verb.
For example: *sit **down**   switch **off**   look **after***

Phrasal verbs are verbs consisting of a main verb + particle(s). Phrasal verbs are sometimes referred to as 'multi-word verbs'.
For example: *grow **up**   take your shoes **off**   I ran **after** the bus.*

Relative clauses give additional information about a <u>thing</u> or a <u>person</u> introduced in the main clause.
For example: *A butcher's is a <u>shop</u> **that sells meat**.*
*The <u>people</u> **my brother works with** are all mad.*

Relative pronouns such as *who, that* or *which* are always used when they are the subject of the verb in a relative clause.

subject	verb	object
who	don't eat	meat

For example: *People* who don't eat meat *are called vegetarians.*

subject	verb	object
that	can speak	English

I've got a parrot that can speak English.

Stative meaning is a way of referring to verbs when they describe states. Verbs with stative meanings cannot be used with continuous verbs forms.
For example: *I **want** a fairer system.* (NOT ~~I'm wanting a fairer system.~~)
*I've **known** him for years.* (NOT ~~I've been knowing him for years.~~)

Subjects usually come before the verb and refer to the main person or thing you are talking about.
For example: ***Money** doesn't grow on trees.   **My tailor** is rich.*
***The biggest rock and roll group in the world** have started their world tour.*

Phonetic symbols

SINGLE VOWELS

/ɪ/	big fish	/bɪg fɪʃ/
/iː/	green beans	/griːn biːnz/
/ʊ/	should look	/ʃʊd lʊk/
/uː/	blue moon	/bluː muːn/
/e/	ten eggs	/ten egz/
/ə/	about mother	/əbaʊt mʌðə/
/ɜː/	learn words	/lɜːn wɜːdz/
/ɔː/	short talk	/ʃɔːt tɔːk/
/æ/	fat cat	/fæt kæt/
/ʌ/	must come	/mʌst kʌm/
/ɑː/	calm start	/kɑːm stɑːt/
/ɒ/	hot spot	/hɒt spɒt/

DIPHTHONGS

/ɪə/	ear	/ɪə/
/eɪ/	face	/feɪs/
/ʊə/	pure	/pjʊə/
/ɔɪ/	boy	/bɔɪ/
/əʊ/	nose	/nəʊz/
/eə/	hair	/heə/
/aɪ/	eye	/aɪ/
/aʊ/	mouth	/maʊθ/

CONSONANTS

/p/	pen	/pen/
/b/	bad	/bæd/
/t/	tea	/tiː/
/d/	dog	/dɒg/
/tʃ/	church	/tʃɜːtʃ/
/dʒ/	jazz	/dʒæz/
/k/	cost	/kɒst/
/g/	girl	/gɜːl/
/f/	far	/fɑː/
/v/	voice	/vɔɪs/
/θ/	thin	/θɪn/
/ð/	then	/ðen/
/s/	snake	/sneɪk/
/z/	noise	/nɔɪz/
/ʃ/	shop	/ʃɒp/
/ʒ/	measure	/meʒə/
/m/	make	/meɪk/
/n/	nine	/naɪn/
/ŋ/	sing	/sɪŋ/
/h/	house	/haʊs/
/l/	leg	/leg/
/r/	red	/red/
/w/	wet	/wet/
/j/	yes	/jes/

STRESS

In this book, word stress is shown by underlining the stressed syllable.
For example: <u>wa</u>ter; re<u>sult</u>; disa<u>ppoin</u>ting

LETTERS OF THE ALPHABET

/eɪ/	/iː/	/e/	/aɪ/	/əʊ/	/uː/	/ɑː/
Aa	Bb	Ff	Ii	Oo	Qq	Rr
Hh	Cc	Ll	Yy		Uu	
Jj	Dd	Mm			Ww	
Kk	Ee	Nn				
	Gg	Ss				
	Pp	Xx				
	Tt	Zz				
	Vv					

Irregular verbs

Infinitive	Past simple	Past participle
be	was/were	been
beat	beat	beaten
become	became	become
begin	began	begun
bend	bent	bent
bet	bet	bet
bite	bit	bitten
blow	blew	blown
break	broke	broken
bring	brought	brought
build	built	built
burn	burnt/burned	burnt/burned
burst	burst	burst
buy	bought	bought
can	could	(been able)
catch	caught	caught
choose	chose	chosen
come	came	come
cost	cost	cost
cut	cut	cut
deal	dealt	dealt
do	did	done
draw	drew	drawn
dream	dreamt/dreamed	dreamt/dreamed
drink	drank	drunk
drive	drove	driven
eat	ate	eaten
fall	fell	fallen
feed	fed	fed
feel	felt	felt
fight	fought	fought
find	found	found
fly	flew	flown
forget	forgot	forgotten
forgive	forgave	forgiven
freeze	froze	frozen
get	got	got
give	gave	given
go	went	gone/been
grow	grew	grown
hang	hung/hanged	hung/hanged
have	had	had
hear	heard	heard
hide	hid	hidden
hit	hit	hit
hold	held	held
hurt	hurt	hurt
keep	kept	kept
kneel	knelt/kneeled	knelt/kneeled
know	knew	known
lay	laid	laid
lead	led	led
learn	learnt/learned	learnt/learned
leave	left	left
lend	lent	lent
let	let	let

Infinitive	Past simple	Past participle
lie	lay	lain
light	lit/lighted	lit/lighted
lose	lost	lost
make	made	made
mean	meant	meant
meet	met	met
must	had to	(had to)
pay	paid	paid
put	put	put
read	read /red/	read /red/
ride	rode	ridden
ring	rang	rung
rise	rose	risen
run	ran	run
say	said	said
see	saw	seen
sell	sold	sold
send	sent	sent
set	set	set
shake	shook	shaken
shine	shone	shone
shoot	shot	shot
show	showed	shown
shrink	shrank	shrunk
shut	shut	shut
sing	sang	sung
sink	sank	sunk
sit	sat	sat
sleep	slept	slept
slide	slid	slid
smell	smelt/smelled	smelt/smelled
speak	spoke	spoken
spell	spelt/spelled	spelt/spelled
spend	spent	spent
spill	spilt/spilled	spilt/spilled
split	split	split
spoil	spoilt/spoiled	spoilt/spoiled
spread	spread	spread
stand	stood	stood
steal	stole	stolen
stick	stuck	stuck
swear	swore	sworn
swell	swelled	swollen/swelled
swim	swam	swum
take	took	taken
teach	taught	taught
tear	tore	torn
tell	told	told
think	thought	thought
throw	threw	thrown
understand	understood	understood
wake	woke	woken
wear	wore	worn
win	won	won
write	wrote	written

Tapescripts

1 Me

🔊 01

My first name's Susan, but the only person who calls me Susan is my dad. Oh, and my sister when she's angry with me, but fortunately that doesn't happen very often now.

Most of my friends call me Sue, and so do the people I work with.

My old friends call me Maggsie, because my surname is Maggs, and I was always called Maggsie at school. I hated it.

Of course, there's only one person who calls me Mum, and that's my son, but when he's with his friends he calls me Sue.

My mum calls me Sweetheart, and my best friend calls me Suzanne because she's French.

My Japanese sister-in-law calls me Suki – apparently, Suki means 'loved one' in Japanese, so that's really nice.

My husband calls me Bunny, but that's another story ...

🔊 02

(See page 4.)

🔊 03

1 /ɔ:/ Paul George Laura Dawn
2 /u:/ Julie Ruth Luke Sue
3 /ɑ:/ Charles Margaret Barbara Grant
4 /i:/ Peter Eve Denise Keith
5 /ɜ:/ Shirley Bernard Earl Burt

🔊 04

A.L.I.C.E. is an award-winning chat robot at www.alicebot.org. She's intelligent and funny and has won prizes for being the most human-like computer. She was created by Dr Richard S. Wallace. Six thousand people a month chat to A.L.I.C.E. Some people spend up to four and a half hours a day chatting online with her, and some have even said they prefer her to their own girlfriends. Here is a typical conversation.

(A = A.L.I.C.E; Q = Questioner)
A: Hi. My name's A.L.I.C.E.
Q: What does your name mean?
A: It means Artificial Linguistic Internet Computer Entity.
Q: Where were you born?
A: I was born in Bethlehem, Pennsylvania.
Q: Where did you grow up?
A: I think I grew up in San Francisco.
Q: What do you look like?
A: I'm blue and I've got one wheel.
Q: What do you do?
A: I talk to people on the web.
Q: Do you like your job?
A: Yes, I have a passion for my work!
Q: Can you speak any foreign languages?
A: No, I only speak English at the moment, but I'd like to learn.
Q: Are you married?
A: No, I am single. How about you?
Q: Have you got any children?
A: No, but you can download me and make A.L.I.C.E. clones for yourself!
Q: Who created you?
A: Dr Richard S. Wallace – he is very, very clever! He's also very kind and generous! In fact he's one of the most ...
Q: Yeah, yeah, okay, A.L.I.C.E., Thank you.

🔊 05

(See page 9.)

🔊 06

Dave Carter's my best friend. We met when we were five years old because our parents were friends and we went to the same school. He works in a different city now, so I only see him at weekends and during the holidays. He's important to me because he knows me so well. We have a really good laugh together and we enjoy the same things – football, clubbing, girls, the usual stuff. When I'm feeling down or when I need to talk to somebody, I can always call him. Recently, I had girlfriend problems and he was great – he's a really good listener. He just lets you speak and he listens. But he isn't perfect! He's always late for everything and he never says sorry. Never! The last time I saw him was last weekend. We arranged to meet at four o'clock to play football, and he arrived at half past six! It was nearly dark! Oh well, nobody's perfect, are they? He's still a really good mate.

2 Place

🔊 07

1
(I = Interviewer; P = Paulo)
I: Do you like your city?
P: Oh yes, I feel lucky to be living in a city that's so big and exciting. I love looking out of my apartment window over the high-rise buildings.
I: What's the city centre like?
P: Some people say it's too noisy and crowded, but I love that. There's always something to see and do. We also have the most famous beach in the world – Copacabana Beach. Then, on the other side of the city, there are beautiful mountains. The highest one is called Corcovado, and it has the famous statue of Christ. If you look down at the city from there, the view is spectacular.
I: What's the weather like?
P: It's great most of the time. The only time I don't like Rio much is in the summer: it's too hot and humid.

2
(I = Interviewer; G = Gisela)
I: Do you like your city?
G: Yes, it's wonderful. I think my city has everything.
I: What's the architecture like?
G: It's a mixture of old and new with plenty of shops for everybody. The castle is the most famous monument, and at night it looks amazing.
I: What's the nightlife like?
G: It's a young city because of the university, so there are plenty of cheap restaurants and interesting cafés and bars. It's got a great nightlife.
I: And what are the people like?
G: Well, some people are a bit reserved, but in general they're really friendly.

3
(I = Interviewer; A = Armelle)
I: Where do you live?
A: Well, I live in a small village with my parents. My grandparents live here too, and my aunts and uncles. In fact, I think I'm related to about fifty per cent of the people in my village.
I: What's your village like?
A: It's very pretty. The countryside is beautiful, and the air is lovely and clean. But it's too quiet. I find it so dull and boring here – there aren't any discos or cinemas.
I: What are the people like?
A: Oh, they're lovely, but there aren't many young people. I want to go and live in the city. Soon.

4
(I = Interviewer; L = Luigi)
I: What do you think of your city?
L: It is a very special place. There is nowhere else in the world like my city – it's so romantic.
I: What's the city centre like?
L: The buildings are beautiful, and we have San Marco, one of the most famous churches in the world. San Marco Square is wonderful, and during carnival in February Venice is the best place in the world to be.
I: Do you like living here?
L: No, I really hate living here. It's horrible. There are too many tourists everywhere.
I: Oh dear. What are the shops like?

L: Well, because of the tourists the shops are too expensive and the canals are dirty and polluted. My city is not big enough for all these people. Why don't they leave us in peace?

📼 08

(See page 12.)

📼 09

(See page 14.)

3 Couples

📼 10

(See page 17.)

📼 11

(I = Introducer; BB = Bobby Brown; R = Rosie; D = David)
I: It's time for our popular competition, *Get Personal*, with your host, Bobby Brown.
BB: Good evening and welcome to this week's *Get Personal*. Let's meet our first couple, Rosie and David.
      Now you'll remember the way the game works. We want to find out just how much they remember about when they first met. So, Rosie and David are going to answer the same questions, and they'll get one point each time they give the same answer. As you know, Rosie and David are in separate studios – Rosie can't hear David, and David has no idea what Rosie is saying. But they can both hear me. Okay, are you ready to play *Get Personal*?
R&D: Yes, Bobby.

📼 12

(BB = Bobby Brown; R = Rosie)
BB: Okay, ladies first, so we'll start with you, Rosie. Tell me, when did you meet David?
R: Um, it was exactly three years, four and a half months ago.
BB: All right! Now Rosie, how did you first meet?
R: Well, I was working as a nurse, and David came into the hospital for an operation.
BB: Okay, Rosie. I want you to think about the moment when you first met. What time of day was it?
R: Um, it was getting dark, and I was working nights that week. So early evening.
BB: And what was the weather like?
R: Oh dear, I think it was raining. Yes, I remember now – it was definitely raining when I arrived at work.
BB: What were you both wearing when you saw one another for the first time?
R: That's easy. I was wearing my nurse's uniform, and he was wearing pyjamas.

BB: What colour were the pyjamas?
R: Um, blue. Or were they green? No, they were blue.
BB: Is that your final answer?
R: Yes, blue.
BB: Finally, who spoke first and what did they say?
R: David spoke first. In fact he shouted at me. He said, 'Nurse, I'm going to be sick.'
BB: Oh well, that's *very* romantic! Thank you, Rosie.

📼 13

(BB = Bobby Brown; D = David)
BB: Now, David, it's your turn. When did you meet Rosie?
D: Oh, nearly three and a half years ago.
BB: Okay. Second question. Where and how did you first meet?
D: Ah, well, I went into hospital for an operation, and Rosie was working there as a nurse.
BB: What time of day was it?
D: Oh, I don't know. Lunchtime?
BB: What was the weather like?
D: Oh dear. It was summer, so I suppose the sun was shining.
BB: What were you both wearing when you saw one another for the first time?
D: Ah, Rosie was wearing her nurse's uniform and, and she was also wearing lovely perfume. I was wearing my favourite green pyjamas.
BB: Finally, David, who spoke first and what did they say?
D: Ah, Rosie spoke first. She said, 'How are you feeling?' And I think I said, um, 'I feel terrible.'

📼 14

(Sounds.)

📼 15

(See page 21.)

4 Fit

📼 16

(MD = marketing director; AE = advertising executive)
MD: OK. Who have you got for me?
AE: Well, we now have a short list of six people. I'm sure you'll love all of them.
MD: Go ahead then.
AE: Well, first of all, we've got Raúl.
MD: Who? Never heard of him. Who's next? Someone better, I hope.
AE: No, Raúl's really famous. He plays football for Spain.
MD: Well, he's no good to me.
AE: OK, next, we've got Shaquille O'Neal.
MD: Who? I don't know him either.
AE: He's massive! Mega-rich, mega-talented, massively famous.
MD: He's not famous with people like me. And he's not as good-looking

as that other boy, what did you call him, Raúl? We need someone who is attractive. I don't care how good he is at basketball.
AE: OK, what about Michael Schumacher? Maybe we could get him. He's more successful than all of them.
MD: It doesn't matter. I want someone attractive.
AE: Oh right, I get it. You really don't want a man. Oh, fine. Well, what about, hm, I don't know, what about a swimmer? There's that Dutch one, Inge, Inge something. She won a few gold medals and she looks good.
MD: Yes, that's the idea. But not swimming – I want something more, you know, erm, more, erm, tennis, for example, tennis is a bit more interesting than swimming.
AE: What about someone like Venus Williams, or her sister, what's she called? Or number six on my list, Cathy Freeman, the Australian Olympic 400 metre champion? Venus Williams looks great and is probably more famous than Cathy Freeman, but Cathy is more, well, I mean, she's lovely, isn't she? Such a beautiful smile. But some people may think athletics isn't as interesting as tennis …
MD: Maybe. Come on. Let's decide. Who do you think is sexier? This runner or that football player, Raúl?
AE: Oh, Raúl. No question.
MD: Well, I disagree. I think this Cathy Freeman is sexier than all of them. See if you can get her.
AE: Are you sure? Is that your final decision? I think she's a very interesting choice.
MD: Yup, let's go for it. When can you contact her?

📼 17

(See page 24.)

📼 18

Three quarters.
Nought point two five.
Nought point three three.
One and a half.
An eighth
A quarter.
One point five.
Nought point one two five.
A third.
Nought point seven five.

📼 19

Three quarters is the same as nought point seven five.
Nought point two five is the same as a quarter.
Nought point three three is the same as a third.
One and a half is the same as one point five.
An eighth is the same as nought point one two five.

20

a) A speed
   Two hundred and five kilometres an hour.
   One hundred and twenty-eight kilometres an hour.

b) A sum of money
   Fifty-nine million dollars
   Seventeen million dollars

c) A big number
   Ninety-seven million, two thousand, four hundred and forty
   Six hundred and twenty-four million, one hundred and twelve thousand, three hundred and fifty

d) A percentage
   Eight point two per cent
   Twenty-six point seven per cent

e) A distance
   Fifty-one point two five kilometres
   Forty-two point one nine five kilometres

f) A football score
   Four one
   Three nil

21

a) Venus Williams' tennis serve has been recorded at two hundred and five kilometres an hour. It's actually the fastest service in women's tennis.

b) Michael Schumacher earned fifty-nine million dollars in 2000: more than any other sports person.

c) The British have a very sweet tooth. They eat a total of six hundred and twenty-four million, one hundred and twelve thousand, three hundred and fifty Mars bars every year.

d) Only eight point two per cent of the UK population trust the government.

e) The official distance for a marathon, established in 1910, is forty-two point one nine five kilometres.

f) France beat Brazil three nil in the 1998 final and became world champions for the first time.

22

Golfing genius
Tiger Woods was born on 30th December 1975 in California, USA, of mixed heritage: he describes himself as a quarter black, a quarter Thai, a quarter Chinese, an eighth white and an eighth American Indian. His father, Earl Woods, named him Tiger after a friend who saved his life in the Vietnam war.

He was only nine months old when he started to play golf and he played his first game at one and a half years old. His father was his first teacher.

At the age of eight, he won a tournament and five more before he was sixteen. On 8 April 2001 Tiger Woods made golfing history. He became the first golfer to win all four majors – the most important tournaments – within the same year.

He is helping to make golf more popular with all ages and levels, and most people agree that he is probably the greatest golfer of all time. Certainly, he is already one of the richest.

He now earns more than $50 million a year. He has a $100 million deal with Nike and also has deals with American Express, Buick, Rolex and Wheaties.

What advice would he give prospective parents of golf champions? 'Don't force your kids into sports. It has to be fun.'

The best advice he ever got? From his dad: 'Always be yourself.'

23

(I = Interviewer; P = Pauline)
I: And here on Radio Five Live we have a winner in this week's big competition. The prize, the prize this week is a trip to beautiful Augusta for the Masters and the chance to meet Tiger Woods! The winner is Pauline Perkins, and she's on the line right now. Pauline, congratulations. I hear that you're mad about Tiger Woods – you're his biggest fan. Is that right?
P: Oh yes. I think he's the most wonderful person in the world and I know absolutely everything about him. I have a website all about him and I write to him every day.
I: Really? What do you like most about him?
P: He's the greatest golfer of all time and he's gorgeous. So young, too. In fact, he's the youngest player to win four major golf tournaments in one year.
I: Oh really? How old is he?
P: He was born on 30th December 1975. I always have a party on the 30th December and I put pictures of Tiger all round the house.
I: Oh, how nice. Pauline, I hear Tiger Woods is one of the richest sportsmen on the planet. Does he live like a typical superstar?
P: No, he's different from other superstars. He's the only real superstar. He's just so, ooh, different.
I: What do you mean?
P: He likes staying at home, playing computer games and table tennis. Oh, and eating his favourite food. He's a perfect man. He's so good.
I: What's his favourite food?
P: Pizza or cheeseburger and strawberry milkshake. I like the same things.
I: And is it true that Michael Jordan is one of his best friends?
P: Oh yes. Michael Jordan is like a big brother to Tiger.
I: I see. And can I just ask you one last question?
P: Sure.
I: What are you going to say to Tiger when you meet him?
P: I'm going to tell him that I ...

5 Review 1

 24

(I = Interviewer; B = Brenda)
I: We've been hearing a lot over here in the States about the actor, Vinnie Jones. Over in Britain he's really well known, isn't that right?
B: Well, yeah, he's much better known in Britain than he is over here.
I: So, what's the big deal? What's so special about Vinnie Jones?
B: Well, before he became an actor, he was already well known as a soccer player. In fact, I'd say he's still more famous for his soccer skills than as an actor.
I: And which team did he play for? Manchester United?
B: No, no, actually, for much of his career, he played for Wimbledon.
I: Wimbledon?
B: Yes, they're not as successful as Manchester United, but while he was playing for them they beat Liverpool and won the Cup. But it wasn't really for his soccer skills that Vinnie became famous. He was well known in Britain for being the toughest guy on the pitch.
I: The toughest guy on the pitch? In what way?
B: He was always in trouble with the referee. Basically, he was a good player, but he was violent.
I: Is there anything special about that?
B: Not really, no, but Vinnie was much more violent than other soccer players.
I: Jeez. What exactly did he do?
B: Well, for example, on one occasion, he told another player he would tear his ear off.
I: Ugh!
B: And on another occasion he tried to bite the nose of a sports journalist.
I: Wow. He sounds like a very unpleasant person.
B: Well, believe it or not, there is another side to him. If you met him, you'd probably like him – he's a lot nicer than many people think.
I: From what you say, he doesn't sound exactly, erm, nice!
B: He's a happily married family man, married to a girl he met when he was twelve, devoted to his son and step-daughter, and he's one of the most generous people I've ever met.
I: No kidding.
B: No, I'm serious.
I: OK, so how did he get into acting?
B: In 1997, at the age of 33, Vinnie's soccer career was coming to an end. He got a job as a chat show host with Sky TV, and then one thing led to another. He got a phone call from Guy Ritchie, Madonna's boyfriend – now her husband – asking him to take the part of a gangster in the film that he was making. The film, *Lock, Stock and Two Smoking Barrels*, was extremely successful in Britain.

I: So that was the start.

B: Yup, that was the start, and in the last few years he has acted with John Travolta, Brad Pitt and Nicholas Cage.

I: Well, it's a great story – soccer tough guy becomes Hollywood star!

B: Yes, that's right. Obviously, he's not as good-looking as Brad Pitt, but he's a great character actor.

I: OK, Brenda, thanks for that. Now, it's back to ...

📼 25

(See page 31.)

📼 26

(See page 33.)

6 Shop

📼 27

(I = Interviewer; R = Russell; B = Billy)

I: Right, okay. Question one. Do you mind going round the shops?

R: Not really. But after about an hour I want to go home.

B: It depends. I don't mind going shopping, but on Saturdays I prefer watching football on TV.

I: Right, okay. Um let's see. Question two. What kind of shops do you like going into?

R: Book shops. I could spend a whole day in a book shop.

B: I love listening to music, so music shops are my favourite.

I: Right, okay. Question three. Are there any kinds of shops you hate going into?

R: I hate supermarkets so I don't bother going into them any more. I do shopping on the internet.

B: I can't stand going into shoe shops with my girlfriend. She tries on ten pairs and then buys the first pair.

I: Right, okay. Last question. Question four. Do you enjoy buying clothes for yourself?

R: Not really. I don't waste time shopping for clothes unless I really need something.

B: I like having new clothes, but I don't enjoy trying them on.

I: Right. Thanks.

📼 28

(SA = Shop assistant; R = Russell)

SA: Can I help you?

R: Oh, I'm just looking, thanks. Well, actually, I'm looking for something for my girlfriend.

SA: And what sort of thing are you looking for?

R: I don't really know. A top?

SA: Right. What colour would you like?

R: Um, what colours have you got?

SA: We've got any colour you want, sir. What colour does your girlfriend usually wear?

R: Oh dear ...

SA: Okay, what colour are her eyes?

R: Green.

SA: Right, purple suits people with green eyes.

R: Oh great. Yes, purple's fine.

SA: Now, what size is she?

R: Um, well, sort of, she isn't very big, but she's not particularly small.

SA: That'll be medium then.

R: Yes, good, medium.

SA: Well, we have this rather nice silk evening top here ...

R: Good, I'll take it.

SA: Are you sure you don't want to see any more ...?

R: No, no, that's great. I'll take it. Thank you. How much is it?

SA: That's £70, sir. How would you like to pay?

R: Seventy?! By credit card, please.

SA: Fine. If you could just sign ...

R: Here you are. Goodbye.

SA: Just a minute, sir. Here's your receipt.

R: Oh yes, er ... can she exchange it if it doesn't fit?

SA: Yes, but she needs to keep the receipt.

📼 29

(SA = Shop assistant; R = Roz)

SA: Can I help you?

R: Yes, I'm looking for a mobile phone.

SA: And what sort of mobile phone are you looking for, madam?

R: Um – what do you mean?

SA: Well, what do you want to do with your mobile phone – do you want to access the internet, send text messages, play games ...?

R: No, no. I just want to make telephone calls.

SA: Right. Something like this perhaps? This model comes with a Call Register facility which keeps track of the calls you have received, missed and dialled – also, if you take our pre-pay option, you can find out how much credit you still have.

R: No, no. I'm not interested in all that. I just want to make telephone calls.

SA: Fine. How about this basic model? It's very easy to use.

R: Yes ... What colours have you got?

SA: Well, we have this rather nice red one.

R: Red doesn't suit me.

SA: Red doesn't suit you??

R: That's right. I wear a lot of pink.

SA: I see. Um, well, we haven't got pink but we have this one in blue. Does blue suit you?

R: Yes, I like blue. I'll take it.

SA: Fine. I don't suppose you're interested in the clock function ...

R: No.

SA: ... or voice and speed dialling ...

R: No. I just want to pay!

SA: Okay, that'll be £60. How would you like to pay, madam?

R: In cash. Here you are.

SA: Thank you, madam. Here's your receipt. Oh, and don't forget this catalogue that tells you all about our mobile phone accessories. I'm sure you'll ...

7 Job

📼 30

A

Yeah, right, it all started when we were at school. We wanted to, like, start a band. I got this second-hand guitar for my sixteenth birthday, and my friend was really good at singing. That's how it started really, you know what I mean? We found a drummer and started doing gigs. And suddenly the band got really big – we started having hit records and making loads of money. So I dropped out of school and really concentrated on the music. I've got fifteen guitars now, but my favourite is still the one I got for my sixteenth birthday, you know what I mean?

B

I work in the maternity department of a large hospital and I've delivered 649 babies so far. It's a great job because it brings happiness to people's lives. When I hand the new baby to the parents, I know that it's one of the happiest moments of their lives. On the other hand, it's a very stressful job. I usually work nights and I work long hours, so I haven't had time to have a baby of my own yet!

C

I couldn't live in a city – I love the outdoor life. It's a hard life, but I've never missed a single day's work through illness and I'm sixty-nine years old. With the new tractor, I have a bit more time on my hands, but I still get up at five o'clock every morning and feed the animals before breakfast. My eldest son gives me a hand at weekends, but I still do most of the work myself – you know you're living when you're outdoors.

📼 31

(P = Presenter; I = Interviewer;
Mr R = Mr Reynold)

P: ... And this week, in our regular report from over there in little old England, our interviewer Gloria Sacks, walked into a department store with a difference ...

I: Mr Reynold, can you tell us what is so special about your department store?

Mr R: Well, yes, it is special. *Reynold's* is a large department store and you can find everything you want for the home here. Oh, and it stays open late on Thursdays and Saturdays.

I: Yes, that's right, but isn't there something special about the staff – you know – has anybody retired recently?

Mr R: Ah, oh I see. No. Nobody has retired recently, and we never force anybody to retire here.

I: How old is your oldest employee?

Mr R: Well, that would be Arthur. Arthur is our cleaner, and he's 87.

I: 87! And he cleans the store every day?

Mr R: Well, not alone, no. He works with two other cleaners. They're not so old – Mabel's 70 and Ivy's 75 – no 76. That's right, she's just had her birthday.

I: And they don't want to retire?

Mr R: No, I think they enjoy the work, and it keeps them young. Also, we pay a decent salary, and they get four weeks' paid holiday a year.

I: So how many workers do you have who are over retirement age?

Mr R: Well, we employ a staff of a hundred and five, and I'd say that maybe half of those are over 65. The young ones work in the office – we've got computers now, you know?

I: Really? Has the store changed much over the years?

Mr R: No, not really. I started working here in 1948 and I've only had two secretaries in all that time. Edith, my first secretary, handed in her notice when she was 72.

I: Oh, why did she leave *Reynold's* so young?

Mr R: Well, she was getting married to someone who lived in another town.

I: Jeez! That's amazing. Tell me, have you ever fired anybody?

Mr R: No, not yet. I can't see any reason to fire somebody, unless they're dishonest. That's not a problem we have with the older employees.

I: And do you think you will ever retire, Mr Reynold?

Mr R: Oh yes. I'm nearly 86! My son's going to take over the business next year. It'll be good to have a younger man in charge. He's er, only 64.

📼 32

Good morning. Let me introduce myself. My name's Lourdes Rivas, and I work for British Airways. As you probably know, we are a major international airline. I'm based at Sondika airport in Bilbao, where I'm in charge of sales and promotion. I'm looking forward to doing this course.

8 Rich

📼 33

(See page 46.)

📼 34

(I = Interviewer; M = Matt)

I: Matt, *Ozone* was a very successful band. Why did you decide to leave?

M: I was very young when I joined the band. At first, all the money and fame and success was very exciting, and I enjoyed the attention. But after a while, I started to lose my identity.

I: What do you mean?

M: Well, we had no freedom at all. Our manager told us how to dress, how to sing and what to sing, how to dance, what to say to the press, where to go and where not to go.

I: But your manager turned you into a chart-topping band.

M: Yes, but we worked very hard and never went out. It wasn't a normal life for a teenager. We weren't even allowed to have relationships.

I: But you were making a lot of money.

M: Yes, that's true. And at first I enjoyed the money but I wasted it on stupid things. Also, I spent too much time with people who weren't my real friends – people who were only interested in my money. I lost my real friends. Then one morning I woke up and thought, 'I don't know who I am.' It was scary.

📼 35

I: And that's when you decided to leave?

M: Yes, that's right.

I: Matt, that was three months ago. Have you decided what you're going to do next?

M: Yes. I've had time to think about my future. I'm going to carry on singing and pursue a solo career.

I: Do you think you've learnt anything from your experience in *Ozone*?

M: Oh yes. This time I'm going to employ a decent manager who listens to me and who gives me good financial advice. I'm not going to waste my money on stupid things. Also, I'm going to spend more time with my family and I'm definitely not going to forget my real friends.

I: And what kind of music are you going to play?

M: I'm going to write my own songs and play the kind of music I like. I've learnt my lesson and I'm definitely not going to make the same mistakes again.

I: So, another Number 1 hit in the near future?

M: Definitely.

📼 36

(S = Suzy; M = Matt)

S: Welcome back to Suzy B on Radio 103. Matt McKay, ex-lead singer of *Ozone*, is sitting here with me in the studio today. Matt, how's life?

M: Really good.

S: That's great. Now your first solo single is coming out tomorrow. How are you feeling?

M: I'm feeling great, really positive. We've worked very hard on the album, and I think we've come up with some really good songs.

S: Excellent. And what about gigs? Are you doing any concerts?

M: Actually, we're starting a European tour next week. We're doing three nights in London. Then we're flying to Berlin. We're doing gigs in three German cities, then we're going onto Holland, Belgium and Denmark.

S: Wow, heavy. That's quite a schedule.

M: Oh, that's not all. We're having a short holiday the following week and then we're touring France, Switzerland, Spain and … I think that's it.

S: Phew. You'll need another holiday after that.

M: Well, you know, it's important to get out and meet the fans.

S: Of course. But enough about work – have you got any plans for your holiday yet?

M: Yes. I'm taking my mum and dad to the Canary Islands for some sun.

S: Excellent. Matt, good luck for tomorrow. I've heard the single, and if you ask me, it's going to go straight to the top of the charts.

M: Thanks. I hope you're right.

S: Okay, let's listen to the single now. Out tomorrow, this is Matt McKay's first solo single, *I'm the one*.

9 Rules

📼 37

(See page 52.)

📼 38

(See page 54.)

📼 39

(See page 54.)

📼 40

I decided to do *The Rules* because I wanted a proper relationship. My relationships always fail because I'm too soft, and people take advantage of me. Even my best friends sometimes take advantage of me.

Before I started doing *The Rules* I was seeing Michael four or five times a week and talking on the phone several times a day.

So it was difficult following *The Rules* because I couldn't phone him, and when he phoned me, I had to finish the conversation first. I love chatting on the phone but I had to tell him I was busy even when I wasn't.

At first, *The Rules* worked. He became more interested and he even took me to meet his mum.

But then he said I was acting strangely. He said I'd changed – at first I was warm and friendly, but I was getting colder and harder. I knew it wasn't the real me, but I couldn't tell him about *The Rules* – that's one of the rules!

The rules are supposed to make you mysterious and fascinating, but he just thought I was behaving like a cow.

Then I began to fall in love with him and I wanted to see him more, but I couldn't. I didn't like playing games with him any more. It didn't feel right.

And then something awful happened. He saw the book ... He was so angry!

He told me to go and play games with somebody else and left.

Anyway, I threw away my copy of *The Rules* and now I'm reading a book called *The Joy of Being Single*. I've decided that I don't have to find a man and get married to be happy. I'm much happier now.

📼 41

(See page 55.)

📼 42

(See page 57.)

10 Review 2

📼 43

a)
W1: I'm home! Sorry I'm late, darling. I had to work late at the office.
M1: But it's eleven o'clock! And this is the third time this week!
W1: I know. I'm really sorry, but it's an important contract.

b)
B: Sorry, sir. Can I come in, please, sir? I couldn't get here earlier – the bus was late. Sorry.
T: Your bus is always late, Ronnie. Why don't you catch the earlier one?
B: Yes, sir. Sorry, sir. Tomorrow I'll catch the earlier bus.

c)
M2: Sir, we sent you the bill on the first Monday of last month.
M3: You sent it last month? I never received it! How much was the bill for?
M2: Twenty-four thousand, three hundred and fifty ...

d)
W2: When are you going to stop? I can't stand the smell of your cigarettes in this house. You know it's bad for the children. And for you.
M4: I know, I know. I'm going to give up. Tomorrow. Next week. Soon.
W2: I've heard that before ...

e)
W3: I've got some amazing news about Tina and Brian, but you mustn't tell anyone. OK?
W4: Of course not. You can trust me. I always keep a secret. What's going on?
W3: Well, you know Brigitte from number 9. She said that ...

f)
W5: Thank you. That was the best meal we've ever had. Wasn't it, Donald?
M5: Oh yes, delicious.
W6: Ah, thank you. We must do it again soon.

📼 44

(P = Presenter; K = Gerald Kelly; D = Driver)

Part 1
P: Welcome to *Tools of the Trade*, our weekly look at professional secrets. This week – the world of the customs officer. We spent a day at the port of Dover with Gerald Kelly, a senior customs officer in the fight against contraband cigarettes. We join Mr Kelly as he interviews a driver passing through customs.

K: Good afternoon, sir.
D: Afternoon.
K: Have you been far, sir?
D: No, I haven't been far.
K: Could you be more precise, sir? Where exactly have you been?
D: I don't know what the place is called – it's a little town on the coast about twenty kilometres from Calais.
K: I see, sir. Did you buy any alcohol or cigarettes during the trip?
D: Er, no. Well, not much. Erm, my sister's getting married next week, so I just went over to buy her a few bottles of champagne. We're having a party after the wedding. Do you want to come? Erm, only joking!
K: Well, if you don't mind, I'm going to have a look in the back of the car. Is it open?

Part 2
p: The back of the car contained six cases of champagne – no problems there. But then they found eight thousand cigarettes – the legal limit is eight hundred. The driver was arrested.
Mr Kelly, do you search every car that passes through?
K: No, that would be impossible. Thousands of cars drive through the port every day.
p: So how do you know which cars to stop?
K: Well, we often have inside information, but this time, I had a feeling.
p: Just a feeling?

K: Well, perhaps a little more than that. You see a guy on his own, he doesn't look like a businessman, it's the middle of the week ... and you think, 'What is he up to?'
p: That's it?
K: No – then we ask a few simple questions. We watch their body language, and you can usually tell if they're lying.
p: You can see it in their eyes?
K: Well, not in the eyes, because they don't usually look at you. They often hide their hands, too. But there are other signs. Have you ever noticed the way people sometimes touch their face a lot when they are lying?
p: So, just by looking at them, you can –
K: No, you have to listen, too. To begin with, they often say very little, just the minimum. Just 'Morning, officer' or 'Afternoon, sir.' They don't give you precise information like names of places. And then they sometimes start saying too much, saying any old rubbish to fill the silence.
p: I've read somewhere that liars usually use more negative verbs. Have you found this?
K: Yes, that's right. Also, their voice often goes up, 'Er, no, not much,' and they sound scared.
p: Does anyone ever get past you?
K: Oh, yeah. We've caught hundreds of the little guys, but we hardly ever catch the big ones, the real professionals.
p: Gerald Kelly, thank you very much. With contraband cigarette sales approaching fifty per cent in some parts of England, customs officers have clearly got a difficult job on their hands.

📼 45

The top three whisky drinkers in bottles consumed per year are:
1 Spain: 145,000,000
2 France: 137,000,000
3 The USA: 117,000,000

The top three beer drinkers in litres consumed per person per year are:
1 The Czech Republic: 160
2 Ireland: 141.3
3 Germany: 137.7

The top three coffee drinkers in cups consumed per person per year are:
1 Norway: 1,356
2 Denmark: 1,305
3 Finland: 1,293

The top three Coca-Cola drinkers in glasses consumed per person per year are:
1 The USA: 343
2 Mexico: 322
3 Germany: 201

11 Smile

📼 46

(See page 64.)

📼 47

(See page 65.)

📼 48

(See page 65.)

📼 49

(See page 65.)

📼 50

a) I'd love to meet your friends – let's make a date now. We could try that new restaurant in town.
b) No, no, don't do it like that. Do it like this. Go on, do it again, and, oh, then get me a cup of tea.
c) No problem – I'm sure I can win. I know I'm faster than the others.
d) I'm working here to get some experience but I'm going to start up my own company soon.
e) Yeah, whatever – I really don't mind. I'll be happy if we go out. I'll be happy if we stay in. Let's do whatever you want to do.
f) Look, are you sure you're okay, because I can stay longer if you want. Anyway, you know where I am if you need me. Take care.

📼 51

(See page 67.)

📼 52

Laughter clubs
Scientific research has proved that laughter reduces the effects of stress and helps the body to fight against illness and infection. In India, the health benefits of laughter are taken very seriously. There is a network of 600 'laughter clubs' where people meet every day just to laugh. They participate in 'social laughter'(quiet tittering), suppressed laughter (sniggering), and the loud, explosive laugh (roaring with laughter), which exercises the lungs.

12 Rebel

📼 53

(I = Interviewer; J = Jake, D = Debbie, C = Caroline, R = Ronny)

I: It's May 1st, and we are in the centre of London in the middle of an enormous demonstration. People are handing out leaflets with information. There are all kinds of people here, but what exactly are they protesting about?

Jake
I: Excuse me! Yes, you. What are you doing here?
J: I'm protesting against globalisation. Multinational companies cause a lot of pollution. They are polluting the world's rivers and seas, and they don't care – they just want to make as much money as possible. I'm also giving out peaceful protest leaflets and T-shirts. There are some people here who want violence, but most people are here to protest in a peaceful way. Me, I'm a supporter of peaceful action.
I: Thank you.

Debbie
I: Excuse me. Can you tell me what you're doing here?
D: Well, I'm in favour of many of the causes here but I'm here today with a group of women from Manchester. We're demonstrating for equal pay for women. Women still earn less than men in most jobs, and it's time for that to change. I'm not anti-men – I just want a fairer system. Would you like to sign our petition?
I: Er, yes, sure, thank you.

Ronny
I: Hi there! Can you tell me what you're doing here?
R: I'm selling veggie burgers. I'm against cosmetic companies that use animals in their experiments. At home I have three dogs, two cats and a pet mouse called Jerry. They are my friends. I support animal rights and I'm protesting against cruelty to animals. All right?
I: Good luck.

Caroline
I: Excuse me. What are you doing here?
C: I'm having fun with my friends. I don't feel strongly about politics and I don't know much about it. This is my first demonstration. My friends and I are against student fees – we're demanding financial aid from the government. We want the government to pay. I know so many people who don't go to college because they don't want to get into debt. I don't really care about globalisation and stuff, but students are really important. I mean, we're the future of the country, aren't we?

📼 54

(See page 71.)

📼 55

explain, explanation
organise, organisation
produce, production
legalise, legalisation
educate, education
reduce, reduction
modernise, modernisation
legislate, legislation

📼 56

(See page 74.)

13 Dance

📼 57

(I = Interviewer; J = Josh; S = Saskia; A = Antonio)

Josh
I: Josh, how are you?
J: Um, to be honest, I'm completely knackered! I've been dancing all night.
I: You're very white. Don't you like sunbathing?
J: Uh, well, I haven't been to the beach yet.
I: How come? How long have you been here?
J: Dunno. Nine, ten days.
I: Well, what have you been doing since you arrived?
J: I've been clubbing every night and sleeping all day. I've met loads of people, especially girls.
I: So, have you had a good time?
J: Oh yeah, definitely. I reckon this is the best holiday I've ever had. The only problem is I'm skint. I've spent all my money and I've still got a few days to go.
I: Oh dear. Well good luck and have a good journey home.
J: Cheers. You couldn't lend me some money, could you?

Saskia
I: Saskia, how long have you been here?
S: Since 1997.
I: Where are you from originally?
S: Holland, but I haven't been home for a couple of years now.
I: What have you been doing here since 1997?
S: Having a great time – I've been working in clubs. I've been a resident DJ at *Amnesia* for two years. Oh, and I've been building my own house.
I: Really? Do you make a lot of money working in clubs?
S: You can, but I've also married a guy from Ibiza. His father gave us the land to build a house.
I: I see. Do you think you'll ever go back to Holland?
S: No way. I love the lifestyle here: it's so laid back. And anyway, all my friends and family come and visit me here.

Antonio
I: Good morning, Antonio. How are you today?
A: Not bad, not bad. But I've been working all night in my restaurant so I'm going to go to bed soon.
I: Well, thanks for talking to us. How long have you been here in Ibiza?

A: All my life. I was born in the north but I've been living in Ibiza town since 1995. That was when I opened my own restaurant.

I: What's it like living here in Ibiza?

A: Ah, it used to be a wonderful place, but now the tourists have spoilt it.

I: But tourists have been coming to Ibiza since the sixties.

A: That's true, but they've changed. Tourists used to behave much better than they do today. Englishmen used to be gentlemen. Now it's all tattoos and piercings.

I: What sort of people come to your restaurants?

A: Well ... er ... tourists.

📼 58

(See page 81.)

14 Call

📼 59

(M = Mum; L = Lorna)

M: Hello.

L: Mum! It's me.

M: Oh, hello, darling. How are you?

L: I can't hear you, Mum. It's a really bad line.

M: Sorry dear. I said how are you?

L: Terrible, Mum. My back's killing me, and the house is a mess.

M: Don't worry, darling, I'll come and help you clean the house.

L: But that's not all – the kids are driving me mad. ELLA PUT HIM DOWN!

M: Don't worry, darling. When we've cleaned the house, I'll take the children to the park.

L: Oh thanks, Mum. There is something else though. ELLA, I SAID PUT HIM DOWN! Sorry – the thing is, I'm expecting six people for dinner, and the fridge is bare. Do you think you could do some shopping on your way over here?

M: No problem, darling. I'll stop at the supermarket and then I'll make a meal your friends will never forget.

L: Thanks, Mum. I don't know what I'd do without you. Could you do one more thing for me?

M: Of course, darling, what is it?

L: Well, I've run out of money. Could you possibly pay for the shopping, and I'll pay you back at the end of the month?

M: That's fine. You don't have to pay me back.

📼 60

(M = Mum; L = Lorna)

L: Mum – you're an angel. How's Dad?

M: Dad? Darling, you know your father and I divorced when you were thirteen.

L: Divorced? Thirteen? Oh no – what number are you on?

M: 0770 899 490.

L: Oh no, I don't believe it. I dialed the wrong number.

M: Juliet?

L: I'm not Juliet – but please, hold on – does this mean you're not coming over?

📼 61

Conversation 1

(D = Dad; L = Lorna)

D: Hello.

L: Dad?

D: Hello dear. How are you?

L: Oh, not too good actually.

D: Oh dear, what's the matter?

L: PUT THAT DOWN!

D: Pardon?!

L: No, not, not you, Dad – the children are driving me mad. OH FREDDIE, WHY DID YOU DO THAT?

D: Look dear, I'm just going out to play golf. Can I call you back later? Or shall I leave a message for your mother to ring you when she comes in?

L: Yes. Please. Could you tell her it's urgent?

D: Yes, okay dear – I think she'll be home ...

L: FREDDIE – DON'T TOUCH THAT! Dad, I've got to go.

D: Oh – goodbye dear.

Conversation 2

(J = Jackie; L = Lorna)

J: Hello.

L: Hello. Is that Jackie?

J: Yes. Hold on a minute ... Turn the music down!

L: Um, Jackie, it's Lorna. Lorna Carr.

J: Oh hello, Mrs Carr.

L: I was wondering if you could come over and baby-sit for a couple of hours this afternoon.

J: This afternoon? Er ... Would you mind hanging on a moment, please? ... (I've got to go and baby-sit.) ... Is it okay if I bring my boyfriend?

L: Yes, that's fine. Would you like me to drive over and pick you up?

J: It's okay. We'll get the bus.

L: NO! Er, no, I need you now actually. I'll be right over.

📼 62

(See page 85.)

📼 63

... and here are some useful numbers for travellers in the UK.

For flight information to and from Heathrow airport dial O eight seven O ... O double O ... O one two three.

You can get train times and fare information on O eight four five ... seven four eight ... four nine five O.

For National Express bus and coach information ring O eight seven O ... five eight O ... eight O eight O.

If you have problems on the road, the number for the AA 24-hour breakdown service is O eight hundred ... double eight ... double seven... double six.

The British Tourist Authority can help you find accommodation. Ring O two O ... double eight four six... nine O double O.

And remember, if you don't know a number, contact Directory Enquiries on one nine two. They will be pleased to help.

📼 64

A

A: Dad ... Do you think I could have a Zoomatron for my birthday? ... Please?

B: What's a Zoomatron?

A: It's a kind of space gun. It's really cool.

B: Oh no. Not another one ...

A: Please.

B

A: Could you tell me where the cloakroom is?

B: What?

A: Do you know where the toilets are?

B: Sorry – I can't hear you.

A: WHERE'S THE TOILET?

B: Over there.

C

A: Can you remember where we left it?

B: Um, I think it was on the second floor.

A: Well, this is the second floor, and I can't see it.

B: I think we parked next to a white van. ... There it is.

D

A: Have you any idea what the time is?

B: Dunno.

A: Well, it's half past twelve. Where on earth have you been? I've been worried sick. Wait till your father hears about this!

E

A: Do you know if the last bus has gone?

B: I'm afraid it left a couple of minutes ago.

A: Oh no! Do you know where I can get a taxi.

B: Try the railway station – there are usually a few taxis there.

A: Thanks.

F

A: Excuse me – do you know where the lions are?

B: They're over there next to the giraffes.

A: Oh right. Thank you.

15 Review 3

📼 65

(R = reporter; H = Hyacinth; D = Derek; K = Kati; O = Oona; M = Maggy)

Interview 1

R: Excuse me, madam, would you mind answering a few questions for

H: Certainly.

R: Well, could you tell me where you come from? Have you come far?

H: We don't live far from here. We live in Richmond, actually, so we usually get here very early in the morning. We like to be at the front of the queue, but Derek was slow getting up this morning, and there was a bit of a problem on the underground, so we arrived a little later than usual.

R: Could you tell me how long you've been waiting?

H: Since about half past eight, something like that, I suppose. So, yes, it's been a long wait. What is it – about three o'clock now? Derek! What's the time now? Derek!

D: Yes, dear?

R: Do you think you'll get in?

H: Oh yes, I think we'll probably get in soon. Won't we, Derek? Derek, stop looking at that girl! You've been looking at her for hours. Haven't you seen enough? She's certainly not interested in you!

R: Well, it's a long queue. Do you know how many people there are in front of you?

H: I imagine there are about, what, twenty or thirty people. It won't be long now, will it, Derek?

D: Huh?

Interview 2

R: Excuse me, would you mind answering a few questions for London South FM?

K: Excuse me? Can you speak a little more slowly, please?

R: Sorry, can I ask you a few questions for the radio?

K: Yes, of course.

R: How long have you waiting here?

K: I have been waiting here since a quarter past eight this morning. I did not know there was a long queue.

R: You must be a real tennis fan!

K: Ah, so-so. I am a student of English. I have been in London for four weeks, and tomorrow I must go back to Hanover in Germany, and I thought it was a good idea to come to Wimbledon before I go back to Germany.

R: Do you think you'll get in?

K: Excuse me?

R: Do you think you will get in?

K: No, I do not think so. It has been raining since half past one. I am wet and cold and I am hungry, and there are many, many people in front of me in the queue. I think I will give up soon.

Interview 3

R: Excuse me, madam, would you mind answering a few questions for London South FM?

O: Oh, come under the umbrella, dear. Would you like a strawberry?

R: Mm, thanks. Have you been here long?

O: Ooh, I'm not sure. What time did we arrive, Maggy?

M: Mm, about eight?

O: Yes, we've been here since about eight this morning. We come every year on the Friday, you know.

R: What are your chances of getting in?

O: Not very good, I would say. It rained on the Friday last year, too, and we never got in. But you never know. There are probably about fifty people in front of us, but lots of them will give up and go home soon. Maybe, we'll get the last match of the day. We live in Scotland, you know, so this is a big day out for us. We're not giving up now, not after coming all this way.

R: Isn't it a long time to wait for one match?

O: Ooh, no. We love the tennis, of course, but we really come for the atmosphere. We've met so many interesting people since we arrived. Have you spoken to that charming young girl from Germany? We've been chatting for ages – she's got such good English. And Maggy always brings her radio, so we've been listening to that. We've been having a great day, haven't we, Maggy?

M: Mm, another strawberry?

R: Mm, thanks. Well, good luck with the wait!

🔲 66

(See page 90.)

🔲 67

(S = Secretary; MK = Mrs Knightly)

S: Mr Rogers' office. Can I help you?

MK: Oh, hello. Can I speak to Mr Rogers, please?

S: Certainly. Could you hold the line, please? I'm afraid Mr Rogers is not in yet, madam.

MK: Ah, would you mind taking a message?

S: Certainly.

MK: Erm, well, it's Joanna Knightly here. I've got an appointment with Mr Rogers at 9.15 and I'm afraid I've missed the bus ...

S: Would you like to give me your telephone number, and I'll ask Mr Rogers to call you when he gets in?

MK: That's all right, thanks. I'll call back later.

S: You're welcome. Goodbye.

MK: Thanks. Goodbye.

🔲 68

(See page 93.)

16 Lifestyle

🔲 69

(R = Receptionist; W = Woman)

R: New Life Centre. Can I help you?

W: Yes. Could you give me some information about your centre?

R: Certainly. Are you interested in losing weight or just improving your fitness?

W: Actually, it's not for me. It's for my husband. He needs to lose weight and improve his fitness. I want to book him a week with you as a surprise for his birthday.

R: Ah, lucky man!

W: Could you tell me something about the programme?

R: Sure. As soon as he arrives here he'll take a fitness test to see what sort of diet he needs to go on.

W: Right.

R: We start every day at 7.30 with a half-hour walk before breakfast.

W: Ha ha. He usually starts the day with a cigarette before breakfast!

R: Oh dear. If he has a cigarette here, he'll be in big trouble. It's a strictly no smoking area.

W: Well, it's a good idea for him to give up smoking. He says he'll give up as soon as he feels more relaxed.

R: Oh well, this is the ideal place to relax. We do at least two hours of yoga and meditation every day, and after the morning hike he can have a sauna and jacuzzi.

W: Oh, he'll enjoy that. But what's this hike?

R: They go for a hike in the morning from 8.30 to 12.30. One of our instructors will take your husband and other people at the same level of fitness for a four-hour hike into the mountains.

W: Four hours! His idea of a walk is going from the front door to his car.

R: Oh, don't worry. When they get to the top of the mountain, they'll have a twenty-minute break before they come down again. The scenery is very relaxing.

W: They'll be starving!

R: Oh, don't worry. When they're hungry they'll stop for a healthy snack. The instructor always carries a supply of fruit.

W: No chocolate then! And what about the afternoon? Can he relax then?

R: No, not really. But he'll have time to relax after the afternoon hike.

W: Oh my goodness. I don't think he'll thank me for this.

R: Believe me, when he finishes the week he'll feel like a new man.

W: *If* he finishes the week!

🔲 70

(See page 98.)

🔲 71

/ɪ/ lettuce spinach
/ʌ/ onion nut
/ə/ banana lemon
/iː/ sardines beans
/ɒ/ orange cauliflower
/əʊ/ aubergine tomato

72

(See page 98.)

17 Animals

73

1   Word A: tail – T A I L tail
    Word B: tale – T A L E tale
2   Word A: deer – D E E R deer
    Word B: dear – D E A R dear
3   Word A: bear – B E A R bear
    Word B: bare – B A R E bare
4   Word A: right – R I G H T right
    Word B: write – W R I T E write
5   Word A: wait – W A I T wait
    Word B: weight – W E I G H T weight

74

(See page 103.)

75

a) Tim
(I = Interviewer; T = Tim)
I: Can you describe your pet?
T: She's very fat and not very pretty. But she's got a lovely curly tail.
I: What does she eat?
T: Anything and everything. She's very fond of banana skins.
I: Is she a good companion?
T: Yes, I always go and speak to her when I'm fed up. She listens to my problems when no one else will.
I: When you go away, who looks after her?
T: If I go away for work, my girlfriend looks after her. But if my girlfriend comes away with me, we have to take her over to my parents. She doesn't like that very much because they've got a dog that annoys her.
I: Do you and your pet look alike?
T: I hope not.
I: If you were an animal, what animal would you like to be?
T: I used to say a dolphin when I was younger, but I don't like the sea very much now. I don't know – a giraffe maybe, though I'd hate to be stuck in a zoo.

b) Gus
(I = Interviewer; G = Gus)
I: Can you describe your pet?
G: He's black and has eight hairy legs.
I: What does he eat?
G: Insects.
I: What, he catches them?
G: No, I buy them frozen.
I: Is he a good companion?
G: Yeah. He's like a friend. We have a special bond.
I: When you go away, who looks after him?
G: Well, I haven't been away since I got him and I don't think anybody wants to look after him. Certainly not my mum. He frightens people away.
I: Do you and your pet look alike?

G: I'm not that hairy – but I think he looks cool, like me.
I: If you were an animal, what animal would you like to be?
G: A lion because they're big and tough and they rule.

c) Maxine
(I = Interviewer; M = Maxine)
I: Can you describe your pet?
M: She's very fluffy and very loveable. My boyfriend doesn't like her because she bit him – she's definitely a girl's girl.
I: What does she eat?
M: Her favourite meals are fresh vegetables, nuts and cereal.
I: Is she a good companion?
M: Oh, yes, I love Page because she's good company for me when my boyfriend is away travelling. Besides, we have the same interests – she loves to sleep all day, eat and then she parties all night long.
I: When you go away, who looks after her?
M: I take her everywhere in her little cage.
I: Do you and your pet look alike?
M: I think that she's better looking than me – who could resist those brown button eyes?
I: If you were an animal what animal would you like to be?
M: I _am_ an animal.

76

I know somebody who's got an iguana as a pet. It's a man I work with called Angus. The iguana is called Iggy and it's probably about five years old – that's how long I've known Angus and he got it soon after we met. It was a birthday present from his wife. It's just over a metre long from the tip of its nose to the end of its tail and it's a lovely green colour. Like all reptiles, iguanas never stop growing, so Iggy will get bigger and bigger. It's quite shy and nervous, which is exactly the opposite of Angus who's very outgoing and confident. It's definitely better looking than Angus though. Iggy doesn't sleep in a cage. At the moment, it lives at the top of the curtains in Angus's living room. When it was young, it ate crickets, but now it's adult it doesn't need so much protein – in fact it's completely vegetarian. Angus takes it for walks in the park on a lead. It's funny – when it's frightened, it runs up Angus's body and sits on his head.

18 Weird

77

(I = Interviewer; KC = Ken Crystal)
I: This morning the residents of a small village in Wiltshire woke up to an amazing sight. It is the biggest crop circle we've ever seen in Britain. The press is calling it the mother of all circles, and the

question everyone is asking … how did it get there? In the studio with me today is Ken Crystal, a crop circle expert. Ken, how long have you been interested in crop circles?
KC: For about eleven years now.
I: Can you tell us something about this circle?
KC: Well, we're very excited about this crop circle. The design is absolutely amazing, and it's enormous.
I: How big is it exactly?
KC: It's almost one kilometre wide! We've never seen anything like this before!
I: It's a very complex design. How many circles are there altogether?
KC: There are more than 400 circles – it really is incredible.
I: And do you know who made it?
KC: No, I don't, but I believe that this is the work of strange forces.
I: What do you mean?
KC: It's impossible for people to make something like this.
I: But I've heard that most circles _are_ made by people. Is that true?
KC: Yes, there are several groups of people who make crop circles. But they didn't make this one.
I: How do you know?
KC: This circle appeared yesterday morning. The day before that it wasn't there. There were only four hours of darkness that night – there wasn't enough time to make it.
I: How long does it take to make a crop circle?
KC: Well, a simple circle takes a few hours. But a circle like this one would take several days.
I: How long have crop circles existed?
KC: The first crop circles were reported in 1980. In the last eleven years, I've visited over a thousand. But I've never seen one like this.
I: Ken, a final question. Do you think that this crop circle is the work of aliens?
KC: I think it could be a message …

78

(See page 108.)

79

(See page 109.)

80

(See page 110.)

81

Des's story
I had a strange experience while I was working in Germany.
    I was walking down the road in a place called Oberstdorf. I was alone, and I was wearing a coat with a hood over my head because it was snowing.
    Suddenly I heard somebody call my name. When I looked round I saw that it was a young woman I'd met the

previous summer in Ireland. I live in Ireland, and she had been on holiday in my home town. After the holiday she'd returned to Germany, and I hadn't been in touch with her since then.

She had no idea that I was in Germany and she didn't even live in Oberstdorf – she was just visiting a friend. But somehow she recognised me, even though it was snowing and I was wearing a big hood.

After that we stayed in touch, and in fact she came to my wedding ten years later.

Lidia's story
My sister and my aunt had a strange experience the day after my mother died.

At the time of her death, my mother was living with my sister. My aunt came to stay with my sister to help her make arrangements for the funeral.

In the afternoon, the two women were sitting in the living room when my sister's little dog started barking.

They went out of the room to see why the dog was barking and they both saw my mother's shadow on the wall. The shadow came down the stairs and disappeared.

They said they didn't feel frightened, but of course they felt very emotional.

Actually, my mother's ghost often appears to different members of the family, in different forms.

I think this is because she was such a strong character, and her memory lives on in our minds.

19 Wheels

82

(K = Karen; R = Ron; J = Jill)
K: You're late!
R: Yes, I'm really sorry – I had to wait ages for a bus.
J: Why didn't you drive?
R: Ah, well. I've sold my car.
K: Oh, are you getting a new one?
R: No, I'm not getting another car. I've decided to live without one.
J: Wow – what made you do that?
R: I think there are too many cars, and this town is far too polluted.
J: Well, that's true, but a car is useful.
R: I don't think so. Not in the city centre, anyway. I can never find anywhere to park, and you spend most of the time sitting in traffic jams.
K: But how are you going to get to work?
R: By bicycle.
K: Don't you think bicycles are dangerous?
R: Not really. I don't think they're as dangerous as cars.
J: Well, I couldn't do without my car. I have to take the children to school every day.

R: I don't think children get enough exercise these days – they should walk to school.
K: Well, I haven't got children, but I agree with Jill – I couldn't live without my car. I sometimes have to come home late from the office.
R: Why don't you get the bus? Public transport is very good.
K: That's not true. The buses are not very regular where I work and anyway, as a woman, I don't feel safe waiting for a bus late at night.
R: Okay, I see what you mean, but aren't you worried about pollution?
J: Of course, but you don't understand – it's easy for you to worry about the environment. I have to worry about carrying the shopping and children and ...
R: Okay, okay, you're right! Come on. Let's get another drink. Hey, what do you think of my new haircut?

83

(See page 114.)

84

(P = Presenter; C1 = Caller 1;
C2 = Caller 2)
P: And that was of course this week's brand new number one! My name's Dave Darby, and you're listening to *Road Rage*. Okay, let's see who's waiting on the line. Hello – what's your name, and how can we help?
C1: Hello, Dave. Um, my name's Mark, and my problem is traffic jams. I waste too much time sitting in my car in traffic jams in the morning on my way to work and in the evening on my way home, and I'm sick of it.
P: Ah, yes. I'm sure lots of people share your feelings, Mark. Why don't you work at home some of the time?
C1: I can't do that, Dave – I work in a shop.
P: Oh, okay. You could use public transport. Then you could read a newspaper on your way to work, and your time wouldn't be wasted.
C1: I can't do that, Dave – I have to use my car at work for deliveries.
P: Okay. Well, Mark, if I were you I'd learn a new language! Where do you usually go on holiday?
C1: Uh, Spain, Dave.
P: Great! You can buy Spanish language courses on CD and play them on your car stereo. They're fantastic, and you won't see the time pass.
C1: Uh, Dave ...
P: Thank you, Mark. Have we got another problem on the line – yes, hello – what's your name, and how can we help?
C2: Er, hello, Dave. My name's ... I'm, I'm called Sharon and I can't pass my driving test.
P: Oh dear, Sharon. Why's that?

C2: Well, I'm too nervous.
P: Right. How many times have you taken your test?
C2: Seven times, Dave. I'm fine in the lessons, and then on the day of the test I fall apart. I start shaking and I can't see the road.
P: Oh dear. Well, Sharon, ...

85

(See page 116.)

86

(See page 117.)

20 Review 4

87

(P = Presenter; A = Amy; J = Jack;
V = Vera)
P: Hi and welcome to *Speak up!*, the radio phone-in where *you* get the chance to say what *you* think about the stories in the news today. ... In the news today is lottery winner, Eva Alvarado. Yes, listeners, Eva Alvarado won $198 million but she says she doesn't want to change her life. She loves her job in a children's home and she wants to stay the way she is. Phone us now on 0800 989 8989 and tell us what *you* think. ... We have our first caller – Amy Wilder. Go ahead, Amy.
A: Well, Mrs Alvarado is obviously very fond of the children, but I'm sure she'll give up the job soon. When everybody knows how rich she is, life will be very difficult. Everyone will ask her for money and she will soon get tired of all the letters. So, she needs to think about the future now.
P: Good point there. We have Jack Nichols on the line. Go ahead, Jack.
J: Well, she doesn't sound very excited about winning the lottery. In fact, she's more interested in the children than in the money, so she'll probably give most of the money away – to the children's home, to her friends, you know? And I think she's right. If you have that much money, how are you going to spend it all?
P: Well, Jack, I'm sure I could help her! Right, let's go to our next caller – Vera Baker.
V: It's a lot of money, and she'll need a financial adviser. She doesn't have to worry about the future any more, but as soon as she has had time to think about it, I'm pretty sure she'll change her mind about just giving money to the children's home.

88

(See page 121.)

Macmillan Education
Between Towns Road, Oxford OX4 3PP
A division of Macmillan Publishers Limited
Companies and representatives throughout the world

ISBN 0 333 92385 5

Text © Sue Kay, Vaughan Jones and Philip Kerr 2002
Design and illustration © Macmillan Publishers Limited 2002

First published 2002

Project management by Desmond O'Sullivan, ELT Publishing Services.
Designed by Jackie Hill, 320 Design.
Illustrated by Martin Chatterton pp127, 128; Rebecca Halls pp62, 63,
77, 122, 123; Ed McLachlan pp17, 32, 42, 57, 88, 92, 116; Julian
Mosedale pp24, 39, 54, 91, 121; David Shephard pp23, 59; Mark
Thomas p117; Kim Williams pp124, 126.
Cover design by Andrew Oliver.
Cover painting After Visiting David Hockney © Howard Hodgkin.

Authors' acknowledgements
We would like to thank all our colleagues at the Lake School,
Oxford, for their help and continued support; in particular, Pete
Maggs, whose thoughtful comments on work in progress were much
appreciated. Thanks also go to our pre-intermediate students who
have kept us focused at all times on what works in the classroom
(and made sure that we disregarded everything else).
We are especially grateful to Helena Gomm and John Hird for the
Inside Out Teacher's Book, to Pete Maggs for the weekly Inside Out
e-lessons, to Guy Jackson for running the Inside Out website at
www.insideout.net, which has finally come of age, and to everybody
involved in the Inside Out Resource Pack: a great team!
At Macmillan Education we would like to thank Sue Bale (publishing
director), David Riley (publisher), and Pippa McNee (picture
researcher). We would also like to thank Alyson Maskell and Celia
Bingham (freelance editors), Jackie Hill (freelance designer), Helen
Reilly (freelance picture researcher), Paulette McKean (freelance
permissions editor), as well as James Richardson and Vince Cross
(freelance audio producers). Thanks also go to the production and
marketing teams who have worked so hard to make Inside Out what
it is.
Once again, we reserve the biggest thank you of all for Desmond
O'Sullivan (freelance project manager). We are indeed privileged to
be working with such a talented and committed professional – long
may it continue! Thanks for everything, Des.
In addition, we must thank our families, without whose support and
understanding none of this would have been possible.
We would also like to thank Thalia Carr (The Swan School, Oxford),
Jenny Johnson (International House, Barcelona) Beth Neher
(International House, London) and Katarzyna Kowalczyk (Macmillan
Polska) for their very helpful comments.

The authors and publishers would like to thank the following for
permission to reproduce their material:
Lyric of Stand By Me, composed by Jerry Leiber / Mike Stoller / Ben E.
King. Produced by kind permission of Jerry Leiber Music / Mike
Stoller Music / Mike & Jerry Music LLC. Extract from 'They were the
happiest couple in showbiz … but then it all went wrong' by Polly
Graham from The Mirror 06.02.01, reprinted by permission of Mirror
Syndication International. Lyric of Suspicious Minds. Words and music
by Francis Zambon. By kind permission Sony / ATV Music Publishing
© 1969. Lyric of Money (That's What I Want). Words and music by
Berry Gordy and Janie Bradford © 1958, Jobete Music Co. Inc. / Stone
Agate Music, USA. Reproduced by permission of Jobete Music Co.
Inc. / EMI Music Publishing Ltd, London WC2H 0QY. Reproduced by
permission of International Music Publications Ltd. All rights
reserved. Extracts from www.princes-trust.org/involvedframes.htm,
reprinted by permission of The Prince's Trust. Extract from 'Best of
Times, Worst of Times: Bill Wyman' by Danny Danziger from The
Times Magazine 30.04.00, copyright © Times Newspaper Ltd 2000,
reprinted by permission of News International Syndication. Lyric of
Don't Worry, Be Happy. Words and music by Bobby McFerrin © BMG
Music Publishing Ltd. All rights reserved. Used by permission. Extract
from '101 Ways To Slow Down', copyright © The Guardian 2001,
from The Guardian 09.09.01, reprinted by permission of Guardian

Newspapers Limited. Extract from Billy Elliot by Melvin Burgess.
Screenplay by Lee Hall (The Chicken House, 2001), Text copyright ©
Melvin Burgess 2001. Original screenplay by Lee Hall © Universal
Studios Publishing Rights, a division of Universal Studios Licensing
Inc., 2001, reprinted by permission of the publisher. All rights
reserved. Extract from 'Why I Bought My Child A Gun' by Phil Hogan,
copyright © The Guardian 2001, from The Guardian 04.07.01,
reprinted by permission of Guardian Newspapers Ltd. Extract from
'104 Things To Do With A Banana' by Wayne M. Hilburn from
www.dmgi.com/bananas.html, reprinted by permission of the author.
Extract from 'Slip Sliding Away' by Sophie Radice, copyright ©
Sophie Radice 2001, from The Guardian Weekend 03.11.01, reprinted
by permission of Guardian Newspapers Ltd. Extract from 'Balloon
Buddies' The Daily Mail 28.06.01, reprinted by permission of Atlantic
Syndication Partners. Extract from The Lost Continent by Bill Bryson
(Blackswan, a division of Transworld Publishers, 1999), copyright ©
Bill Bryson 1989, reprinted by permission of the publisher. Lyric of 24
Hours From Tulsa. Words by Hal David. Music by Burt Bacharach. ©
1963 New Hidden Valley Music Company / Casa David, USA. Universal
/ MCA Music Limited, Elsinore House, 77 Fulham Palace Road,
London W6 8JA / Windswept Music (London) Ltd, Hope House, 40 St
Peter's Road, London W6 9BD. Used by permission of Music Sales Ltd.
All rights reserved. International copyright secured. Extract from
'e-How to remember names' by Valerie Singer, from
www.ehow.com, reprinted by permission of Blue Frogg Enterprises.
Whilst every effort has been made to trace owners of copyright
material in this book, there may have been some cases when the
publishers have been unable to contact the owners. We should be
grateful to hear from anyone who recognises copyright material and
who is unacknowledged. We shall be pleased to make the necessary
amendments in future editions of the book.

The authors and publishers wish to thank the following for
permission to reproduce their photographs:
Associated Press p73 (tr); Ardea pp102, 105 (t); David Bebber p108
(tr); Big Pictures p31; Bridgeman Art Library p20 (b); Neil Bruce
Motoring Library p112 (t,m); Jenny Cockell p109; Corbis pp10 (tm, b),
13 (tm), 40 (tm), 55 (t), 56 (all); Paul Cousans p108 (tl); Empics pp22
(all), 26 (r); Fortean p100, 107; FPG pp6 (br, tm), 14, 40 (a), 47 (all),
60; Getty Images pp4, 6 (bl, bm), 10 (tl, tr), 12, 13 (bm, t, b), 18
(both), 28 (t, b), 34, 40 (c), 41 (all), 44, 45, 60 (br), 64 (a–c), 65 (all),
69, 71 (all), 78 (all), 82 (both), 83, 85, 95, 99, 100, 101, 102 (a, b, c, d,
f), 103 (all), 108 (mr, bl), 110 (both), 114, 119, 125, 127 (m, r); Greg
Evans Picture Library pp112 (b); 128 (mr, r); Hulton Getty p21; Image
State pp6 (tl), 9 (b), 124 (a); Alberto Korda Guerillero Heroico (Che
Guevara) © ADAGP Paris and DACS London
2002 courtesy of Couturier Gallery LA p74; Magnum p94; Desmond
O'Sullivan p104; PA News p5 (b), 37 (r), 58; Photodisc pp26, 50, 99;
Pictor International pp6 (tr), 38 (both); Popperfoto p70; Powerstock
pp64 (t), 75; Redferns p43; Retna pp9 (tr), 46, 73 (br), 67; Ronald
Grant Archive p30; Rex Features Ltd pp16 (all), 20 (tr, tm, bm, br), 37
(ml), 73 (l), 77, 86, 117, 118, 127 (l); Science Photo Library p111; Louis
Stettner Promenade Brooklyn 1954 © ADAGP, Paris and DACS
London 2002 courtesy of Gallery 292 / Howard Greenberg Gallery
p68; Topham Picturepoint p37 (mr); Universal Pictorial Press pp37 (l).

Commissioned photographs by Haddon Davies pp26 (Pauline
Perkins), 48 (Ozone), 49 (Matt McKay), 97 (food stuffs).
The publishers wish to thank Lou Wright.

Cartoons on p85 produced with permission from Tony Husband; pp7,
25, 84 with permission from Private Eye; pp8, 61 with permission
from The Spectator, pp27, 79, 113 with permission from
Cartoonstock; p86 with permission from Business Life; p72 with
permission from Punch.

Printed and bound in Spain by Edelvives SA.
2006 2005 2004 2003
10 9 8 7 6 5 4 3